The *Desire* of All Ages

How to Make Money

Dr. Kawuma Kayiwa

Copyright © 2011 Kawuma Mugabi KAYIWA

All rights reserved. No part of this book may be reproduced in any form, except for the inclusion of brief quotation in review, without permission from the author/publisher.

ISBN: 9889855550
ISBN:-13: 978-988-98555-5-0

Kayiwa Foundationst
P.O.Box 91185 TST,
Hongkong.
Tel: 852-27392743
Email: cares@kayiwa.com
Website: www.kayiwa.com

Additional copies can be obtained worldwide from bookshops and online stores.

Dedication

This book is dedicated to Kayiwa Foundations.

Kayiwa Foundations is a Community Agency for Relief and Educational Services. It was established as a poverty relief charity to help the poor in their suffering and to protect oneself from being corrupted by the World.

The mission is to offer poverty relief and income generating programs, encourage local business communities by linking them to overseas investors, supply back-to-work tools, offer job-training and employment opportunities, and provide health and housing services.

Kayiwa Foundations provided the vision and information that this book has used to lay the case that one can move from poverty to prosperity with no possibility of falling back.

Contents

Dedication		iii
Acknowledgement		vii
Preface		ix
Introduction: Blessed are young men.		xi
1	Money: How can you grow rich without it?	1
2	Dar Es Salaam: Abode of Peace.	19
3	Poverty: Condition wherein a person cannot satisfy basic needs.	29
4	Attitudes: Distinguishes a fool from the rest.	41
5	Prosperity: Wisdom to enjoy wealth.	51
6	Starting : Moving the first step is the hardest.	53
7	Dream: When issues are becoming complicated.	67
8	Fences: Attitudes that deter one from going Forward.	73
9	Goal: How to overcome forces to which you have no control.	83
10	Climb: Can you start a family without a girlfriend or from nothing?	95

11	Accountability: How to resolve conflicting thoughts.	105
12	Thoughts: How to control your own mind.	117
13	Doubt: Why change your mind?	129
14	Experience: How to take advantage of what we know.	139
15	Failure: How to handle disappointments.	153
16	Decision: How to choose the right option only.	167
17	Blessings: Is prosperity a result of hard work, a gift or both?	191
18	Curses: Is there anything like Bad Luck?	209
19	Disbelief: How to stop trusting your fears.	221
20	Prostitution: How to resist enticements.	235
21	Corruption: How to take responsibility over ideas from other heads.	255
22	Gold: How to regain lost opportunities.	291
23	Memory: How to fight forgetfulness.	307
24	Success: How to cement your victory.	315
Index		329

Acknowledgement

I wish to acknowledge the service of my wife Letty Kawuma and of my brother Prof. Simeon Kayiwa who have spared no effort in editing the manuscript. The book cover was designed by Faith Kayiwa.

I wish also to acknowledge people whose names have been mentioned and those individuals who identify themselves with the story. Of course efforts have been made to disguise the characters but where you can be identified just thank God that your name or character has been used to drive someone from poverty to prosperity.

PREFACE

Four old friends met. The four hadn't seen each other for a long time though they were neighbours. One was very Godly, another Godless, the third 'goldly' and the fourth was you. We meet here not talking of the old good days of girlfriends or boyfriends but of the reality of the world we are living in and what to leave grand children with.

One was honest about his life. He had taken full charge of his income but he hated his job, wives, looks and practically everything around him. He felt hopeless and resigned himself to being poor and never managing to get ahead or enjoying his life.

His friend had a different story to tell. He hoped for better things to come. He loved his job and family He was thrilled of what the future might bring.

The third guy was lying in between. These guys had the same background but were living different lives. As these three discuss their own lifestyle you will find much that you can identify with. Use their stories to map out the remaining part of your life. Many life answers are in this book. Read on and you will find the point in life where myth meets heartbreaking reality.

It is not hard work that brings prosperity. The world is full honestly of hard-working men and women trapped in the very life they hate. On the other hand, some people are satisfied in general but bleeding in particular areas.

While everyone else wishes for money or success, the desire of all ages is prosperity. Your destiny is predetermined but you are the only one to determine how to get there. This book gives you a guided tour on how to move from poverty to prosperity and how to avoid falling back.

Introduction

"Yes, a person is a fool to store up earthly wealth but not have a rich relationship with God."

Those in italics are not my words. You may believe them and prosper or reject them and perish. The basic cause of poverty is being in a bad relationship. It could be relationship with God, government, family, neighbourhood or self. Out of a sense of hopelessness, inadequacy or failure comes disliking or despising yourself. You then cannot trust you. You cannot trust God either. You develop resentment to others. You earn self-pity. This very mood invites feelings of guilt, depression, sluggishness, doubting, complaining, murmuring and worrying. Eventually, you feel trapped in an inescapable mud with seaweed wrapped on your head, swimming around in circles and unable to see the escape route.

It is what you believe that determines your feelings. As for me I'm glad and thankful to God that I'm alive to give you reason to live. People may search for their life time to get what you have in this book. You do not need to keep anymore in nakedness, trouble, hardship, persecution, sickness or famine. Conquer your poverty but not freely; you have to read this book.

I regret the hours I have wasted in reasons, excuses and pleasures I have lost in searching for happiness. I now confess that although there was wisdom in me, it never kept around when competing desires fought for me. My wisdom just turned into foolishness. I have no one else to blame. I now return and repent the advices I rejected, feel remorseful to the people I hurt and express regret for all the selfishness behind me in the way I led my life. If I were to pay back I would pay the world back with this book. I sincerely envy the young men and women who are reading the Desire of All Ages. Here are old, proven strategies to reclaim your time and feel less rushed and less stressed. Yes, there is a chance to move from poverty to prosperity with no possibility of falling back.

CHAPTER ONE

Money

Suppose God told you…….
No. My idea drops. I can't believe that as my mind thinks of this as the first page. What a scaring thought to begin a book with! Just think of this.
    A friend of mine changes his character, belief system and his life style every time he meets a new girl. Changing girlfriends can make men crazy. That is not to mention the complex psychology of prostitutes. Prostitutes learn a new culture every day, week, month etc. They get affiliated with mind after mind, day by day! Are they real?
    "Why are you doing that?" I asked one such friend of mine. He said, 'God said to us to multiply'. Then he asked God, "With what?"
    I asked, "Is sex for gratification of a basic human need, procreation or both?"
    I might have laughed his answer funny but well, well, well….. Forget about my friend. Charlie is just a crazy business friend of mine in Jerusalem. He is one of those people who work hard for money. Like any other person poor in spirit he never has enough money; he is never satisfied with his income. Charlie proposed the title of this book. He said that the desire of all ages is to make money. How can you grow rich without it?
    The prostitutes I have in mind are such ones as I saw on Freedom Road night after night hanging out for any man who comes by, walking, cycling or driving. One prostitute (Jane--not her real name) told me that she strongly believes in God, believed in God, and will believe in God. She told me so, so many times. So says Charlie as well.
    Do they ever pray to Him?
    Charlie answers, "Yes" and his prayer every morning is: "Lord, give me this day another woman."

To him variation is a very important human need. He changes every day. I am surprised he has been my friend for a bit of while. Still the question is, 'What is in his mind? Is it satisfaction of a human need or obedience to God?'

Jane's prayer is, "Lord, give us this day our daily bread. Do not take us into salvation but protect us from the police."

Talking about variation, if you were ever given a chance to live your life again, would you ever consider marrying the same woman or man again? Would you ever cast your vote for the same politician again? Would you ever go back to the same school again? Would you be an African, British or Japanese traditional ruler again? Would you be born to the same parents again? By the way, do you realize that no one wants to remain the way he is for long? That is why beauticians and surgeons have earned so much from women and men who want to alter their shape, skin pigment etc. Think of Mike Jackson.

If you are worried for living in some illicit relationship but then in another ear you hear God loud and clear offering you a big money fortune, at the pain of breaking that relationship, would you say, "That must not have been God speaking?" Would you pray, "Dear God, give me one more day or one more weekend? I think I will drop dead if I quit now."

Let us go deeper. I am a coward in a lot of ways. I am a baby jelly, I think. Thoughts are troublesome. Looking for prosperity, for example, can be scary. For how long will I hold to this wealth? Poverty too scares me. Thinking is rough and tough. I know that sometimes my pen stammers but people stand me all the the time. People are kind to stammerers. What I mean is that when I began sharing my mind with you by this book, like a stammerer, I would go back, back, editing and editing it a number of times. Stammerers are not sure whether to say this word or that but they know the goal of their mind. The more I read my pages the more I got scared. Writing makes thinking clearer. New realities are established with clear edges. The more I write the more I am sure what to say when giving a speech. It is the same about life. To have money or not to bother about working for more is the question. I stagger under thoughts like that but when I write, in the end I know what to do. It becomes all clear. My reader will surely have a clear mind about life by the time this book ends.

Meanwhile, like breathing for the first time makes the baby cry so loud while being born, I am all of a tremble as ideas drop. It all scares the hell out of me.

Yes, you can be scared of your own writing as parents can be of their own children! Every new born they hold is a way of touching a future which they may not live long enough to see. How will we be by the end of these lines of mine? Every author knows that his book will be read by people he will never meet and by generations he will never live in. Ask the Bible and the Koran where their writers are! Scaring!

What would you do if you had said, "It is futile to serve God. What do we gain from obedience when instead He appears to be blessing the arrogant more? Yes, we will go to heaven but what about our human needs? It appears we cannot survive without begging from people who got their wealth the wrong way? It appears evil doers prosper more, and those who insult Him walk free. What will I do? Challenge God? Escape from Him and go berserk like a wild terrorist? There is money in that too. I am sure no one wants to know. Why did I write this? I think we need ethics.

This is the second part of the above question. What would you do if you had consulted your pastor and he told you, "Malachi 3:16: Then those who feared the Lord talked with each other and the Lord listened and heard"?

Would you consult that pastor again or would you look for a doctor or a lawyer? Tell me. Would you say that you are running crazy? What would you think? Would you say you might have been dreaming or these are works of great imagination?

I know this God-thing is scaring and might not do well to the marketing of this book. I am not a preacher. Somehow however I found out there is a God. I cannot easily explain how easily I came to know this. When rival thoughts came battling for control of my mind, I asked peace to be the umpire. I followed neither emotions nor feelings. I followed peace. I say this to you so that in future you do not let your hearts be troubled nor be afraid. The formula works and works at all times.

There is a choir which everybody tells me sings like angels. It seems everybody knows angels. They surely sing very well. At least everyone knows how well they sing, without really, really being sure if they ever sing at all. You know what I mean? It is better to believe than to doubt.

I know without asking for laboratory proofs that God lives. I get peace thinking he exists. Thinking 'God' is simply an abbreviation for 'gold-oil-diamonds' or thinking that there is no god gives me confusion and a feeling that I am a fool. Elsewhere, the name God gives somebody a brain damage. Anyway every name gives somebody somewhere a brain damage. That is non-issue. I challenge those who feel put off by a scary debate that wouldn't they go to a cinema if they are told that the film showing is scary?

Let's get back! Suppose God told you, "Go into the world and prosper", what would you do? Would you remain skeptical and say, "Show me the money!" Would you rise up and walk? Would you continue in your slumber? Or would you say, "I will not believe it was the voice of God until my bills are paid? I will not believe until I have a new house or a new dress. I will not believe until my children are out of college. I will not believe until I have got a job. I will not believe until I am healed. I will not believe until my problem is solved! I will not believe until….I die"

If you ever felt that you would like to put off that silent voice for another day; or if you felt that acting upon such a voice immediately might ruin your reputation or hurt other people's feelings, or if you ever felt that the message might be alright but the timing might be wrong, trust me you are reading the right book. If you are not convinced yet check it up in Malachi 3:16: "A scroll of remembrance was written in God's presence concerning those who feared and honoured his name". Verse 17 says, "The Almighty saw the list and remarked, 'They will be mine in the day when I make up my treasured possession. I will spare them, just as in compassion a man spares his son who serves him.'"

I do not know about you. You may be the guy who thinks prosperity is determined by fate at birth. You may think some people are created to be happy and others are there to suffer. You may think one cannot change one's fate. What I am saying here is different. I know that suffering teaches perseverance and perseverance teaches patience and patience teaches faith and faith leads to action. Having said all that I do not mean there is no Gain without Pain. You can surely turn from poverty to prosperity by reading this book.

In my earlier book, <u>Face to Face With Grief</u> (A Psychological Approach to coping with suffering) (ISBN-13: 978-988-98555-1-2) I made a great statement. I said, "You are what you think" I have been humbled by the great number of people who have called me up to say how much they have been helped by reading that book. I want to suggest to those who have not read the book yet to get a copy right now. If you can do it today, why wait for tomorrow? This I am making might be the biggest advertisement for <u>Face to Face with Grief</u> but I owe no one any apology. It is on record. You can turn your life around from surviving to thriving by simply changing your thinking. I am standing on that ground to add an afterthought. It is not what you feel that matters. It is what you believe.

You may argue otherwise but you do not have to feel good to be good. To be good just do what is good. If you think it is hard just try it. Practice makes perfect. The process has nothing to do with your feelings! Feeling angry shouldn't make you angry. It is just like hearing insults. You choose when to call an insult an insult. Sincerely you can feel hungry yet have no desire to eat. You do not have to feel forgiving before forgiving or feel forgetting before forgetting. Do you want to do it? Just do it.

A few minutes ago I felt like licking my elbow. I tried it and failed. I tried so many times and failed as many. So I came to the conclusion: One cannot lick one's own elbow. You may feel like doing it yet you cannot. Our actions cannot be directed by our feelings.

If you want to change your belief do not allow your feelings to control your thinking system. You can write this down: "My feelings, you are mine. That does not make me yours." It is just like falling in love. Loving someone does not make him or her love you.

If you want to gain understanding seek knowledge. Do not walk in step with the wicked or stand in the way that sinners take nor sit in the company of mockers, but keep company with those who delight in the law of God, and who meditate on his law day and night. You will be like a tree planted by streams of water, which yields its fruit in season and whose leaf does not wither—whatever you will do will prosper.(I love this promise from Psalm 1:1-2). You will surely see the distinction between the righteous and the wicked; between those who serve God and those who do not. What I promise by reading this book through is that you will see ways of walking to prosperity through your circumstances. You will not listen to those who discourage you. You will not listen to those who criticize you. You will listen to those who know that as you prosper they too prosper. You will not surrender your joy to distracters.

Just as I was writing this book my nephew sent me this text message: "Uncle please send me U$ 500 being school fees. Send to this account Fred …… (Surname withheld) Ac No:295120987001, Trust Bank."

I called my sister and asked what Fred was doing lately. She told me he had just got married and was working as a primary school teacher. His wife was a perfect price for those who love carelessly.

I therefore knew why he needed the money. I sent Fred this message. "Sorry I cannot help you at this time." I left out the reason that led me to this decision. You know what? I did not believe him.

Face to Face with Grief presented a psychological approach to coping with suffering. As it was at the time of writing so it is today 'a wonderful title for people recovering from tsunami, terrorist attacks, floods or earthquakes. It restores self confidence into people who have lost loved ones, friendships, jobs or sources of income. It shows the way forward after some devastating news. Without belittling your feelings for the loss of your loved ones, demeaning the pain of joblessness and poverty and blaming you for your circumstances, it uses the counseling and experience of others to dig you out of your own grave. It helps the reader to modify and control ones anger, doubts , hatred and helps one to think through one's goals, guide one's life course decisions and let one think and design one's lasting relief from one's problems'. The quotation is from the book cover.

Many people have been helped by this book. Rising sales could be a measure of this success story. I am not writing this to pat myself on the back but to say that if you missed a boat that could take your life from surviving to thriving, do not worry another boat to take you to the land of richness, money, overflowing joy, wealth and prosperity is ready to sail.

I am talking to people who have ever lost an opportunity. Do not give up. Close to where I am there is an advertisement. It reads, "If you lost a rainy day," says God, "Do not worry I will create another one for you another day". In the same city I saw another signboard reading, "Pray before you are prayed for." Suppose you were divorced once or twice or let us say you have ever been divorced or you are contemplating divorce,… and …..a beautiful woman or this awesome guy comes along and says, "This is me to dry your tears" what would you do? Wouldn't you marry him or her?

I am a counselor by profession. I asked a friend of mine Hosef (you will read about him later) this question and he answered, "I would marry her."

I said, "Hosef, one woman almost made you crazy and another one almost made you take your own life. You have just been divorced not once and not twice. Would you consider marrying again?"

This book, "The Desire of All Ages: How to Make Money and move from Poverty to Prosperity with no possibility of falling back", is a practical guide to changing one's life from poverty to prosperity. I call it the guided tour from poverty to prosperity. In this book you will find a practical plan on how to market yourself and your services. You will find the common causes of failure in life and how to conquer those circumstances. Those who have lost their fortunes and those who are just beginning to make money will appreciate the value of having a guided tour.

Writing this book has not been easy. I started with great excitement but after writing a few chapters I realized that I was not writing what I wanted to write and instead I was writing what I did not want to write. For months I gave up the project then I had a dream and I saw words clearly inscribed on a wall: God, Gold, You and Godless. I stayed hours in bed half awake and half asleep trying to interpret my dream. This book is the result of that vision. If I were to title it anything else, I would have called it: God, Gold, You and Godless.

Once this is said you feel, "Oh God I have just landed myself on those other "Make it Rich schemes." *If you feel this way, my advice is: Throw this book right away and ask for a refund.* I am writing this in italics for your easy reference. Anyone who reads this book this far and stops here is entitled to full refund with no questions asked. Quote Page 8 for your reference.

I know there is a great wall between poverty and prosperity. In fact this is what I saw in the dream. I saw a picture of a world. In this world there was an economic ladder on which was tied the fruits of prosperity. Everyone was trying to climb this ladder. Some people ran in teams called countries and some people ran on their individual merit. The entire human race was competing. Developed countries were right at the top of the ladder and developing countries were right down on the base. The division was so big that one could see the ladder as covered in different colours. What however made the greatest difference between the rich and poor was the point at which some people would quit. The poor quit at any one time but the rich never quit.

There was also another difference. The poor, I mean those who stayed permanently poor, were down the ladder complaining and abusing their situation on the exploitation by the rich. The rich however, I mean the rich who got to the top and remained there, were always grateful to the poor who pushed them up and were always helpful to the poor. It is kind of silly but they were not worried that if the poor grew rich (they the rich) would lose their prosperity. The only people I saw rise and fall were the mean who grew rich and remained mean. I saw an ex-millionaire who had been so hard on himself. He had been too mean even to put food in his own mouth. He fed on chips and fast foods. He knew it was better to give than to receive, yet he could not follow through.

Poverty is multifaceted. Not every person was on the ladder. The people in extreme poverty were stuck away in the mad far from the ladder. To these even to live was an act of courage. The hardest part of their struggle was getting to the first step. In fact some of them were not even looking in the direction of the ladder at all. They were not resting either. They seemed to be running in circles. There are moments they appeared to be going towards the ladder but either they stopped short of it, bypassed it or just changed direction and swam away. They looked trapped in an inescapable mud with seaweed wrapped on their heads swimming around in circles and unable to see the escape route.

In front of this lot were those who were at the bottom rungs. These survived because they had some ray of hope. Though their development was sometimes uneven and slow, they were generally making some progress. They reminded you of that guy who said, "Jesus, if only I could touch your garments, I would be healed"

I'm quoting this guy because he was as desperate as most of us could be; yet he survived the circumstances. He did not wait for his circumstances to change but worked through his circumstances. Read the story for yourself in Luke....You will see what I mean. In fact his story ranks among those in which Jesus was quoted saying, "Your faith has healed you." He believed that the end justifies the means and that kept his hope alive.

The greatest challenge of our time is that one cannot go up unless one starts climbing and to start climbing one needs to reach the ladder. The first mandate of this book is to encourage the poor to move up to the ladder. We shall start by redressing the poor.

Poor people are men and women who are struggling to get rich. A man is ridiculed for starting building a house and failing to finish it. Not finishing is not where the fault is. I quote Luke 14:28, "Suppose one of you wants to build a tower. Won't you first sit down and estimate the cost to see if you have enough money to complete it?[29] For if you lay the foundation and are not able to finish it, everyone who sees it will ridicule you,[30] saying, 'This person began to build and wasn't able to finish.'

In the same way, those of you who do not plan ahead cannot get rich.

Poor people are not failures. A poor man of today (particularly after reading this book) might be the rich man of tomorrow. There is hope. Moreover, failing once or twice does not make you a failure. Succeeding once or twice does not make you a success. You have to fail repeatedly, persistently and convincingly to be called a failure. I repeat. Failing 0 times, 1 time, 2 times does not make you a failure. The number of times you fail does not matter. It is the time you fail to get up that counts.

It is the responsibility of everybody (particularly the rich) to assist the poor find the bottom of the ladder. Remember a man commits adultery not only when he sleeps with a married woman but the moment he winks an eye onto her. Adultery does not start with action but with imagination. So it is with prosperity and so it is with poverty. We need to help the poor just think through their situation.

The poorest of the poor will never get out of the pit unless they get to the bottom of the ladder. The upward movement starts at the bottom of the ladder. The thinking part or the planning part is the beginning of all wisdom. You can spoon-feed poor men or you can forgive African countries of their foreign debts but they will never get out of poverty unless they start thinking on their own of what crisis they are in, how to overcome the crisis and what they want to be after the crisis. Man's greatest enemy has always been man himself. It is not the devil that devours man; it is the pride in man that devours man. Poor people are fond of saying, "I cannot do that" yet prosperous people say, "Everything is possible…(To those who believe)." To get out of your hardship you need to participate actively in the struggle. You cannot sit and stare. The time of "Pray for me" passed away two thousand years ago when the apostles of Jesus begged, "Teach us how to pray." (If you want to check out my story, go to Luke Chapter 11). I have bad news for every poor man and every poor woman. The upward movement starts at the bottom of the ladder but the thinking part comes before that and no one can do the thinking for you.

There is so much confusion in this world. I do not want to frighten you but there is rent to pay when you live on planet Earth. There are people who keep on shaking the ladder to stop others from going further up. You may hate such people. You may hate yourself. Welcome to planet Earth. Here all you can change is your thinking otherwise I would advise you to go and live elsewhere. Here you cannot change the environment. This is a crab race. Crabs fail to climb over a wall not because they do not have strong hands or legs. Each crab is pulling the other down!

Wow! What has happened to 'the guardians of civilization'? The strong should be lifting the weak to the ladder. Look around you and see what is happening. Poverty affects individuals, groups and is not confined to developing nations or to people with poor backgrounds. Life is not easy but you can make life easier by changing the way you look at it. Stop blaming your circumstances.

I am writing this book from a country where more than 60% of the people earn less than a dollar a day. More than half of the country has no electricity and more than half the population has never seen a mobile phone. I am not talking about having a nutritional diet. I am not talking about hospitals without medicine or doctors. I am not talking about schools without books. I am not talking about malaria or HIV. I am talking about a people where Moslems and Christians lie together like a lamb and a cub and none goes at the other or runs away from the other.

Lack of money breeds grievances but that is only when you think about it that way. I have seen Christians marrying Moslems and the other way round. I have seen Moslems with their veils in churches and Jesus healing them all alike without saying, "Change your name first." Life is not easy but you can make life easier by changing the way you look at it.

I am in Tanzania. If you look at this country as one of the poorest places in the world you will see starvation, poverty and disease. You will think of supplying fresh water and toys for Christmas. You may perhaps donate your second hand clothes to your favorite charity and claim or not claim tax rebate. You will see a desperate people and you will find excuses for resigning on the fate of this race.

If you are lucky you may watch a TV program about marriage of underage children or recruiting child prostitutes and you will feel some bit of sympathy in your heart. However, if somebody told you that the people of this country might be poor but the country is rich you may think about this place with some degree of interest. Let me be that person to tell you. This country is rich. It is rapidly developing. Its main city is the third fastest growing city in the world. I may go this far at this moment to catch your interest but I could have added the third dimension here.

Deuteronomy 8: 7-9. "The LORD your God is bringing you into a fertile land that has rivers, springs–a land that produces wheat barley, grapes etc. There you will never go hungry or even be in need. Its rocks have iron ore in them and from its hills you can mine copper". If this is a true description of this country would you like to invest in here?

You have read this far but still you may not be able to see yourself in the picture. You may not be able to define your position on the ladder. Your position might be like that of a man who had been sick for 38 years. He lay on the bank of the river in pain for all those years. Every year there was a specific time when the river water would turn medicinal. Whoever would fall in the river first at that specific time would have ones illness healed. He lay there, tried every time but never succeeded to be the first one because he was lame. He tried for 38 years but he never succeeded. In the 38th year he however succeeded. Watch your critics. Never allow them to walk away with your hope.

Before you leave however I want to encourage you with one story. There was a man who was so sick. He could neither talk nor walk. He could neither live nor die.

Reports came around that Jesus was in some house in the city. Relatives and friends carried him there only to find the whole place over crowded. They tried to push through the crowds but they could not break through. They pushed 0 times, 1 time, 2 times, 3 times, 4, 5, 6, 7 times but they could not reach Jesus. Winners never quit, losers do.

They said to one another. "Let us lower him down through the roof."

I imagine they had no ropes. They had no reason for having come out with ropes. They looked for the ropes anyway. They climbed up the roof. I can personally see these men with hammers removing the roof of someone else's house. Wow, that was courage!

Piece by piece they removed the roof and lowered their patient through. They did no not drop him on the floor. This is why I argue that they had long ropes.

You may be stunned at the driving power behind their success. Jesus was stunned too. "Man, your sins have been forgiven. Your faith has healed you." The Bible says, "The man was made whole." He did not need further the assistance of his relatives and friends. He carried his own bed back home.

Now I repeat to you: A man is not judged brave by the number of times he falls but by the number of times he rises. It does not matter how many times you have been on that yoyo swing of yours. It does not matter whether you have tried 0, 1, 2, 3, 4, 5, 6, 7, 8, 9 or 10 times. It is your faith that heals. Do not let this go out of your head

I want to take you away from this figment of your imagination. I want to make another disturbing statement and you may hang me for it if I do not turn out to be right. Before I do that I want to renew my refund pledge and even extend it to cover this page. Go back to Page 8, check what is written in italics. The offer is extended to Page 13.

"We can overcome poverty and the entire human race is destined to prosper. This is another bold statement and I am saying, "It is a true statement" and throughout this book I am going to say it again and again and I am going to urge you to believe and practice it and I promise you that your life will move from poverty to prosperity with no possibility of falling down again. I am going to say there are no hidden secrets on the journey to prosperity and there is no hidden formula either. Prosperity is more than money, more than riches, more than wealth. It means to be whole. Prosperity therefore is more of a public asset than it is a property of the rich.

When you see trees swaying or when you see water swirling do not say you have seen the wind or the storm. What you have seen are the results of the storm or of the wind. The real wind or the real storm is that energy that empowered the water or the tree to move. Without that energy the water or the tree would have stayed in one place. In the same way do not count the cars, the beautiful houses, the jewels as prosperity. The real prosperity is that energy that enables you to move from misery to success. I have now exposed all there is in this book and all that is left is for you is to make a choice whether to read on or not. (The refund pledge terminates).

I am making another offer here and I am putting it in italics. *If within your heart you hear a voice telling you that you can never grow from your state of poverty to extreme prosperity particularly because prosperity is not for you, send an email to the author at cares@kayiwa.com with the words DISBELIEF in the Subject column and your money will be refunded.* It will not pay you to read this book and it is not fair that I charge for a service you cannot get.

I say all this because I have come to believe (and belief is the central theme of this book) that if all gods came together, the only thing all would agree about is their desire to help the poor. All religions preach against poverty and have institutions designed in heaven to assist the poor. Look at the Koran. In the Book of the Cow, Chapter 1, Verse 2 Article 110: "And keep up prayer and pay the poor-rate and whatever good you send before for yourselves, you shall find it with Allah; surely Allah sees what you do". Then look in the Bible. Luke 4:18 "The Spirit of the Lord is on me, because he has anointed me to preach good news to the poor. He has sent me to proclaim freedom for the prisoners and recovery of sight for the blind, to release the oppressed." What is the good news to a bankrupt? What is the good news to a hungry man? What is the good news to a prisoner? What is the good news to a sick man?

There are many more examples that can be quoted from other religions. The fourth Noble Truth of Buddhism says, "Everyone can be enlightened (or enriched)"

I will continue with this theme. Deuteronomy Chapter 15 verse 4-7. "4 However, there should be no poor among you, for in the land the LORD your God is giving you to possess as your inheritance, he will richly bless you, 5 if only you fully obey the LORD your God and are careful to follow all these commands I am giving you today. 6 For the LORD your God will bless you as he has promised, and you will lend to many nations but will borrow from none. You will rule over many nations but none will rule over you. 7 If there is a poor man among your brothers in any of the towns of the land that the LORD your God is giving you, do not be hardhearted or tightfisted toward your poor brother". I guess what I am saying here is there in Verse 4 that prosperity is for all.

Let me quote the Koran again: The Family of Imran, Chapter 1, verse 3, Article 181 "Allah has certainly heard the saying of those who said: Surely Allah is poor and we are rich. I will record what they say, and their killing the prophets unjustly, and I will say: Taste the chastisement of burning."

I am saying these things because there are some people who want to keep the poor in the sorry state by quoting Jesus saying, "Blessed are the poor" and justify laziness, lack of accommodation, hard life, suffering as if it were from the Lord. They preach that Jesus was humble and poor because he was born in a cowshed! Rubbish. Rubbish. Rubbish. How many poor men need treasurers to keep their finances? How can one who owns the universe be poor? Look at property owners. They own so little yet they are so rich! Those who say such things start and finish the argument themselves. Jesus could have started as a poor man but he died as a King (Undeniable. There was a banner on the cross).

And think again: Psalm 22:18 and John 19: 23 "When the soldiers crucified Jesus, they took his clothes, dividing them into four shares, one for each of them, with the undergarment remaining. This garment was seamless, woven in one piece from top to bottom.

24"Let's not tear it," they said to one another. "Let's decide by lot who will get it." This happened that the scripture might be fulfilled which said, 'They divided my garments among them and cast lots for my clothing.' So this is what the soldiers did".

My question to you dear reader: Did soldiers share out Jesus' rags? Was it rags they shared? No! He was dressed like a king. "They took his clothes, dividing them into four shares, one for each of them." These are historical records. The undergarment alone was better than what you or I are wearing today. Compare: This garment was seamless, woven in one piece from top to bottom.

Be deceived not. You can turn from poverty to prosperity. You were created to live a prosperous life. If God is on your side no one can be against you. Rise up and walk.

What I am going to tell you next is a life changing message. It is a strong message requiring changing your thinking. Every computer expert knows that before you do any editing to your computer registry it is critical that you make a backup of the current registry. The temptation to make "one little change" without backing up is great. It can also be deadly. I am telling you to backup all your reasons and excuses because I do not want you to come back and say, "I tried this and that. It did not work for me yet I could not recover my old thinking." I am speaking from experience and most likely you are going to ignore this warning just as most people do. Hopefully you will be a little smarter than other people unless you are ready for real change.

Genesis 47:14-26

There was a great famine in Egypt. Prime Minister Joseph collected all the money that was to be found in Egypt and Canaan in payment for the grain they were buying, and he brought it to Pharaoh's palace.

When the money of the people of Egypt and Canaan was gone, all Egypt came to Joseph and said, "Give us food. Why should we die before your eyes? Our money is all gone."

"Then bring your livestock," said Joseph. "I will sell you food in exchange for your livestock, since your money is gone."

When that year was over, they came to him the following year and said, "We cannot hide from our lord the fact that since our money is gone and our livestock belongs to you, there is nothing left for our lord except our bodies and our land. Why should we perish before your eyes—we and our land as well? Buy us and our land in exchange for food, and we with our land will be in bondage to Pharaoh. Give us seed so that we may live and not die, and that the land may not become desolate."

So Joseph bought all the land in Egypt for Pharaoh. The Egyptians, one and all, sold their fields, because the famine was too severe for them. The land became Pharaoh's, <u>and Joseph reduced the people to servitude,</u> from one end of Egypt to the other. However, he did not buy the land of the priests, because they received a regular allotment from Pharaoh and had food enough from the allotment Pharaoh gave them. That is why they did not sell their land.

Joseph said to the people, "Now that I have <u>bought you</u> and your land today for Pharaoh, here is seed for you so you can plant the ground. But when the crop comes in, give a fifth of it to Pharaoh. The other four-fifths you may keep as seed for the fields and as food for yourselves and your households and your children."

"You have saved our lives," they said. "May we find favor in the eyes of our lord; we will be in bondage to Pharaoh."

So Joseph established it as a law concerning land in Egypt—still in force today—that a fifth of the produce belongs to Pharaoh. It was only the land of the priests that did not become Pharaoh's."

The moral of the story is that while money may save you it can enslave you as well. Wisdom is a shelter as money is a shelter, but the advantage of knowledge is this: Wisdom preserves those who have it but Money …. No wonder then Jesus said the love of money is the beginning of evil. This is not to say that you must not hunt for it. Do not make it your number one priority. Wisdom, food, shelter, wealth, prosperity are all better than money. To cut the long story here: Charlie was wrong. The desire of all ages is prosperity not money.

If you want to make real money—I mean money that lasts—money that can make you really rich, with no possibility of falling back into poverty- save 10% of your wake up time and give it to God's ministry. If you are the poor in spirit guy sleeping 4 hours a day, give God 10% of your 20 waking hours. This calculates to only 2 hours per day. It is perhaps even less than the time you spend on TV, or watching one movie, or surfing the web or you spend busy idle. I am not asking you to spend these two hours reading the Bible, singing hymns or praying. Spend these two hours talking about God to your children. Talk about Him when you sit at home and when you walk along the road, when you lie down and when you get up. I assure you God will pay you more than double for your trouble. If you spend 2 hours, God will reward you with at least 4 hours of rest. You will have then 4+4 hours of rest every day. That length of sleep will take care of your stress, anxiety and depression. You will get up with a smile when you rise up and you will go down with a smile to sleep. You will go to bed without fear expecting a night guarded by angels. Yours will be a land without tears or sorrow. That is what it means to live in the Kingdom of Heaven. You will not have to prostitute your body for daily bread nor be enslaved by money lenders anymore. You will live like a prince or princess. Those who will see you will surely remember that blessed are the poor in spirit for theirs is the kingdom of heaven. That is the true prosperity and that is the very desire of all ages. That is the good news to the poor. Once you get that you will never look back.

Note: If at the moment you are sleeping more than 4 hours a day, less time will be demanded of you.

CHAPTER TWO

DAR ES SALAAM

I am writing this book from the Butterfly Beach (Kipepeo), Dar Es Salaam, Tanzania. I am not very fond of fishing and I am not the sort of person you would describe as a "Fisher of Men." I am on a beach site because it is hot everywhere else in the city. I happen to be here. If you want to do anything, or make any move, you must start from where you are. This is common sense science. If you are in bed you do what is done in bed. If you are in office you do what is done in office. Right?

Do you want to be a missionary? Do not wait until you go overseas. Do you want to give your property to the poor? Do not wait till you die. Do you want to grow rich? Do not wait until you grow rich. Start right now from where you are to behave rich. The guiding principle is one: Wake up and wake up others too.

If you want to ruin your day I have a free prescription for you too. Sleep in church during the sermon, read your Bible in bed, pray in hospital, run a negative commentary on your cooking as you serve, gossip, murmur and curse. You will get the same result if you lend money to the poor with interest or accept a bribe against the innocent. Whoever does these things will be shaken.

If you want to enjoy your life this is for you too. Rid yourselves of all evil; no more lying or hypocrisy or insulting language and above all else show love even when you have none. Love those who love you and those who hate you. The only exception to this rule is: Do not be a womanizer (whatever sex you may confess).

So far said is true if you were seeking happiness. If however you were searching for prosperity, the motto is, "Happy is a person who lives while still alive."

There is something about fishing I came to Dar Es Salaam not knowing but I am proud to have learnt and I want to tell it to you. You can 'hook' a woman with cream and strawberry but you cannot catch a fish with cream and strawberry. For some strange reason, fish prefer worms. You have to bait the hook with some dangling worm and tell the fish, "How about that for dinner, Darling?"

Perhaps of more interest to me than the fishing and the kissing that is going on around here is the discovery that Dar Es Salaam is the African version of Jerusalem. Dar es Salaam is an Arabic word meaning "Haven of Peace." The bay formally called Mzizima is the largest and richest city in Tanzania. It has a population estimated around 2.5 million according to Demographia.com. It is increasing at a rate of 4.47% annually (the 3rd fastest in the world) and the metro population is expected to reach 4.06 million by 2015.

Though officially Dar es Salaam lost its status as the capital city to Dodoma in the mid-1970s, it has remained the centre of the permanent central government bureaucracy and continues to serve as an economic centre for the East African Federation.

I hear Dar Es Salaam is planning to regain its capital status. There are arguments that transferring the capital to Dodoma was ill conceived. By birth-right Dar Es Salaam was the capital city of Tanzania and neither suffering nor tribulations should take away this right from her.

History has it that in 1859, Albert Roscher of Germany discovered Mzizima the way Columbus discovered America. In 1866 Sultan Seyyid Majid of Zanzibar renamed it, 'the Haven of Peace', in a way of touching a future which he never lived long enough to see but in contrast or mockery of its position as a slave trade post at the time. Within a short period however, the fame of the city spread to as far as Europe. Dar es Salaam grew and grew from glory to glory. To cut the long history short, Majid died in 1870 and the city fell with him.

In 1885 Europe realized that invading, attacking, occupying and annexing Africa was leading to a European World-wide war. They sat down on a table and decided to scramble Africa up. "Let's tear it," they said to one another. "Let's decide by lot who will get each piece." Dar Es Salaam fell to the Germans. In 1887 the German East Africa Company was established and put its headquarter here. Dar Es Salaam threw off its Arabic garment and changed its role and grew into an administrative and commercial centre of the German East Africa. By early 1900 Dar Es Salaam had expanded into an industrial city with a rail line.

Then World War One came. Rules of diplomatic relationship changed to "Might is Right." German East Africa was captured by the British and renamed Tanganyika. Dar Es Salaam was retained as the territory's administrative and commercial centre. Under the British rule slave trade was replaced with apartheid. Dar Es Salaam was divided into separate European high fields (Oyster Bay) and African homelands (Kariakoo and Ilala) with a buffer zone of "Coloureds"- Indians and Arabs at the City Centre. The homelands and the high fields developed at a distance from each other. You could refer to Chapter One to understand why Europe would ever scramble for this land. You may have to change your thinking that the description did not refer to Israel but to Tanzania.

The Second World War brought a new era to Tanganyika and to Africa as the whole. The veterans returned with a new spirit of rebellion and were not ready to take everything from their masters for granted. Kenya was burning with a pro-independence movement codenamed MAU MAU (Mzungu Aende Ulaya, Mwafrika Apate Uhuru) (literally translated British Back to Europe Africans Get Freedom). To make the long story short again Tanganyika, Kenya and Uganda were administered as one country under the British East Africa Company.

For some reason, just as some women prefer cream to strawberry, Tanganyika did not pick up war slogans as fast as Kenya did. Soon after World War II, Kenya was on fire but Tanganyika was experiencing a season of peace. Dar Es Salaam was enjoying rapid growth but Nairobi was going down.

Economists tell me, "There is no prosperity where there is no peace". You can say it the other way round and you remain 100% right. If you want to have peace in your home stop the battle cries. Wives submit to your husbands so that your conduct alone will win them over to you. It will not be necessary to say a word or to dress yourselves in jewels and perfumes but those men will see the purity and reverence inside of you and they will work their way into your hearts. They will recognize you as weaker and necessary compliments. They will want to share in your glory and they will treat you with respect. They will do this otherwise they would miss having a share of your gift. For the same reason children obey their parents. For the same reason bosses treat their employees as equals and consequently increase company profits. For the same reason employees serve their masters in the same way no matter whether the employers are seeing or not. Where there is peace there is prosperity.

Towards the end of the 1950's political developments, agitation against British rule and demand for independence started gaining momentum. Tanganyika African National Union (TANU) was created out of a teachers' union. From a simple idea TANU became an action and a force that overthrew the mighty British Empire and led to Tanganyika overturning the colonial rule by December 1961. TANU was stunned. They were demanding independence by 1975 but got it by 1961!

This is a lesson. If you want prosperity, keep your eyes focused onto it. Work towards it. It will not come later than expected but earlier than expected. They may call you a "Teachers' union" but if you have ever walked without shoes you could recall the power of a little thorn. A little thorn in the foot could stop an elephant from walking. A little thorn in the foot could stop you from running. A little thorn in the foot brought down the Empire of Great Britain.

Tanganyika ever since has guarded her independence jealously and has never lost it. Tanganyika made three important declarations. She swore never to interfere in other countries' affairs. She swore to live in peace with her neighbours. She swore to be self-reliant.

This is for you who want to prosper. Swear to get along with your brothers. Swear to make friends with your neighbours. Swear to keep your marriage happy. I know there are some of you who have taken it as their habit to broadcast whatever you hear about your bosses, companies and friends. Thanks be to the internet and mobile phones. You speak out what you ought not to have known and pretend you could have done better or perhaps differently if you were in your superior's position. Tame your tongue. Some of you want to settle your neighbours family problems. Why do you look at the speck of sawdust in your brother's eye and pay no attention to the plank in your own eye? Some of you want to live on borrowing this and that from your neighboour. Live within your own budget (financial budget and time budget). Poverty comes to hypocrites. You condemn others for what they have achieved and yet you do not want to go through the same struggles they may have gone through. Do not move your boundaries. Guard your independence jealously. Treat others as you want them to treat you. Life is not easy but you can make life easier by changing the way you look at it. St. Paul learnt to live in contentment whether he had plenty or scanty. He said that when he was in a dungeon. Throw out your pack of reasons and excuses. Format it. Be born again.

Dar Es Salaam has a story to tell. In 1961 Tanganyika became independent. In 1964 Zanzibar became independent too. By 1964 both countries were independent but looked very different from each other. Zanzibar was some prosperous tiny city-state lying in the waters of Indian Ocean, with Arabic culture and away from its African hinterland. For it to imagine surviving for a few years was but far-fetched. On the other hand, Tanganyika was an empty piece of land with nothing to show. Dar Es Salaam was there as her capital but there was nothing in her if you compared her to Zanzibar.

President Nyerere of Tanganyika looked at Zanzibar and it looked to him like a beautiful necklace lying in the sea. He told President Karume of Zanzibar, "Let me give you a neck to hang on."

In 1964 Tanganyika and Zanzibar married and chose Tanzania for their new name. You could have thought that as Zanzibar's wealth was to be managed by Tanganyika the capital of Tanzania would be Zanzibar. Marriages have traditions of their own. In union the winner takes it all and in divorce the couples share. This was a marriage in which Tanganyika played husband. Dar Es Salaam therefore was kept as the capital of the United Republic of Tanzania. (Zanzibar was recognized by having a 'Za' in the name of the Republic the way Mr. and Miss share S in Mrs.).

Dar Es Salaam has clang to its title as the capital city by keeping to the peace in her name.

There is power in a name. No parents ever give a child a bad name. If you want to know what your parents were meditating about at the time of your birth study your name. Your name is more than simply a label to distinguish you from another. A person's name identifies a specific, unique and identifiable individual person. With a pen in hand, paper on table (and eyes closed), write down what your name means to you.

To those who are single marriage is a bed of roses. I will keep the experience of the married to the end of this story. I will only mention in passing that some partners only come to realize the true nature of their spouses after putting on the wedding ring. They wake up and grumble, "Had I known that is what you are I would never have married you!"

In early 70's complaints arose that Tanzania was too big to administer effectively. It was a scarcely populated piece of land stretching from Zanzibar to Rwanda, from Kenya to Malawi and that Dar Es Salaam in particular lying at the remote end of the country had outlived its usefulness as the capital. Its position at the outskirts of the country was named as its worst disadvantage. In 1973 provisions were made to relocate the capital to Dodoma, a more centrally located city in Tanzania's interior. Zanzibar too voted for the move because Dar (as Dar Es Salaam had become to be known in contrast to Zanzibar's Zar) had become too near for comfort. The situation had become like two neighbours sharing the same man.

At the time of writing this sentence (2008), the relocation process had not yet been completed, and Dar Es Salaam remains Tanzania's primary city and is growing stronger. This is why I said, "I hear Dar Es Salaam is plotting to regain its capital status". There are arguments that transferring the capital to Dodoma was ill conceived. By birth right Dar Es Salaam is the capital city of Tanzania and neither suffering nor tribulations can take away this right from her" but do not quote me please. In any family quarrel the best third parties can do is to zip their mouths. I have learnt and now I confess that a loose mouth is a trap to its owner.

Dodoma may be in the centre of Tanzania but Dar Es Salaam boasts of having a port. Dar Es Salaam has guarded its position jealously. Dar Es Salaam has not been deterred by competition but instead has invigorated its strength towards growth. Rumors have it that Dar Es Salaam is offering one of its suburbs (Kigamboni) to be the new seat of Government.

There is a secret why Dar has clung to its position. As I said earlier that there are no secrets to prosperity, I will open Dar's secret. Yes I know wounds can be bandaged and insults can be forgiven but confidence betrayed cannot be repaired. I will go ahead and tell you that Dar Es Salaam secret lay in her name. Note: I am not bringing out a new idea. This information is in public domain. God has given fathers authority over their children and given the children the obligation to obey their mothers. The people in Dar Es Salaam believe that if you respect your father, one day your own children will make you happy and God will hear your prayers. This is what is called the Dar Es Salaam spirit.

In the same Dar Es Salaam spirit, accepting but not envious of other people's developments, your resolving never to be left behind economically, actively agitating against poverty and demanding prosperity at all costs can turn you into a whole person (with nothing missing). Forces like competition may come to destroy you, fear not, you will instead grow and grow stronger because you have a unique "emotional gene". Call it an inborn gift (Temperament). Just identify your temperament and seek to satisfy its needs. Usually the needs are love, power and association. This is the tip of the iceberg!

I sincerely envy the young men and women who are reading this today. You bought a book to show you a way to prosperity but in addition I have given you a free history account of Tanzania and of Dar Es Salaam. If I knew what I am telling you now in this lesson before I got grey haired; if I knew the art of living when my body was strong enough to go on falling in love with the best girl in town; if somebody had told me what is in this book or if when I was told I had the guts to listen I would have grown richer than I am today and I would have done it long ago. I would have had many days to enjoy prosperity and I would not have struggled so much to make a living.

I now know that what is good for grand-parents is not necessarily good for grand children. Grand-parents are bold headed in the middle. Grand children are bold headed in the sides. I know if I were given the chance to live my life again, I would never spend a bit of my life in sorrow. I now know that my actions should have been led by my beliefs not by my feelings. Imagine losing your promise simply because love has lost its zeal!

I was told but I never believed nor see the relevance then that the grey hair elders wear is a crown of wisdom. Now I add that happy are the elderly who boast of nothing than their respect of their creator. Wisdom is the power to do today what will benefit you in future. Unless you learn what you can while young, you will never be wise when you reach old age. Similarly unless you enjoy your poverty while poor, you will never enjoy your life even when you prosper. Do not say, "I will be happy when I get this or that." That way you may die without enjoying a single day in your life. Life is just like a metallic mirror, it only shines as you keep it polished.

If you heard God telling you to go and prosper, you would not ask him to send someone else. You would not excuse yourself that you were not a good communicator or that you did not have enough money.

You would fear God and would hear him say:

- I am your father, listen to me.
- I have heard these excuses before; your grandfather Moses told me the same things,
- I never take an excuse for an answer.

You would simply say, "Here I am Lord, send me."

I have been at this beach for many days now. I still prefer ice cream to worms. It is not that I have tasted the worms and felt them slummy. I just believe that what our hands do is predetermined by our brains. If I were to eat worms I would start by changing my thinking to that of the fish. I would not need to turn into a fish but I would need to reason out the nutritional value of the dish the way the fish does and my action would be based on that judgment. I say this again: "I would not need to change into a fish but I would change my attitude to that of a fish." My appetite would not be determined by how hungry I am. It would be determined by something deeper than mere feelings. It would be determined by a decision not to excuse my weaknesses by saying, "I am just human" or "I am not Jesus Christ."

As I learn fishing I realize how we have got life wrong all along and how to make it right as we go along. Count yourself blessed among people, for you are reading this book. You do not have to see your dream turn to dust. Remember peace breeds prosperity and peace in spirit brings prosperity in spirit. This is an after-thought added to blessed are the poor in spirit....One reinforces the other.

CHAPTER THREE

POVERTY

Talk to me about poverty. Are you complaining of eating bread without butter? Some people have butter but no bread and others have neither bread nor butter. Are you complaining of a thorn in your foot? Some people have no limbs at all. That is what I call poverty. The economic state of lacking something in life is abbreviated as poverty. If you have a house but you cannot sleep in it….. You are married but you are living as though you are not married….. You have children but you do not enjoy them….. You go seeking for help and you get none…. You are a millionaire but you eat chips and fast foods…. It isn't right for someone rich to be selfish. What use is money to a stingy person? Some people are too stingy to put food on their own table. To be stingy with oneself brings own punishment and glorifies greed, Mr. Rich Fool! To seek God and do not find him….. That is poverty. To buy this book and do not read it…. That is poverty. The condition wherein a person cannot satisfy his or her basic needs is poverty.

It does not matter what state of poverty you are in to make your life turn around. I do not know your name or where you are coming from. My best guess is that you are reading this book. You might be suffering from a stinking level of poverty as found in Africa conveniently termed "Extreme Poverty" or what medical cycles describe as "Coma" or in numerical terms "Earning less than a dollar a day". You might be that paralyzed man neither able to talk, walk nor cry. You might be an occasional sufferer who only pays bills on demand or when you receive the final notice. You may be this guy who earns from hand to mouth; eats to live or you may be the rich fool.

(Luke 12:16 *"A rich man had a fertile farm that produced fine crops. [17]In fact, his barns were full to overflowing. [18]So he said, `I know! I'll tear down my barns and build bigger ones. Then I'll have room enough to store everything. [19]And I'll sit back and say to myself, My friend, you have enough stored away for years to come. Now take it easy! Eat, drink, and be merry!'*
 [20]*"But God said to him, `You fool! You will die this very night. Then who will get it all?'*
 [21]*"Yes, a person is a fool to store up earthly wealth but not have a rich relationship with God."*

 Those in italics are not my words. You may believe them and prosper or reject them and perish. The basic cause of poverty is being in a bad relationship. It could be relationship with God, government, family, neighborhood or self. Out of a sense of hopelessness, inadequacy or failure comes disliking or despising yourself. You then cannot trust you. You cannot trust God either. You develop resentment to others. You earn self-pity. Self pity invites feelings of guilt, depression, sluggishness, doubting, complaining, murmuring and worrying. Eventually, you feel trapped in an inescapable mud with seaweed wrapped on your head, swimming around in circles and unable to see the escape route.

 It is what you believe that determines your feelings. As for me I'm glad and thankful to God that I'm alive to give you reason to live. People may search for their life time to get what you have in this book. You do not need to keep anymore in nakedness, trouble, hardship, persecution, sickness or famine. Conquer your poverty.

 Did I tell you I stammer sometimes? I regret the hours I have wasted in reasons, excuses and the pleasures I have lost in searching for happiness. I now confess that although there was wisdom in me, it never kept around when competing desires fought for me. I have no one else to blame. I now return and repent the commandments I rejected, the idols I worshipped, the selfishness behind me in the way I led my life. I want to pay the world back with this book. I sincerely envy the young men and women who are reading this book today. Here are old, proven strategies to reclaim your time and feel less rushed and less stressed. Yes, there is a chance to move from poverty to prosperity with no possibility of falling back.

What comes to my mind to illustrate my case is this story of a marriage that went wrong (and was repaired). The writer's name has been removed.

RE: "My Husband has become Manual,"

"I have lived with my husband for the past 15 years and our eldest son is now in Form 3. When we first met I was a young girl and all that experience I have today is a result of his humble teaching. He was patient with me till I graduated (and I mean it).

"After six years in marriage and birth of my second child my husband committed a terrible sin. All night long on my bed I waited for the one my heart loved. I woke up and went about the city, through its streets and squares but did not find him.

"The watchmen found me as they made their rounds in the city.

"Have you seen the one my heart loves?"

"Scarcely had I passed them than I found him. I held him and would not let him go till I had brought him to our house–to the room where all our children were conceived.

"At first I forgave him because I thought he had fallen into bad company, or he had been drunk, or he had taken drugs, or he had been depressed, or, or, or, or but now I realize my husband did not 'fall' into sin, he 'worked" himself into it. My husband had all his movements recorded in the messages sent on his cell phone. He slept and worked on his plans with steadfastness. He made sure everything worked fine for him and if I caught him he sounded not sorry for what he had done but for being caught.

"My husband degenerated further. One who used to come back home early eventually could not be back until late by one hour, late by two hours, late by three hours and until after midnight, very early in the morning, next day and next week.

I forgave him seven times, seven by seven times, seven by seventy times, seven hundred times, seven thousand but he could not repent once. I complained to him but the more I did the more he insisted on hurting me. He later told me what I had feared all along. He had a new lover and she would either move in or he would move out. My husband's problem was not how I felt about this arrangement but how he could take a second wife without annoying God. He was such a good Christian and the only obstacle between him and happiness was the church that could not marry him.

"Calling his concubine his "Unlawfully Wed Wife," he told me that he had made "Special arrangements" to see me on the even days of the week. He saw her on Mondays, Wednesdays and Fridays. He said Sunday was his Sabbath (Day of Rest) and I could never question where he took his rest from.

"On my days my husband goes 'manual.' I do not know how to say this but I have had to practically push him to stand and if he does I have had to hold him 'lest he falls down.' At first I thought it was my co-wife who was sucking him dry but now I realize the situation is not that bad. It is worse.

What should I do?"

(Name and address withheld).

When I got this letter I decided to be slow to judge lest by the same standards I am judged. I thought to be in love and yet not loved is some kind of poverty. To be married and live as though you are not is some kind of poverty. To have children and not enjoy them is some kind of poverty. I sent out a blog and these were some of the answers. I tell you: If you do not put this book down, it will put you up.

Sarah: He might be sick.
Pross; Life is like that. You swore to stay with him in 'good and in bad times till death does you apart.' Sorry this is the sour part of the deal.
Chris: Get a spare tire.
Phoebe: You do not sleep with a snake. Pack up and go. You have nothing to lose.
Resty: The man is yours and no one has a right to take him away.
Betty: **PUSH. P**ray **U**ntil **S**omething **H**appens but do not give up the fight.
John: It could be entirely your fault. Perhaps when he comes to you he finds you no longer love him as you used to. You are either cold or lukewarm.
Gina: Poverty makes men lose their fire power.

Cate:	You are just in your early thirties. You might live another 30 years. Are you going to spend the rest of your life in sorrow just because you married a wrong boy when you were at school? Get out and live again.
Peter:	These **trial**s are only to test your faith, to show that it is strong and pure. It is being tested as fire tests and purifies gold–and your faith is far more precious to God than mere gold. So if your faith remains strong after being tried by fiery **trial**s, it will bring you much praise and glory and honor on the day when Jesus Christ is revealed to the whole world. If he wants to leave, let him go but if he wants to stay do not chase him.
Paul	Read my Second Letter to the Corinthians Chapter 7
Brenda	When you're dating a guy, you can forgive him for some indiscretions, but when you are married and that is your position, it is nearly impossible to turn the other cheek if he strays. You cannot turn to the church or the police. The guys who run these institutions themselves are guilty even before trial. I suggest you walk out on him before he walks out on you. Withdraw whatever services you offer him and if he is not hurt enough, get out. Stay out for a night. You can stay at your auntie's home for a night or at any place but out of his roof. He will come back screaming. Men are mean and jealousy.
Barbie	The truth about love is that you do not need a man's love to love him. You can love him unconditionally and this is the love that lasts. No matter what he does to you love him anyway. In the end you will win him over. All love types have been tested and found defective under strain but unconditional love has survived. Try it.

One of the most intriguing responses came from Miro and I quote his response in detail.

He wrote:

Dear Friends

Here is a good thing about life. You will never look at a cup of coffee the same way again.

A young woman went to her mother and told her about her life and how things were so hard for her. She did not know how she was going to make it and wanted to give up. She was tired of fighting and struggling. It seemed as one problem was solved, a new one arose.

Her mother took her to the kitchen. She filled three pots with water and placed each on a high fire. Soon the pots came to boil. In the first she placed carrots, in the second she placed eggs, and in the last she placed ground coffee beans. She let them sit and boil, without saying a word.

In about twenty minutes she turned off the burners. She fished the carrots out and placed them in a bowl. She pulled the eggs out and placed them in a bowl. Then she ladled the coffee out and placed it in a bowl.

Turning to her daughter, she asked, "Tell me, what you do see."

"Carrots, eggs, and coffee," she replied.

Her mother brought her closer and asked her to feel the carrots. She did and noted that they were soft. The mother then asked the daughter to take an egg and break it. After pulling off the shell, she observed the hardboiled egg. Finally, the mother asked the daughter to sip the coffee. The daughter smiled as she tasted its rich aroma. The daughter then asked, "What does it mean, Mama?"

Her mother explained that each of these objects had faced the same adversity ... boiling water. Each reacted differently. The carrot went in strong, hard, and unrelenting. However, after being subjected to the boiling water, it softened and became weak. The egg had been fragile. Its thin outer shell had protected its liquid interior, but after sitting through the boiling water, its inside became hardened. The ground coffee beans were unique, however. After they were in the boiling water, they changed the water.

"Which one are you?" she asked her daughter. "When adversity knocks on your door, how do you respond? Are you a carrot, an egg or a coffee bean?"

Think of this: Which am I? Am I the carrot that seems strong, but with pain and adversity I do wilt and become soft and lose my strength? Am I the egg that starts with a malleable heart, but changes with the heat? Do I have a fluid spirit, but after a death, a breakup, a financial hardship or some other trial, become hardened and stiff? Does my shell look the same, but on the inside am I bitter and tough with a stiff spirit and hardened heart? Or am I like the coffee bean? The bean actually changes the hot water, the very circumstance that brings the pain. When the water gets hot, it releases the fragrance and flavor. If you are like the bean, when things are at their worst, you get better and change the situation around you. When the hour is the darkest and trials are their greatest, do you elevate yourself to another level?

How do you handle adversity? Are you a carrot, an egg or a coffee bean?

May you have enough happiness to make you sweet, enough trials to make you strong, enough sorrow to keep you human and enough hope to make you happy.

The happiest of people don't necessarily have the best of everything; they just make the most of everything that comes along their way. The brightest future will always be based on a forgotten past; you can't go forward in life until you let go of your past failures and heartaches.

You have to consider that when you were born, you came crying and everyone around you were smiling. Live your life to the brim, even to spill over, so that at the end, you're the one who is smiling and everyone around you is crying.

You might want to send this message to those people who mean something to you (I JUST DID); to those who have touched your life in one way or another; to those who make you smile when you really need it; to those who make you see the brighter side of things when you are really down; to those whose friendship you appreciate; to those who are so meaningful in your life.

If you don't send it, you will just miss out on the opportunity to brighten someone's day with this message!

It's easier to build a child than to repair an adult. (Unquote).

Now stop and meditate on what you have read above. Please do not go onto the next page until you have taken a position on the issue. You have looked at what the blog said. You have read what Miro wrote. If you were the lady who sent the problem to me in the first instance and then got this page for an answer what would you do?

SPECIAL INSTRUCTIONS: DO NOT READ ON. MEDITATE ON WHAT YOU HAVE READ ABOVE. GO BACK AND READ FROM PAGE 31.

Our feelings are determined by what we believe.

How many continents are there in the world?

Depending on how you count them, there are anywhere from 4 to 7 continents. The difference of opinion arises because some people consider Europe and Asia to be one continent Eurasia. Some people consider North and South America to be one continent America, and a few people even consider Europe, Asia, and Africa to be one huge continent called Eurafrasia. Now following their belief you will get:

#1 - Seven Continents : Africa - Antarctica - Asia - Europe -North America - South America - Australia

#2 - Six Continents: Africa - Antarctica - Eurasia - Australia - North America - South America

#3 - Six Continents : Africa - America - Antarctica –Asia - Europe - Australia

#4 - Five Continents : Africa - America - Antarctica – Eurasia - Australia

#5 - Four Continents : Eurafrasia - America - Antarctica - Australia

Let me summarize it all. We are what we think. Our thoughts follow our belief pattern. If you think you are doomed to fail, your fear will certainly get you to what you fear most.

Jane was a case in a point. Jane was a young lady with low self esteem. She had a constant fear of rejection. Most people did not regard her that way but deep in her mind she was constantly looking around her surroundings to confirm that everyone hated her. In fact she had vowed to be always the first one to reject others. She acted rude, mean and negative to other people. When they hated her in turn, she said to her mind, "I told you…" In fact her negative attitude earned her the rejection she feared most. Her husband left her. She turned to praying, "Lord, give us this day our daily bread. Do not take us into salvation but protect us from the police."

If however you are determined to succeed and you work towards success, nothing, absolutely nothing will deny you your success. Tribulations, temptations and trials will come but hope and courage will standby you up to the battle's end.

I give another example of a man called Job. He wrote:
"I loathe my very life. Therefore I will give free rein to my complaint and speak out in the bitterness of my soul. I will say to God: Do not condemn me, but tell me what charges you have against me.

"Does it please you to oppress me, to spurn the work of your hands, while you smile on the schemes of the wicked?
Do you have eyes of flesh? Do you see as a mortal sees?
Are your days like those of a mortal or your years like those of a man that you must search out my faults and probe after my sin- though you know that I am not guilty and that no one can rescue me from your hand?

"Your hands shaped me and made me. Will you now turn and destroy me? Remember that you molded me like clay.
Will you now turn me to dust again? Did you not pour me out like milk and curdle me like cheese, clothe me with skin and flesh and knit me together with bones and sinews?

"You gave me life and showed me kindness, and in your providence watched over my spirit. But this is what you concealed in your heart, and I know that this was in your mind: If I sinned, you would be watching me and would not let my offense go unpunished.

"If I am guilty—woe to me! Even if I am innocent, I cannot lift my head, for I am full of shame and drowned in my affliction. If I hold my head high, you stalk me like a lion and again display your awesome power against me. You bring new witnesses against me and increase your anger toward me; your forces come against me wave upon wave.

"Why then did you bring me out of the womb? I wish I had died before any eye saw me. If only I had never come into being, or had been carried straight from the womb to the grave!

"Are not my few days almost over? Turn away from me so I can have a moment's joy before I go to the place of no return, to the land of gloom and deep shadow, to the land of deepest night, of deep shadow and disorder, where even the light is like darkness."

That was quite courageous of a man talking to God! But the same author later on wrote, "I know my God lives" and he was given back double for his trouble.

Now here is an assignment for you. In your own handwriting, write a letter to God using the very words of Job. Simply go to page 37 and start writing,

"Dear God,

"I loathe my very life ……………." Copy down everything and end the letter with "Are not my few days almost over? Turn away from me so I can have a moment's joy before I go to the place of no return, to the land of gloom and deep shadow, to the land of deepest night, of deep shadow and disorder, where even the light is like darkness." Sign your name and put the letter in an envelope ready for posting.

Believe right now that success delayed is not success denied. If you could figure out how to commit suicide and yet go to heaven you can determine your course of action when you are in trouble. You see our action should follow our feelings. Our feelings should follow our thoughts. Our thoughts should follow our beliefs. We are what we think. We think what we believe. We feel what we believe. We do what we feel. If we are to prosper…. let me start all over again. If we have to change from poverty to prosperity we have to change our beliefs, we have to change our thinking, we have to change our feelings and we have to change our actions.

Jane later on realized that her marriage was her problem and solving it was hers too. In this world we may have to suffer but we have to cheer up. Some people have suffered worse than us and in reality though our position might be bad today it could have been worse or this is not where we used to be.

Can we do that or how can we do that?

Look at the statement above, "Can we do that?" See how by simply adding the word, "How." We have been able to change the sentence meaning. By saying, "How can we do that?" we have changed our doubtful, "Can we do that?" beyond recognition. Our action now is going to depend on this new feeling. It is no longer a question of whether we can or we cannot but a question of how. How can we do that?

Swim straight to the ladder. Do not go in circles. Straighten up your life by lining up beliefs, thoughts, feelings and action in one straight line. I have used the words or 'straight', 'line', repeatedly for a purpose. Get a pen . I have some exercise I need you to complete. I have left the next page blank for the purpose.

EXERCISE.

Draw a ladder. At the top of it write the word "PROSPERITY" At every step of the ladder write fruits of prosperity like house, degree, debt-free, and all those things you would like to have and be called 'Prosperous.' At the bottom of the ladder, across the page draw an arrow. The arrow should come from the left end of the page to the very bottom of the ladder.

Hint 1: You can make your ladder as long as you want for it to accommodate as many fruits as possible.

Hint 2: The arrow head should touch the ladder. On the arrow write the words, Thoughts, Action, Beliefs and Feelings in the right order.

Now that you have been able to read this far when you see a dress you desire, do not say to your mind, "I cannot afford that" but question, "How can I afford that?" Do not say, "I cannot enter eternal life" but "What can I do to enter eternal life?" Do not say, "They cannot understand me" but "How can they understand me?" Not "He cannot love me with all these mistakes of mine but "How can He not love me with all these mistakes of mine." Not: "Can I make money?" but "How can I make money?" "Not: 'Can I get out of poverty' but 'How can I get out of poverty?'

Sincerely, it does not matter what state of poverty you are in to make your life turn around. It is never too late. Did you write the letter to God?

CHAPTER FOUR

Attitudes

We are now dealing with the question of attitude. What makes one a fool is not what he does in the end but what he does in the beginning. If you choose to believe a lie in the beginning and act faithfully in the darkness of that lie, you will bear fruits of your thinking. If true a tree is known by its fruits you will be called a fool. Given a choice a fool chooses to believe a lie and denies the truth. Similarly a poor man chooses poverty and denies prosperity. A poor man may be shown ways of getting rich but scorns the way because he thinks, "That's difficult. I cannot do it". He leaves his natural desire to make money unattended to. He does what he doesn't want to do and does not do what he wants. Isn't it foolish to act that way? You may not want to be called a fool. What should we call you if you are such a man?

God created man in his own image. That is why when we cry, "God save my face!" he is quick to act. Wholeness or Prosperity is the image of God. In this image we were all created. It is a state of being whole with nothing missing, broken or lacking. The sole purpose of our existence is to give God his glory. We have to live here on earth and in life thereafter praising this state. I am talking about praising the prosperity of God. So God created our forefathers and told them: Go in the world I will show you and there you will prosper. You and your offspring will prosper.

Since man started walking on this universe he has been looking for this prosperity. Some have gone up the mountains, others have gone down the valleys; some have surveyed the seas, others have gone in the skies; some have gone to the moon, others have gone to Antarctica and Oceania. The purpose of all of them is one: Prosperity.

The reason you wake up every morning and go to work is to make money. The reason why you want to marry a rich man is to make money. The reason why you want to send your children to college is that they may make money. Tell me anything that you do and I will show you that the hidden motive is money.

The desire of all ages is making money. From the Biblical times to the present day we live to make money. To test this theory try out on any child (aged between 1-100) ask what he/she wants and offer the alternative but in monetary terms, even if the offer is 80% lower in value to the child's desire, he/she will choose the money. This was Charlie's argument.

Money is not prosperity but the unit in which prosperity is measured. To our American public, let me put the record straight. Not all money is measured in dollars. There are Euros, Francs, Shillings, Yens and Yuans. Some see money in the number of zeros the note carries. Some see money in the picture the note bears. Some see money in the security features in the print. Some see money in the number of women it brings. Some see money in the number of cars it buys. Some see money in the number of children it bears. Some see money in the problems it creates.

Jesus held a coin and asked his disciples, "What do you see?"

They looked at it and read, "Pay taxes to Caesar."

It does not matter what you say you see in money. When you hold the American dollar do you see the zeros or "In God We Trust'? What really matters is the motive, the driving force that makes you search for money. I could tell you that there is a country with a one billion dollar note in circulation. Would you go to that country so that you may be called a Billionaire? If you were intent on going anyway and discovered that one billion dollars can only buy you a loaf of bread, would you still go? The desire of all ages: Make Money (but worthwhile money).

I want to say one thing before I close. Not all that glitters is gold but all that makes you whole is prosperity.

In this chapter however I did not want to talk about prosperity but about attitude. You have read what I told you before. I want to do one thing but I stammer into another. This is the poverty of the matter. When you seek something and miss it that is poverty. When you keep broken tea cups in your storerooms, keep clothes you cannot wear in the closet, money in a bank you cannot use, ideas in the head you cannot share, then you have it: Poverty.

Poverty hurts and by how much it hurts depends on the way you value yourself. It is this attitude that will determine your course from poverty to prosperity. You said it all in your picture.

Some people thought of the picture. They did not draw because they could imagine what it was all about. They rushed through life. They excused themselves because they had no pen nearby. They jumped the opportunity to analyze their circumstances. They were in a hurry. Listen to what I am telling them to do now. "GO BACK TO PAGE 20."

Life should not take you in circles. It is said the children of Israel walked for 40 years a journey that could have taken them from Cairo to Jerusalem 11 days. They walked in circles. They were walking from slavery to a land of milk and honey. They took 40 years full of wrangling, criticism and quarrels. This story appears in the Bible to teach us what we should never do. You may have thought it faster to jump the exercise but now you need to go back and straighten up your life. We can move from poverty to prosperity by straightening up our thinking. "GO TO YOUR PICTURE AND NAME THE TAIL OF THE ARROW, 'POVERTY'." Your picture shows how to move from poverty to prosperity.

I want to add a special word for those who might feel victimized by being ordered to return to page 20. There are many people who still fly from Cairo to Jerusalem via London. Just feel happy that it is never too late to start straightening up your thinking. I confess being one of the people who regularly need to go back and think life through. I am not the only one. Jane told me that before she straightened up her marriage she used to go on for days and days worrying about her husband, house and children and yet solutions to her worries came in seconds. Imagine worrying for days and days about a meeting and when the issue is raised, the discussion lasts only one minute!

Forget it all. You can move from poverty to prosperity by simply changing your attitude. Suppose a wise person goes to court with a fool, and the fool rages and scoffs, who wins the case?

Attitude is everything. I believe attitude is the key to success. It is also the key to failure. Really! Turn a key one side it locks the door and turn the other way it opens it. How have you used this key? Our attitude is much more important than money, than circumstances, than failures, than what other people think or say or do. Our attitude has a remarkable impact on our lives. We have the choice every day regarding the attitude we embrace for that day. We cannot change our past. We cannot change the fact that people will act in a certain way. We cannot change the inevitable or things that are bound to happen. It's like that saying "Life is 10% what happens to you and 90% how you react to it." So in fact, it's true life is what you make it. Our attitude determines choice, and choice determines results. This means that if you choose to work for the future, you have chosen the results you want to achieve. So are you a winner or a loser? Are you an egg, a carrot or a bean? You are what you choose. It's all about attitude.

Some people choose not to worry about anything; they go through life happy-go-lucky and they are rewarded for it. Others choose the hard road to life and they die under pressure. They may be sleeping in the same bed, parenting the same children yet one sleeps and snores and another does not rest. It is the attitude. One chooses to live today, today, and another chooses to live tomorrow, today or even yesterday, today. When one is told to leave tomorrow to itself one does not listen! Then he/she complains of confusion, depression, anxiety…….. divorce, prostitution, debts, poverty and the greed of the rich.

Where does your heart lay? What is it that you truly want to achieve? Is your heart set on making money, passing exams, becoming a star, traveling the world, going to heaven or maybe even something like opening a restaurant or starting your own fashion brand? It's important that we know what we want, that we know where our heart lays, so that we can set a goal and strive to achieve it.

I started writing this book in the year 2006. The Second World War was over and Germany had returned to the so called International Community. We take the story when Germany is hosting the Soccer World Cup games.

I told you about fishing but there is a lesson here from football. I am not a football player and all I know about football is what I have learnt from watching TV (from Dar) but I think what I can say about football is true. In football, the ball is not kicked aimlessly. There are rules, aims and goals. It is a lot like life. A footballer sees his target which is the goal posts. He maneuvers through his opponents just like we have to when faced with a problem. At the same time, he knows in the posts is planted a devil to swat his success.

The man with the ball is not discouraged by that but he drives straight towards the goal posts. He keeps focused into that direction. The only time he kicks the ball backwards is when he is trying to confuse the goal keeper otherwise his target is one– that his ball must touch the net. Even though it takes skill, practice and time, the footballer has eventually to make a goal. What is even more interesting is that it does not matter how rough or smooth you play but the winner is the one who scores more goals.

Who said life is as easy as that? Actually it might be easier depending on how you look at it. Also like in football, life has penalties, failed attempts and falling face first. At times the footballer is almost at the goalposts when he gets tripped and the chance just like that (twinkle of an eye) slips away. In life, we also face obstacles that take us back to the start. This is when we need to "start a new life" I wish to emphasize that our attitude determines our choice to get up and continue battling or stay fallen and fail.

I think I have explained my point. I have written something like this in <u>Face to Face with Grief</u> but it does not bother me if I write it again. "You know where you have been. You know where you are and you probably have an idea of the life you want to live in the future. What you need now is not to wait for opportunities but to go out and search for them". If you are poor it is especially important we think carefully about what it is that we want. If you have got your thinking straight and you want to get your life from poverty to prosperity – you have to realize that you have all it takes. This chapter you are reading has been named for all good reasons: The Question of all Ages: How to modify attitudes.

Paul in a parallel reflection says,

"Philippians 3:[13] Brothers and sisters, I do not consider myself yet to have taken hold of it. But one thing I do: Forgetting what is behind and straining toward what is ahead, [14] I press on toward the goal to win the prize for which God has called me heavenward in Christ Jesus." *(what I am set out to do). Brackets are mine.*

I want to establish here that to become prosperous we need to forget the woes of the past and focus all our energy and attention to the goal. We fear to invest our present resources because we fear we might lose our investment as it happened before. That is one way of sticking ourselves in poverty. The fear of the future which actually stops us from investing today comes by reminding us of the past. You cannot doubt unless you consider the past. Forget the past and walk firm into your future.

Paul continues:

"[15] All of us, then, who are mature should take such a view of things. And if on some point you think differently, that too God will make clear to you. [16] Only let us live up to what we have already attained".

You do not count your past failures as your past attainments, do you? Forget your past and start a new life focused on your goal and not based on your past fears. I want you to throw out your old self. Dress yourself up in a new body. Give your body a new spirit. Do not choose to be a baby again. Dar Es Salaam, take off that Arabic veil. You now belong to Germany East Africa. You are called mature. Do not go back in your mother's womb but be born again.

"[17] Join together in following my example, brothers and sisters, and just as you have us as a model, keep your eyes on those who live as we do".

Get a piece of paper and write down five people whose example in life you would like to follow. They should all have one thing in common. They are all rich and they are all honest.

"[18] For, as I have often told you before and now tell you again even with tears, many live as enemies of the cross of Christ. [19] Their destiny is destruction, their god is their stomach, and their glory is in their shame. Their mind is set on earthly things".

Cross out and replace those names who fit in this description. Think and add someone who befits the remarks in verse 20.

"[20] But our citizenship is in heaven. And we eagerly await a Savior from there, the Lord Jesus Christ, [21] who, by the power that enables him to bring everything under his control, will transform our lowly bodies so that they will be like his glorious body".

If we want to make money, real money, we would not want to be the rich fool. We are not prejudiced against the rich. We aspire to be one. We just want to get rich right. Jeremiah says,

"17 [11] Like a partridge that hatches eggs it did not lay are those who gain riches by unjust means. When their lives are half gone, their riches will desert them, and in the end they will prove to be fools.'

I have to make it clear. In drawing plans on how to prosper we must make sure we will not later on be haunted by our own actions. We will not be haunted by our own desires (feelings). We will not be haunted by our own thoughts. We will not be haunted by our own beliefs. We will enjoy our wealth abundantly.

I do not want to come in with a heavy hand of crick-cracking criticism or with a stick to bend your thinking. Many people live simply like this. Tell me what I want to hear and I will listen to you. Give me what I want and I will be your friend. I will do what you say as long as you allow me to be me. Treat me the way I want and I will approve your ways. Everything in life is looked at from this self-perspective. This book has you at the centre as we answer that great question: How to modify attitudes. It is this simple self-centred, corrupt attitude that needs changing.

Let me remind you. I am at Kipepeo Beach. The song in the background fits my thoughts. It is by Jimmy Cliff. It says: You can get it if you really want.

> You can get it if you really want
> You can get it if you really want
> But you must try - try and try - try and try
> You'll succeed at last - mmmm yeah
> You can get it if you really want

"You can do it if you really want".

How? "Try and Try". The question lives on. How do you try? How do you make money? How do you get out of poverty?

- Develop a desire to succeed.
- Choose to win.
- Encourage yourself.
- Celebrate your victory even if there is nothing to show.
- Praise God and give thanks for what you believe.

There is something especially lovely at this beach. It's the trees. I say this to shy away from the point. Trees make such a lovely contrast to the endless blue waters and to the endless white sand. Beyond that they provide shades. From my shade I am looking at the water waves. In the water there are beautiful people. They are half swimming, half running, half jumping, half galloping. If I had the poetry of Solomon as in the Song of Songs 4 I would have described them as young gazelles. The difference between Solomon and me is the angle from which we are looking at the girls. To illustrate my point read this .Song of Solomon 4

Lover : How beautiful you are, my darling!
Your eyes behind your veil are doves.
Your hair is like a flock of goats.
Your teeth are like a flock of sheep just shorn,
Coming up from the washing each with its twin;
Your lips are like a scarlet ribbon;
Your mouth is lovely.
Your temples behind your veil are like the
Halves of a pomegranate.
Your neck is like a tower built with elegance;
Your two breasts are like twin fawns of a
Gazelle.
You have stolen my heart, my sister, my bride;
With one glance of your eyes,
With one jewel of your necklace.
How delightful is your love!
How much more pleasing is your love than wine,
And the fragrance of your perfume than any spice!

> Your lips drop sweetness as the honeycomb,
> Milk and honey are under your tongue.
> You are a garden fountain,
> A well of flowing water streaming down.

You see the difference with me. I am not talking about anyone woman in particular. In fact from where I am seated I cannot see these ladies to Solomon's details. I cannot see their faces clearly (and I do not care). It is within my own imagination that they have beautiful legs and once I have formed this concept in my head I begin to see what I want to see. I do not want to sound vulgar but I see all the bikinis in their different styles and colors. We are what we think. We think what we believe. We feel what we believe and we do what we believe. Belief is at the centre of our journey of turning from poverty to prosperity. If we are to change our attitude this is where we are and it is where we must begin.

As I stand at this beach and look at the girls or the gazelles, I hold my breath and say, "It is good and desirable to be rich!" I can however change this picture by assuming that these girls are the ones the local people here call Chang Doa (prostitutes). Once I do this all the beauty vanishes and they start looking like fish that can never fill its stomach until it is hooked.

Which attitude will carry you through the day? I do not know about you but for me the moment I imagine this chapter is about prostitutes then I feel like putting the book down. Surely there are better things to do in life than thinking about aids, orphans, misery, tears and pain.

On the sandy side of the beach there are groups of children. Some are building castles but none is building any grass-thatched huts as those that symbolize poverty in Africa. Children have it right in their brains. If you are to grow rich, think big! If you want true prosperity, think like these children.

I notice another group of people on this beach. They are mostly men and women looking like some kind of pensioners. They are all speaking out loud (hardly listening to each other) but hearing each other. They seem to be interested in one thing: Beer and BBQ. You do not need to read this on their faces. Their stomachs show. I could confirm this with a photograph. Most of these people have their shirts off. From my standpoint I can draw a new theory on losing weight. It is not what you eat that makes you fat but what you play. The guys who are lazing about in chairs have bigger stomachs than those who are running about. I assume they are eating same lamps of meat. Yes there is obesity as a disease of the rich but neither ugliness nor health risks shall destruct us from growing rich. I am convinced it is good to be rich and we all have to work towards it. It is quite possible to grow from poverty to prosperity. All you have to do is:

(1) Master how to deal with people.
(2) As you read this book stop and ask yourself how to apply the suggestions made to your life and do this as often as you read each page.
(3) Keep notes of what you are reading. Highlight those points you certainly need to remember even if it means writing in this book. Put a date and signature as you highlight ideas which stand out as good for you.
(4) Continuously assess your progress by looking back and meditating on the highlights.
(5) Read each chapter again and again before you move forward.
(6) Do not worry. That will not make the book bigger.
(7) Read on.
(8) Design a motto: Sticky thinking sickens, hurting people hurt.

That is how to modify attitudes.

NOW here is another exercise. Go back to your ladder picture. Arrange your goals (steps) in the order you want your life to go. What you want to get immediately should be on the bottom of the ladder. What you consider the best fruit of prosperity should be at the top most rung. The ladder signifies your attitude. I am reminded of what my teacher told me. If I were given a choice what to do first playing my computer games or doing my calculus I would have to start with the one I hate most.

CHAPTER FIVE

Prosperity

We now come to the real gist of the matter. What does man really want?

Prosperity.

One dictionary defines prosperity as wealth, affluence, opulence, riches, success, or the antonym of poverty. Using these many words shows that prosperity is bigger than any one of these but all of these. The human race has all along from the beginning or creation of the world been aspiring to have this form of prosperity. God knew the thoughts of his people and revealed them in this passage I am quoting from Prophet Isaiah

Isaiah 65:17-26:

17 For, behold, I create new heavens and a new earth; and the former things shall not be remembered, nor come into mind.

18 But be ye glad and rejoice for ever in that which I create; for, behold, I create Jerusalem a rejoicing, and her people a joy.

19 And I will rejoice in Jerusalem, and joy in my people; and there shall be heard in her no more the voice of weeping and the voice of crying.

20 There shall be no more thence an infant of days, nor an old man that hath not filled his days; for the child shall die a hundred years old, and the sinner being a hundred years old shall be accursed.

21 And they shall build houses, and inhabit them; and they shall plant vineyards, and eat the fruit of them.

22 They shall not build, and another inhabit; they shall not plant, and another eat: for as the days of a tree shall be the days of my people, and my chosen shall long enjoy the work of their hands.

23 They shall not labor in vain, nor bring forth for calamity; for they are the seed of the blessed of Jehovah, and their offspring with them.

24 And it shall come to pass that, before they call, I will answer; and while they are yet speaking, I will hear.

25 The wolf and the lamb shall feed together, and the lion shall eat straw like the ox; and dust shall be the serpent's food. They shall not hurt nor destroy in all my holy mountain, saith Jehovah.

(American Standard Version (ASV) Copyright © 1901 by Public Domain)

I shall not add another thought on this. I want to leave you meditating on the real prosperity. Meditation to reading is digestion to eating. The two must go together. Any plan made must be meditated upon otherwise it would be like building a house without constructing a foundation. Build yourself a habit of meditating on your plans and the rest will go well with you. If you want to gain wisdom, contemplate, meditate, think over, mull over, turn over in your mind, ponder, deliberate, consider and reflect on the issue. What is prosperity?

CHAPTER SIX

Starting

I got this story from Dar Es Salaam but listen carefully this might be a story about you.

"When Abed gets up each morning, he thinks of all the gloomy day ahead of him. He has trained himself to think that all that can come to him is a landlord kicking him out of the house, children falling sick, wife caught sleeping with a neighbor and all other sickening ventures."

This certainly is a bad start for a man who is poised to succeed. By what you have read so far you know Abed is on a path to fail.

Abed is a Form 6 lever, jobless and penniless. The 27 year-old lives in Kariako.

This is a suburb area of the city of Dar es salaam in Ilala district. Administratively Dar Es Salaam or Dar for short comprises of three districts Kinondoni, Temeke and Ilala.

In earlier centuries Kariako was a small village that was frequently raided by slave traders. Thousands of people were kidnapped from Kariako and forced into slavery in the Americas. This is part of history the Tanzanians have learnt to forget when applying for visas to USA. There is no benefit in living in ones' past just as there is no benefit in living in one's future. Enjoy today to your best and that way you will make your life good for the rest of your life. Tomorrow has enough of its own problems and yesterday is passed.

Today Kariako is mainly known for its extensive market that consumes numerous city blocks. Agricultural goods, house wares, clothes and many other items at bargain prices can be found in small shops and on the floor of the streets. Kariako is one of the fastest growing towns of Dar but also can boast of its lion share of hawking and crime.

Starting

We bring in Abed's story after he has tried his luck on several employment opportunities and failed.

In one of his many attempts to get a job, Ismail (Abed goes by many names) was given a welding job which could pay him Tsh(read Teesh or Tanzanian shillings) 25,000—equivalent to US$ 25—per month, working 13 hours per day for seven days a week. He budgeted. His rent was Tsh 5000 so he had Tsh 20,000 left. The daily bus fares were TSH 400. This multiplied to Tsh 12,000 a month. He was left with Tsh 8000. He could have to spend TSh 266 a day on his meals, his family and everything else if he had to survive. He declined the offer and sought out another venture.

(Attention reader. By printing time the exchange rate between a Tanzanian shilling and a US dollar had changed such that TSH 25000 could only come to US$ 20. If the current fall of Tsh continues by the time you read this book Abed might need to work 26 hours a day to earn the same amount of US dollars!)

Many people over here do not count their money in these terms. They consider what money can buy. The cost of a street prostitute has moved from US5 to US 20 per "Shot." The number of foreign tourists pouring in Dar has gone up folds these years! The cost of a beer bottle has kept to US$ 1.00 but in local currency has moved from Tsh 1000 to TSh 1300. Abed was a good Muslim. He did not count his money in terms of how many beer bottles his salary could pay for. His religion abhors taking alcohol.

He went to a place called Ubungo Bus Terminus

Ubungo is a ward in the western part of Kinondoni district. It is known throughout much of the country as the central hub of transportation. All roads in Dar lead to Ubungo. Its bus terminal is massive.

The Kinondoni area is regarded as home to the city's high and middle income earners, privileged in terms of infrastructure improvement, living accommodations, social service provision and security. Most top government officials prefer residing here to Oyster Bay. It attracts more visitors than the rest of Dar es Salaam city area all combined.

(Jane read through this manuscript and corrected me. She said it is in this area where prostitutes charge US$ 20 not in

Kariako. She seems to think that the right price for Kariako is still US 5.00 "plus a free meal of chicken and chips.")

The Ubungo bus terminal serves as a transportation link to most large Tanzanian cities such as Arusha, Moshi, Morogoro, Dodoma, Mbeya, Iringa, Mtwara, Lindi, Singida, and Mwanza. It as well links to Nairobi of Kenya, Lilongwe of Malawi, Lusaka of Zambia, Lubumbashi of Congo and several other East African cities.

Abed wanted to be a taxi driver but he had no car to drive. Taxi drivers are required to provide their own vehicles. His way out was to befriend a number of drivers.

Abed Ismail's duty was to approach potential passengers with his new name Charlie Bongo tagged on his neck as Taxi Driver No: 140. He would sit on a steering wheel and negotiate in clear English with the passenger the rates. Once agreed he would jump out of the taxi and appoint some driver to take the passenger with stunning and special instructions, "Take this one to Liiban Hotel Tsh 7000."

He would then wittingly turn to the passenger and say, "Sir, taxi drivers here are not trustworthy. He should not cheat you. Pay Tsh 7000 and only that. Pay no more nor less and have a nice journey.

"Do you have change? You do not have to give tips but whatever note you will give the Taxi driver will take your balance as his tip.

"Welcome to Tanzania.

"Do not trust any Tanzanian. I am telling you this because I am a Tanzanian and I know Tanzanians. There is no Tanzanian who can tell the truth. This is true because I am a Tanzanian and I know what I do and what I say".

Abed/ Ismail/ Charlie, the driver and everyone else except the passenger would know that the price has been inflated. By this one deal Ismail (or whatever you choose to call him) could earn Tsh 5000 off one passenger. Abed justified his action by saying he was getting a refund for his school fees. Tanzania national language is Swahili and one would have to pay for special tuition to learn English. Abed did.

This sense of justification where you find arguing with yourself indicates the very point where change must start.

We see Abed justifying his practice of cheating customers by arguing that he paid for English language tuition. If we were to call for change we would start by dismissing this claim. We justify waking up late that we went to bed late. Identifying this point where justification has built its stronghold is the first step in mounting our upward journey. This is the first step and it is the hardest of all hidden weaknesses to find. Just as all roads in Dar Es Salaam lead to Ubungo, all thoughts lead to this point. It forms the basis of our desire to stay where we are or to take off from. You often hear someone saying, "I cannot change, suffering is but my fate." Then such justify their poverty on the colour of their skins, the politics at the time of their birth, the strength of their enemies. If you are going to get out of the mud, stop looking at how strong is your destroyer but focus at the strength of your redeemer. I do not know whether this is true but someone told me that there was a man who died and on reaching Heaven told God that he had escaped from Satan. God asked, "How is Satan?"

"He is on earth looking for whom to devour. He is about to take it over. He is destroying everybody. Unless you do something, God, the earth is finished!"

God sent the man back to earth!

You cannot live by praising the strength of the devil. I warn you. If after reading this story you resolve never to use a cub in Dar Es Salaam you will never go anywhere. Do not even attempt to disbelieve what is said about Abed.

I know this story to be true because the passenger was me. I later came to learn that Bongo is the commonly-used nickname for Tanzanians. The use of the word can be traced to the mid-1980s. Bongo is Swahili for 'brains'. It is thought that due to the hard economic times during Nyerere's rule, the only way one could survive and prosper was by possessing a keen streetwise intelligence. Those who acquired this special intelligence made Bongo their surname.

The next day I got a taxi from Liiban Hotel and asked it to take me to Ubungo Bus Terminus. It charged me Tsh 2000. I went straight and looked for Charlie Bongo (Taxi Driver No: 140). I had noted his details in my Daily. The taxi driver came but he had never been Charlie Bongo and he never looked like one. Taxi Driver No.140 was a woman this time!

As Ismail he moved on. He sold drinking water in plastic bags, tried to work as a houseboy, a wheel barrow pusher or even a comedian at stage.

For his troubles he cursed the day he was born. He used never to put it this way. He used to say that he was not born but according to the Evolution Theory he came out of a great bang. 'Why would God create me and give me up like an old piece of rug or a bad piece of clay?' Bongos are not born but 'banged'.

If you were given a choice to be rich or to be poor and that to achieve either you need the same effort, what would you choose? If you can answer this then you can answer the great question of all ages: How to start?

Let me help with the answer. Rich people have no more in common with the poor than hyenas have with dogs. You get into this picture when you visit Serengeti National park, or any place where animals live in the wild.

The rich hunt down the poor just as lions hunt down donkeys in game reserves. The rich scorn the poor. When a rich man stumbles, his friends will steady him up but when a poor man falls, his friends desert him. When some rich man makes a mistake there are some people ready to cover him up and explain away all things he should never have done and demand unconditional forgiveness. Let some poor man make the same mistake and all he gets is rebuke and criticism. No one listens to a poor man. Poverty never makes sense but prosperity earns praise even from the heavens above.

Now choose: Do you want Poverty or Prosperity?

There is nothing wrong with prosperity if you never sinned to get there but there is nothing glamorous in being poor. I know in Beatitudes Jesus said "Blessed are the poor" but you do not embrace poverty to earn blessings. Do not blame God for your poverty. Do not say he was teaching you humility. He does not cause what he hates. He does not need your service to accomplish his purposes. If a person achieves with a clear conscience success in life he certainly has to be congratulated. The choice between poverty and prosperity is a choice between beauties and wrinkles. Your answer will always show on your face.

I have guided you to making your choice. I have already told you where to start from. Once you hear debates in your head, interpret them to be a wake-up call. Take your position that is where to start from.

A man came to Jesus and asked him what he could do to attain eternal prosperity. Jesus told him to sell all he had and give the proceedings to the poor. The issue is not about giving alms to the poor but the issue of starting from where you are. Another man replied, "Let me go home and burry my father and then I will come and follow you". Jesus' answer was, "No start right now."

I have heard there are many people called by God or by bishops to go and serve in foreign missions but many answer, "Wait let me retire first; let my children finish college, let me make enough money first…….then I will follow the will of God". The experience of these people tells us what a risk and a task to disobey God. Reasonable delay may be but the call to prosperity says: Start right now and start from where you are.

The writers of the Bible recognized this importance and they put the story of Adam and Eve in the opening chapters of the book. The first question God asks Adam is, "Where have you been?'

We cannot presume God did not know where Adam had been. He meant if you know where you have been, you know where you are, then you can plan where you are going.

Your restoration from poverty to prosperity begins from where you are. There is no time for procrastination for those who are bound to prosper. Start from where you are by counting your blessings one by one. Put on paper every good thing about you. Do not compare yourself to others. This is your own story. Do not wait until other people breakdown the fences for you. You reach the fence and decide whether to climb it, break it down or let the gate be opened to you.

Look at your life this way. Suppose you want to get out of debt, what do you do first? You name the debt. If you go to a debt counselor and say you want him to help you get out of debt he will start by asking you how much your debt is. You must know to whom you owe and how much. You need to know where you are. Getting out of debt is like getting out of sin. Getting out of poverty is like getting out of debt.

As I write this I am looking at my secretary, Jane. Today she has no phones to pick and no letters to post. She came this morning with her threads to make a dress in case I have no errands to give her. She is doing exactly what I have described above. She is designing her own dress from a collection of rugs. She cuts an old cloth piece by piece and does not pull the rug with excessive force. She could tear the whole piece up. She picks up the needle with her teeth and carefully passes her thread in the needle hole. She pulls up the thread and twists and turns her fingers. She looks so mentally absorbed but even after many twists and turns there is nothing much in terms of size she can show. You may wonder why she tortures herself this way. Wouldn't it be better she went to a supermarket and bought herself a sweater instead of going through this knitting process?

I asked Jane and she responded, "That would not have sentimental value."

Look for those tiny bits of your life that have been good. Put them on paper and perhaps head it: The Old Good Days. Meditate on these old good days. Find out what was so good and common among all of these fruits. Break down the fruits and look for the seed. What is it that planted all these good days? There must have been a seed somewhere. Good days are not created but made. Days are good if they are accompanied by success in them. Plant a seed to success. Plant it where you are. That is why you start from where you are, not where you would be or you will be. You will never find an answer by looking at a problem. The answer is not where the problem is. The answer is where you are. Start from where you are. In prosperity we look for happiness, success and joy that over flows. A record of your miseries will not drive you forward. That is why the starting point is at a point of success not of failure. That is why we start with the good old days. Find one old seed that made your old days good and plant that seed again where you are.

You are not the first person to be confronted with this question of how to overcome obstacles. Abraham asked himself the same question. God answered him," Stand here. Look to the east and the west. Look to the north and to the south as far as you can see. All that you can see I will give you."

The same God was talking about prosperity. He was showing Abraham the way to start. This is why this chapter is filled with examples on how to breakdown inferiority complex. For you, stand where you are and look at all the opportunities before you. Start with the idea that is closest to you. Act quickly on that idea before it slips away. That is where to start from. Start from where you are with the first possibility. Take it from me. If you go to a restaurant buy the first menu that you choose. Given two ideas follow the first one that comes. You can discard the first option and take to the second one but reversing from the second choice to the first one will leave your heart wounded.

Luke 10:"When you enter a house, first say, Salaam Alek um ('Peace to this house.') If a man of peace is there, your peace will rest on him; if not, it will return to you. Stay in that house, eating and drinking whatever they give you, for the worker deserves his wages. Do not move around from house to house.

"When you enter a town and are welcomed, eat what is set before you. Heal the sick who are there and tell them, 'The kingdom of God is near you.' But when you enter a town and are not welcomed, go into its streets and say, 'Even the dust of your town that sticks to our feet we wipe off against you"…….. I have given you authority to trample on snakes and scorpions and to overcome all the power of the enemy; nothing will harm you". Wow, Isn't that gift Prosperity?

" However, do not rejoice that the spirits submit to you, but rejoice that your names are written in heaven." Isn't that prosperity?

At that time Jesus, full of joy through the Holy Spirit, said, "I praise you, Father, Lord of heaven and earth, because you have hidden these things from the wise and learned, and revealed them to little children. Yes, Father, for this was your good pleasure."

How to start?

It was this very question Abed asked me. I told him: Money is knocking every day at your door but you refuse to open. Wake up every day and open your doors. Listen to the door and keep expecting. Eventually money will show up and enter. The first step however is in answering the question, "Are you ready to change?" If you are, take a walk around the house or jog around a track but keep listening for the call. It may come with the bang of thunder, with the light of fire or in a silence of a whisper. What is true is that prosperity is not a reserve of the rich but a gift on offer for whoever may want to pick it up.

Money comes to your pocket. You refuse to let it stay and live there. The poor tolerate holes in their pockets and crazy enough they expect money to keep in the pockets. If you were money and you came to a person who does not want to host you, would you stay for a night?

Where ever you go in Dar, be it in a shop, home or office, you are greeted with "Karibuni" meaning , "You are welcome and feel free to do whatever you want here." In the rare event of landing in a wrong place or being greeted with "Whom are you looking for?" or "May I help you?" you would certainly know that the next thing is to escort you out.

You have to distinguish between the rich and the poor. When the poor get money they spend it immediately. They buy food, travel in buses and other public transport vehicles, pay for water, pay for electricity or school fees. The truth is that by the time money comes in it has already been spent up. The poor who are lucky to meet these expenses remain as broke as they were before money came in except that this month's rent is paid up. It is immaterial to say that the poor live beyond their means or spend more than they earn. They always do and they will always do.

The rich are different. They always eat out in big and expensive hotels and they are always invited for free dinners. They fly from place to place but their air tickets, hotel expenses and entertainment bills are taken care of by somebody else. The very rich do not even sign (I do not mean to pay) their hotel bills. They drive in limousines and they do not care a dime whether diesel is cheaper than petrol. They are rich and all they care is to attract money. They do not spend money. They save it. They do not call it saving however. They invent a new word: Invest.

Are you ready to change from poverty to prosperity? If you were given a choice to be rich or to be poor and that to achieve either you need the same effort, what would you choose?

When you stay with poor people you realize one other factor why they never move out of poverty. I said it before but I can repeat it here. They move in circles. When a rich man consults you and you give him an advice he values, he immediately leaves whatever he is doing and implements the advice right away. The poor are not like that. They go away as if determined and then they start thinking negatively of your advice. "What if this problem arises?" they say. The next day they will be having complaints and excuses. We must not grow weary of helping others or better put we should not be worn out by others.

Abed moved from one question to another. To help myself out I sent him an email.

"Abed, I do not condemn you that you are poor because you are lazy. I am a great defender of the poor. If I were in court I would stand firm and say, "Lord Justice, The man standing before me can do so many things at the same time. That is not an act of a lazy man".

"You push barrows, run errands for different masters, wait for money, chase business lines in all directions, and sell everything from apples to zebra skins. You do much of this on an empty stomach and yet you do not complain or lay down. On the charge of being called, 'Lazy', you are acquitted. You are not lazy in the slightest sense of the word.

"I however have this against you. There are moments when you are engaged in too many things. If you try to do too much, you hurt yourself. You are not able to finish your work and you are not able to get away from it either. You work like a slave, you get paid as a slave but you get behind all the time. This is called 'Momentary Insanity'. In a court of law all you can plead for is leniency not forgiveness. We cannot blame your poverty on you except on the choices you make.

"Well, let one who has never sinned be the first one to condemn you. I said it in the last pages of Face to Face with Grief that our life is not determined by the reasons we give but by the choices we make. I know where I have been. I have no right to condemn you. I however have the experience to tell you that in a world there is always someone who is very poor and not up to any task. He may be slow, ignorant, sick and in need of help. God himself finds this man worth helping, pulls him out of the mad, puts him on his feet and pushes him up the ladder. And this man could be you.

"I have learnt my lessons. When you analyze it all you see that in one way or another that poor man pleased God. Do not make fun of someone who has fallen on hard times and is dressed in rags. Bees compared to other insects are very small but the honey they make is the sweetest of all foods. It is very easy for God to make the poor person suddenly rich. He could see the bee in him and he may love that quality. Sometimes God's wisdom is man's foolishness. We might be looking at the same thing. I might be thinking of your lack of focus but God might be looking at the juice.

"If success or failure is up to God to make, I do not suggest you go home and sleep waiting for God to make up his mind. There is a choice for you to make meanwhile. If you were given a choice to be rich or to be poor and that to achieve either you need the same effort what would you choose?

"Which one is easier to borrow one million dollars or to save one million dollars? In whichever choice you take, how many people do you need to know before you achieve your goal?

"I believe you have made up your choice. I can even guess that you have chosen prosperity over poverty. Yes you have made a good choice but you cannot start moving unless you take the first step. You cannot however move to prosperity unless you know what you are doing. The first step is to admit that prosperity or poverty is all a matter of personal choice. You choose your goal and then you determine your path".

I admit I gave Abed quite a long lecture. You will be glad to learn that Abed moved from poverty to prosperity. He does not accredit every bit of his success on my teaching but I am grateful he did what I said. You can succeed if you really want. All you have is to try and try. Getting rich is the same as getting in shape. You do not try this diet and this and that. You follow one menu up to the end.

(1) Get a piece of paper and pen.
(2) Write your name or choose a pen-name that implies not how good you are but how good you want to be.
(3) Complete this declaration.

'I ...... (penname)........................... Do declare of my own free will, having been cautioned that I am free to say nothing and do nothing but whatever I may put in writing could be taken in evidence against me, hereby state my desire to change/keep the status quo# Delete as appropriate. This is my choice at the moment. Later on I can add, alter or correct my thinking.

(4) If given a choice to be rich or to be poor and that to achieve either I need the same effort I choose …………..

(5) I recognize that though I am entitled to growing rich, prosperity cannot come to me effortless. I therefore undertake to love and to show love habitually to others starting from those nearest to me outwards. I will always keep my heart happy and commit my mouth to reflecting this feeling. I write down on this paper 5 attitudes I hate and I undertake to remove from my life and swear to replace them immediately with their corresponding opposites. These are:

Old Attitude	New attitude
1	1
2	2
3	3
4	4
5	5

I tell you we do not need to go beyond this point. You have now whatever it takes to grow from poverty to prosperity. It is not the talks but the walks that changes a man's position. I know this prescription works because it worked on Abed. I know the story to be true because the doctor was me. I have further checked on it and I found that St.Peter too gave a similar prescription to his disciples. In his letter marked 1 Peter 2:1 he wrote, "Put away all malice and all guile and insincerity and envy and all slander."

I have changed so much since then. My joy is not so much that Abed prospered (that is for him to enjoy) but that as he went up I climbed further up. I now do not have to give long lectures. If a man challenges my principles, I just say, "Look at Abed." I no longer try to understand things which are too hard for me, or investigate matters which are beyond my power to know. I do not compliment a person on his good looks basing myself on his height or weight. On the other hand I do not look down upon the poor, prevent them from making a living or keep them waiting in their need. Many are presidents who have ended their careers in jail while their offices are taken over by people never heard of before.

I told you that I envied young men and women reading this book. On the other hand I admire old age. When you are old or know you are getting old you realize there is no more time to waste in sorrow, failed ventures, regrets, gossip, quarrels or conflicts. You have to use the remaining time enjoying yourself. You no longer look for money but prosperity. You become conscious that if you touched tar it would soil your hands. You strive to keep in good company. "Hurting people hurt."

You do not try to lift things which are too heavy for you. That is called stress. Stress leads to depression. That is a real sickness. "Sticky thinking sickens".

When people come asking, "What can I do to prosper?"
You answer, "Seek wisdom."
You do not go into giving long lectures like I gave Abed but you simply say, "You do not have because you do not ask".
Then they say, "What do you mean?"
" Isaiah 65"

Then they go and find it themselves.
"The Lord says," I was ready to respond, but no one asked for help. I was ready to be found, but no one was looking for me. I said, 'Here I am, here I am!' to a nation that did not call on my name. All day long I opened my arms to a rebellious people, but they followed their own evil paths and their own crooked schemes".
It is up to them to read on and on and so on. They check and they find they are the people being talked about. Every author knows that his book will be read by people he will never meet and by generations he will never live in.

In my old age I have no time to complete the sentence, "Seek yee first the kingdom of God and the rest shall follow."

What do I say?

"Seek wisdom (full stop)".

Old age has taught me that when you do a good deed know who is benefiting from it otherwise your effort would be wasted. Now when someone asks: How to get started my answer is simple and clear: Cast away your fear……

I say it this way because I have grown to learn the language of the devil. This is what I call any opposing spirit. When I want a man to prosper because he works like a bee, I respectively ask myself why God would want this same man to prosper. Then I discover it is because he makes honey. When I get this, I out of duty decide to change my reasoning. I then want him to prosper because 'he makes honey'. Yes, God's wisdom is man's foolishness but it is more foolish to think oneself wiser than God. It was God who knit me in my mother's womb and that is a challenge no one can dare overthrow.

It happens many times I take this attitude to life situations. There is always a voice on my mind that says, "Bees can sting and it bloody hurts. Whoever has known bees would testify how deadly these insects can be. Honey may be sweet but bees' life style violates any reason for loving honey."

When I hear this, my answer is one, "Get behind me Devil. You are standing in my way!"

Now when someone asks: How to get started my answer is simple and clear: Cast away your fear……starting from where you are.

CHAPTER SEVEN

DREAM

Last night I had a dream. The setting was some time about two weeks after Christmas but certainly before the New Year. Do not be bothered about the timing because the author of miracles is still at work. Unless someone created a 4-6-year-day how did we jump from 4-6BC (being Before Christ) to 1 AD (Birth Year of Our lord) in just one night? When issues are becoming complicated, confusing and argumentative the solution is to take one choice and be satisfied with that. Actually the BC/AD dating system is not found in the Bible. This system for numbering calendar years was invented by Dionysius Exiguus in 525 AD on assignment by Pope St.John 1 to determining the correct date for Easter for use by all churches.

Yes history confuses me too. Why did one who was commissioned to fix Easter ended up fixing Christmas?

It is interesting to note that Dionysius intended to make the birth of Jesus Christ the dividing point of world history. However, when the calendar was being calculated, the year of Jesus' birth fell around 4-6 BC, not 1 AD. Whatever happened, it is fitting that Jesus Christ is the separation of "old" and "new." BC was "Before Christ" and since His birth, we have been living "In the year of our Lord." Philippians 2:10-11. What is important for one to start his journey from poverty to prosperity is to believe that one mind is better than two. The main issue is I had a dream.

It must have been hard economic times for my family. We rented out one of our bedrooms to a holiday tourist Latvin by name. I do not know how long she stayed with us or where she came from because the dream started just as I mentioned earlier 'some time after Christmas'.

My wife Letty was out either shopping or out at church. For sure I do not know where she was. I was alone in the sitting room and then this lady Latvin walked to me. Of all things I noticed first was her elegant beauty in her long blue dress. She was in her mid-thirties.

My house was well in order. I felt some kind of pride and comfort as you get when visitors come to see you and find your house clean. This is exactly what I felt when Latvin came to see me. I cannot explain this feeling since she was now living with us. Anyway feelings are feelings and this is one feeling I never dismissed. She came in and I felt happy.

I noticed one thing however. There was nothing on my dining table except one old visa card. She did not talk about it but I felt like hiding the card. I did not. It was too late. She had seen it. I felt ashamed. Again I did not understand why I should have been ashamed of having a credit card.

She asked me how I was planning to go through the new year. She was particularly concerned with how I would raise school fees for my son Justice. She had mercy in her eyes and she offered to help. She said she would write me a cheque meeting all my son's expenses. This was a grand new year gift. I thought I had come face to face with an angel. We all believe in angels, don't we? I did not think it at that time but you can start growing rich by opening your door to strangers. Some opened their houses to angels that way.

The show kind of moved quickly forward. My wife was standing behind me in awe of this visitor. She was beating her chest shouting, "Praise God, Praise God."

My daughter Faith was seated opposite me explaining to Latvin how we had survived the hard times up to the moment. I felt beaten by her and I wanted her to keep quiet. I think it is a normal parental feeling to think that children sometimes talk too much. Oh my God, oh my God how I longed for her to keep quiet but the more I gazed at her the more she talked. My parents had a rule that children should greet visitors but should never talk to them. I had not passed this training to my children.

Faith explained to Latvin that I had two credit cards: one a Master Card and the other a Visa Card. What we used to do is to borrow money from the Master card and pay the Visa card and then vice versa. As money became scarcer we stopped paying back the whole sum borrowed but used the other card to pay off the interest rates. By Christmas we had gone beyond the credit limit on the visa card. That is why it was lying discarded on the table. It would not be long before the Master Card was cut too. Then we would all eat our last meal and die.

The rich young lady handled me four cheque leaves. I do not exactly know what she was paying for but I recall she was meeting all my debts, paying off her dues and commitments. She was making me debt free.

I grabbed the cheques and passed them over to Letty. Latvin resisted a bit saying I had to sign for them first. She asked me how much I was in debt. How much was the principle amount I owed on my cards. How much I had paid back so far and how much was due. How much I had paid in interest rates alone. To all these questions I answered, "I do not know."

Latvin went on to explain that if we had to move out of poverty we had to take responsibility for our progress. We had to start by opening books of accounts. We had to record each and every coin that came in or went out. We had to know on our finger tips our income and our expenses. We had to run profit and loss accounts and we had to have a balance sheet every month. The poor are poor not because they do not have but because they cannot account for their wealth.

Latvin taught us a very important principle in book keeping. She taught us that if we were spending Tsh 500 per day on our meals it is not enough to know that we spend that much each day. If we spent TSh 500 yesterday we would need to record it down and forget about it. Today we would not have to worry about where the Tsh 1000 went but we would know that today's burden was worth Tsh 500 not Tsh 1000. We would not worry ourselves of raising today's Tsh 500 and tomorrow's Tsh 500 because tomorrow's record is made tomorrow. This principle of keeping our books in order would improve our income by minimizing our worries. A worried mind is always a disorganized mind.

She repeated what I already knew. She said if I were to prosper I would start by

(1) Deciding to prosper,
(2) Casting away my fear, and
(3) Opening a book of accounts.

Latvin took me out for a walk.

Just about 50m from my home was a big tree and down there in its shade was lying a street sleeper. I may have ever seen him before but I had never paid much regard. This time Latvin stopped and greeted him. They looked like acquaintances. My heart said, "Why should this young lady sit down with this lunatic?"

I saw Latvin remove her high heeled shoes and climb the tree. The beggar was leading her up. In my mind I criticized her not only because I thought it was culturally incorrect for women to climb trees and more so when they are wearing dresses. I stayed down at the trunk of the tree and I saw them going up and up and up.

There was a mixture of anger and disbelief in my head. Latvin was my visitor and surely she should have had the courtesy to tell me of what she wanted to do or where she wanted to go. She did none of these and she was just climbing and seemingly enjoying herself and leaving me in pain down. If all she wanted was to hurt me she could have left me home. It was like walking a friend to a beach and she joins another company and leaves you there alone to do whatever you may want. I am writing this book from Kipepeo and I have documented the pain men endure when they bring Changu Doas to the beach. When the music starts the Changu Doas stand up and dance with whoever. When the song ends they just move on with the new guy as if nothing had happened. I did not want to live the pain of the men who walk them in but here I was deserted at the bottom of the tree.

Latvin went up and more and more beggars came and climbed the tree and went to her company. I saw the tree covered with beggars. Each and every bit of tree had beggars on it. I wondered where they all came from. I then realized there were so many beggars living in that tree only that I had never paid any attention to them. This was different from those men climbing up the economic ladder. These were beggars coming in with a spirit of joy and celebrations and all of them dressed in kind of blue jean uniforms. I knew they were beggars but they were not begging. They were not fighting. They were not dirty. They were not stealing but somehow I knew they were street sleepers. They adored Latvin and she loved them so much. This hurt me so. How did Latvin find them? How did she develop such a binding relationship with them? Putting envy aside, I kept on wondering how come there were so many street sleepers in my neighbourhood and yet I had never seen them or perhaps seen only one?

The answer came to my mind. I had not searched. When you look for money it comes to you. These beggars flowed in numbers to Latvin because she searched for them. She went to where they were and more and more flew to her. She extended her helping hand to them and so they went to her. True with money we have to go to the market and offer our service and money will flow into our pockets. Latvin showed me beggars in my neighbourhood the way I show you money in your neighbourhood.

I woke up.

CHAPTER EIGHT

FENCES

I explained in Chapter Six (sorry if I didn't) that attitudes are the fences that deter one from going forward.

Ismail is not the only man of his kind. The Butterfly is fenced off to cut away men like him from the peace and tranquility of the beach. Poverty and crime are closely associated. At the time of going to print it had not been clearly established who breeds the other.

There is a high fence and a big gate at Kipepeo. The entrance is guarded by strong men with guns. Whoever wants to enter must pay a dollar. None can come to the beach unless he has gone through this gate. There is an unwritten inscription on the gate:

"I was built to separate heaven from hell, the rich from the poor, the full from the starving, and the healthy from the sick. Come through me if you have a dollar or Tanzanian shillings 1000 and I will give you rest—not as the heavens promise but as the world gives.

All ye who are heavily indebted and burdened, look through the fence and see how good it is to be rich. If you are naked or half naked inside the fence that is civilization but if you are naked or half naked outside the fence that is primitive. Decide today to get rich and civilized.

The rich are never wrong but mistaken.
The rich are never late but delayed.
The rich are never angry but upset."

We are talking about this fence that separates the rich from the poor. At one part of the fence the wall is built in concrete. The wall shades the rich from onlookers. It gives the impression that the poor are poor because they are either lazy or cursed. Interestingly gathering the data for this book I have interviewed a lot of people. I have come to the conclusion that the rich in fact do not think that way. It is the poor who think that the rich do. I have also found another truth. There is nobody called, "They". When someone comes warning you not to do something because, "They may misunderstand you or blame you or whatever......;" firmly ask: Who are they?

Nevertheless, there is some truth in the statement the poor make of themselves. The poor are stinky and dirty. They spend all their life disturbing the rich begging for alms. Instead of looking for work they stand outside the fence gazing and staring all their life out. They are usually sick and full of problems. They are either stealing or about to steal. When I speak this way I sound as if that dream turned me against the poor. No. I stand in defense of the poor though I strongly agree they should keep their books monthly.

Some poor people are worse than the way that description puts it. They are too lazy to put food in their mouth. They cannot feed their families and cannot send their own children to school. The little money they get they feed prostitutes. Isn't poverty a curse and if it is, aren't poor people cursed?

So the rich say, "Let them be fenced off".

Outside the fence is a parking lot for the rich man's cars. No one except the driver is allowed to come near this spot. The poor yes may not steal the cars but may steal the driving mirrors or the side lights. If they do not do that they may write insulting remarks on cars. No one but the poor-at-heart writes on another man's car, "Clean me please!"

The rich want to save money. They have had this park designated as a free parking lot. Ironically this is called a return on their investment. The way they look at it is, "One by One makes a bundle".

I understand it was difficult for the management of this beach to offer this space for free. It was called free parking but the signboard read, "Parking on your own risk." Abed tells the story. I recorded the conversation and I quote it verbatim.

"If you want to ask somebody to do something for you, before you speak pause and ask yourself, 'How can I make him or her do it?' You do not need to go to university or be a womanizer to learn this, do you?

"I had just returned from Japan with a new Prado and of course a new girlfriend. (Prosperity comes with good things! Prosperity means getting one good thing and many others added. Prosperity is a package; Richness+ Health+ Happiness+ Joy+ Peace+ Shalom and everything to the full that there is nothing broken, missing or leaking).

"There was a strong urge in me to impress my girl that I truly belonged to the New Breed of Gentlemen. I wasn't white alright but my wealth had removed my collar bars and I could mingle with people of all races. Despite the risk of losing her, my struggling mind wanted to take her to the Paradise Beach which was frequented by whites only (and a handful of super rich Indians). I aspired to belong to such a 'race-less' community because I believed prosperity is wealth without borders. On the other hand bank managers, politicians, the people with influence or those who can lend you a million dollars sit in such places.

"I pulled in my cruiser like any other. I noticed on parking that all available space had been marked, "Specially Reserved". To me this was revolting. I had read that President Nyerere had decreed that with independence Tanzania had embraced the principle of 'Prosperity without Boarders'. Kariako, Oyster Bay and Central belonged to all peoples.

"I knew right away that this guard was just following orders. There was no way I could fail to find space on the beach. I was not asking for a stool or some special seat. I wanted some safe space to park my car knowing that at the end of the day tires will not be inflated, side lights vandalized or side mirrors removed. I was simply going to swim about in the sea and walk about the beach, naked or half naked. What was this nonsense that the beach could be full?

"I decided to park in one of the marked spaces and face whatever music could arise. There is something I identify with as a man and I cannot tolerate. I cannot stand someone who belittles me in front of my lover.

"I was ready for a fight but my girlfriend asked me to consider if I had thought out all other options. She actually suggested going to the Butterfly Beach (Sunrise Gate) instead.

"I swore some words against the guard I later learnt never to repeat. I will not say those words to you because I now know that using bad language or not taming one's tongue frustrates your life up. I pulled out my keys and drove to the adjacent entry making sure that with my power drive I had covered the guard well in dust.

"Butterfly Beach has two entries. The one I tried to use first is rightly called VIP Gate and it is for members only. About 100m away from here lays the Sunrise Gate that admits everybody who is not a 'very important person'.

"I was just parking and a guard (similar in color and uniform to the one before) appeared. He told me that I could park but I would be charged one American dollar or Tsh 1000 for entrance and park on my own risk. I felt like driving off again but chose to see the manager instead. Naturally I did not want to pay for what I could get for free but more than that what was the point of discussing such a thing with a guard?

"Poor people are not accustomed to free service. He would certainly simply say, "I'm only a guard". If I talked to the cashier, she would say, "I'm only a cashier". If I talked to the gateman he too would answer, "I'm only a gateman". Employees the world over are only interested in keeping their jobs. They are not interested in doing their work. If they did what they were interested in many of them would grow rich , move on to prosperity and quit their donkey work. They work themselves to retirement and when asked what they liked best about their job they cannot name any. These retire poor and old.

"The guards were not interested in whether I ate beans or beef. They were not interested in my job or colour or in my girlfriend. They were interested in themselves. They were interested in living cheque to mouth. They were interested in paying their utility bills. They were not interested in prosperity. They were only interested in surviving. They thought prosperity is for the top 5% of any nation and poverty is for us all. As far as I am concerned they were mistaken in their thinking, mistaken in their belief, mistaken in their feelings and mistaken in their actions. Their desire to grow to prosperity has been numbed by the false sense of security.

"What can I do for you, Young Man?" the Manager greeted.

"I took his hand with a hard grip, sized him up from up, down, down and down to his shoes and up to his badge and back to his eyes. I did this all along holding his hand.

"I saluted: 'Salaam Alek. (May Peace be With You) Mr. Manager' (then I remembered that what people love best about themselves is their names) and I started again. 'Mr. Buxter, God Bless You, listen to me. You know John (his badge read John Buxter but addressing him in this way was for cooling him down. I was turning him from a stranger to a friend).

'I was a bit shocked when I was told I had to pay for parking here. I have been to places like Tokyo, Yokohama, Kumaguchi but I have never seen the like here. Anyone beach in Tokyo has more cars than we have in all our beaches combined and have much less of parking space than we have. The Japanese would be justified if they charged entrance fees but they do not and they ensure that parking is safe. Where is the basis for this surcharge of yours?'

"I do not blame you John. Perhaps if I had been in your position and took your job and found the policy in practice I wouldn't have changed it. No. If I were the real boss I would have changed it. If I were a new manager and did not find the policy in position I wouldn't have introduced it. I hate employing last century's methodologies to run this age. You know to me this surcharge stinks like an outdated income tax. It does not raise revenue but sucks it.

"You know John I am a Manager too in my enterprise. It might be smaller though. What makes a difference between you and me is that I invest my energy and time in minding my own business but you spend your time and energy in someone else's business. When I am thinking of making my business grow you are waiting for promotion. I wonder who is not wasting time!

"But this is not about you or me. A duty of all managers is to make money for the firm and the more money they bring in the better they are appreciated. They are then promoted until they reach the top of the ladder and that is when they aspire to run the business and then they are pulled down 'lest they stand on their own". I am not frightening you but if the path to prosperity you have taken means work and more hard work, promotion and more promotion , think of the time it takes to grow rich. You might retire before you grow rich. Now let's take a piece of paper and figure out what it means to you to have a free parking lot".

Abed took a piece of paper from the file the manager was carrying. He folded it into two halves and one column he headed 'ADVANTAGES' and the other he called 'DISADVANTAGES.' Under <u>Free Parking</u> he wrote, "You will have many more cars on average. Assuming four passengers per car, your Gate Collection from individual visitors will increase to more than double the present capacity.

Under Disadvantages/Charged Parking he wrote," You are going to wipe out your income from people like me. I will not park here and I will not visit your beach either. The added income from me will be zero.

Under advantages he wrote: Many cars, many visitors. That is good advertisement. TV and poster advertisements are expensive these days. This is a big investment, isn't it?

The third advantage said that many families will be able to bring their children along. Children are big spenders, aren't they? Businesses grow with big spenders. If you had a choice between running a wholesale shop and retail shop, which one would you choose?

He scribbled more advantages and disadvantages and handed the sheet to the manager. He then returned to his car and told the manager to consider both scenarios. The manager walked back to his office but Abed stayed in his car talking to his girlfriend and playing music.

After ten minutes or so the manager returned and said, "For this time only I grant you free parking. The Board will decide on the overall policy later."

Three days later Abed received a letter in his mail from the Butterfly Beach Management Company thanking him for his patronage and informing him that from then on the parking lot would be free and secure.

Abed concluded, "Taking a choice is not enough in itself. You must follow the choice with an action. Choice without action like faith without action is dead. Take it for granted that god seen or unseen is with you all the time and will fight for you. I just sat resting in my car and God's spirit went with the manager to the office."

Note that Abed got what he wanted not because of what he did but the way he did it. He never mentioned what he wanted. He concentrated on what the manager wanted and would be able to hear. The management wanted not to entertain people but to make money out of them. In fact none of the managers on the Beach Board was a professional entertainer–musician or comedian. They were money makers. They saw the opportunity and wanted to make money out of it.

Having mentioned that, I want to point out that this truth may be relative to whom you are talking with. The Chinese world seems to be handling things differently. I am told the Chinese method is for one to lay out what is in his best interests in disregard of what the opposite end may want. They advise to mark up your personal needs to 125% until you wear out the other party with your demands. As a matter of compromise, you both lower your interests and this way you achieve at least 100% of your needs. Shake hands and call this a "Win-Win Solution."

The position of this book is that if Abed had gone in claiming his citizen rights to move freely in "Bongoland" and organized strikes for open access to beaches he would still be camping out up to this day. The choice to adopt the Win-win system is up to you. What we are pointing out is that some people might be shaking the ladder to stop you from climbing up and others might be fencing off the ladder to stop you from reaching it but these obstacles must not numb your drive to prosperity.

To breakdown fences that are standing in your way, learn three things from Abed.

(1) Realize you are on a mission;
(2) Have confidence in your techniques; and
(3) Believe God is with you and will not forsake you.

Man is not self sufficient. You will always need the assistance of another to climb over the fence. It is not necessarily true that because you are in need you will obviously get assistance. In fact your greatest obstacle may be the one with the key to assisting you. You cannot therefore go into an open argument with one with authority over you. Arguments never win. Even if you get what you want given that you have got it on the expense of hurting someone else's pride, dignity, reasoning and capacity, this is not victory. You did not get it in good faith. A good action done with bad attitude is bad.

Put it this way: When we are wrong, we may feel it within ourselves and perhaps be even ready to confess it to others. We may be ready to change or follow the right path. What we may not be able to accept is to changing as a point of weakness. If some outsider comes to feed us with force on some facts, we are bound to defend our self esteem. Most mothers know it that babies would rather choose sleeping to feeding by force. You remember a man who went manual? People demand their dignity. Rich and poor people do. Poor or rich we all walk with two legs. We all belong to the same body. We all belong to the same human race and we all subscribe to the same principle: You cannot change a man against himself. A man convinced against his own will is like one who confesses under duress or who sleeps with a quarrelsome wife. His opinion stands but changes at the earliest opportunity.

Abed's approach is based on seeing life in the other person's point of view. We often fail to work with the rich because we emphasize what we want not what the rich want in us. Of course you know what you want and that defines your starting point. It is in your heart not in anybody else's. Understand your position as a poor. Understand your dependence on the rich. Communicate to the rich how helpful to him you could be and seek to develop that relationship. Handle your interests as your personal property. Do not force others to lead your thinking and then condemn them for neglecting your feelings. Arrogance, dirt and hooliganism cannot earn you your daily bread. Share each other's interests. Tell them what they want to hear. Respect every moment you talk to someone richer than you as if you were on a job interview. The only way to influence other people is to talk about what they want to hear and show them what they have to get.

I know what I am talking about. I want to make more money by selling Face to Face with Grief. I do not say that straight to you.

I tell you how you could benefit by reading my book. I envisage the reader saying, "If I wanted to read Face to Face with Grief I could have bought it. I want to read The Desire of All Ages: How to make Money and move from Poverty to Prosperity with no falling back". If you are that reader I give you some extra bargain. Send me a mail at <u>Kayiwa Foundations, P.O.Box 91185 TST, Hongkong</u> and state your complaint. Tell me that you have read up to page 81 and that still you have no hope of getting prosperous. Tell me why. Based on your recommendation I may remove a number of pages in the next edition. I may not give your money back but I may make you glad by following your advice and I could somehow mention your name in the acknowledgement page. As for making so much money that you may move from poverty to prosperity and remain on top of things all depends on the choices that you take. You choose to be poor or to be rich. You choose to trust those who encourage you or those who discourage you. You choose to follow your weaknesses or your strengths. You choose to walk by plan or by accident.

If you were given a choice to be rich or to be poor and that to achieve either you need the same effort, what would you choose?

If you were given a choice to borrow one million dollars or to save one million dollars which one would you choose?

If you were given a minute to define yourself in your own words or to give five excuses tying you in poverty what would you do?

If you were told that all your life is going to be destroyed but you were given one piece of it to choose to be preserved what would you choose?

If you were told that the road to prosperity begins at the mark immediately after procrastination how long would you wait before taking action?

I said it in the beginning of this book that on the road to prosperity there are no hidden secrets or formula. If there were any hidden secrets or treasures I would have given them away and be hanged for it. All I can quote to you, "Blessed are the eyes that see what you see. For I tell you that many prophets and kings wanted to see what you see but did not see it, and to hear what you hear but did not hear it."

In this chapter I have mentioned two ways of holding an argument. You need knowledge to keep on talking but you need wisdom to keep on reasoning. What distinguishes this book from many other "Prosperity Ministry Series" or "Get Rich Schemes" is that it believes in the existence of absolute truth. That absolute truth is called Wisdom and it is God's copyright. That is why we included above, "(3) Believe God is with you and will not forsake you."

In fact this is an important strategy in overcoming poverty. I could call it the fourth principle in breaking down fences. This is the principle of idolizing Christ. Talk like him. Think like him. Act like him. This is in line with the principle of matching man's wisdom with God's wisdom. This cannot be foolishness! When walking on roads, seated in your houses or talking to your children, talk about him.

The fourth principle seems to be an expansion of the idea, "Believe God is with you and will not forsake you". Yes all these principles work together for the good of man. So when you 'Believe God is with you and will not forsake you' you are effectively 'casting away your fears'. On the other hand you are testing and putting 'confidence in your techniques' which in turn 'fulfills your mission'.

This chapter however will not be complete if I do not point out that it is not the responsibility of those who build fences to take them down. It is your responsibility who is fenced off to break down the barriers. Remember these barriers are not actually as physical as they may appear. They are spiritual. They are within your own thinking. You cannot touch and feel your attitudes. You cannot see them but you can hear them. You can enlist them yourself. In addition someone may come and point them out to you. Do not be hard-hearted or hot-tempered. Simply ask who is there to blame you. If there is none, rejoice for prosperity is within your grasp. The fences that deter you from going forward are broken.

CHAPTER NINE

GOAL

"Alright" you might say, 'I might change my attitude, my beliefs, my thinking pattern but what shall I do to those forces to which I have no control?"

This is a very good question. You may be broke, sick and homeless but you realize none of these has anything to do with your journey except that these are the things–reasons and excuses– to get rid of as you prosper. Their only purpose is to discourage you.

As you were born the world gave you a choice to live or to die. Babies choose crying to laughing. Nurses and mothers interpret this as tears of joy. It is hard to live but you picked courage and lived anyway. Living is a matter of picking choices. You have to choose to be happy or sad. You hear people say, "I cannot forgive you". Whoever says so does this because one has made up a choice to be unhappy. One knows pretty well that if one forgives you, you will be happy and your happiness might overflow onto him. He might become happy too and this might oppose his first choice. We do not forgive others lest we are forgiven. The hardest part to recite with meaning in the Lord's Prayer is, "Forgive our sins as we forgive those who wrong us." It loses meaning before you mention it. We may not be able to change our history but we may be able to forgive it. The question is: Do you want to be a prisoner of your past, a pioneer of your future or a passenger of your presence?

You cannot live by carrying all your yesterdays. You will end up in hospital. Stress is a disease for those who carry more than they can lift. If you cannot manage carrying your baggage of today, do not add on that of yesterday. Yesterday could have been such a burden. Today has its own burden. Why do you load yourself with two luggages? Make your suffering easy. Carry today's baggage today. Carry tomorrow's luggage tomorrow. You either do it this way or you will lose your salvation, suffer rejection, get depressed and lose forgiveness as you will not be able to forgive others and above all else lose your promised prosperity.

I met one disorganized man. His theme song was Olivia Newton John's "Hopelessly Devoted To You." What I like about this song is the idea, "My head says, 'Fool forget him' and my heart says, 'Do not let him go.'

I propose an exercise here. Go to www.youtube.com and play this song. Again I admit some people who move in circles might prefer to jump this exercise because they know the song in their heads anyway. I guess you will not be the first to be heartbroken and your eyes not the first to cry! He rejected my advice and he has remained disorganized.

If two people are to walk together don't they have to agree? Let us agree then that those issues that put one into trouble are not the same issues that have to put one out of trouble. Let us agree that your belief system determines your sight. Let us agree that our tongue is creative and whatever we say to ourselves comes to pass. Lets us agree therefore that when we talk to our bodies positively they react positively and vice versa. Let us agree not to listen to those who try to discourage, to criticize or to condemn us. Let us not be concerned with what we cannot do but with what we can do.

Look at your skin. It might be showing signs of a perishing body. Your wrinkles might be showing what you have gone through. Your skin might be dry and even giving away. These are real symptoms of body decay. Your hair may be talking about the time you are left with on earth. Despite all that do not say, "I will be happy when my debts are paid or when my life changes." That will not take away your wrinkles. That will not take away your gray hair. That will not take away your dandruff. However a little dye on your head will take away your gray hair. A little foundation will bury your wrinkles and a little oil will take away your dandruff.

I agree feelings and actions should go together. On the other hand I am glad they usually do not. If we had to wait to be happy until our desires are met how many people would die in sorrow? Eat even when you are not hungry. Rejoice even when you are unhappy. In the midst of all your troubles, while you are still buried in your bills, still being tormented by your poverty and being enslaved by your creditors find one good reason to thank God for the day. Cheer up yourself even if you find nothing to celebrate about. One method works. When you cannot find anything to encourage you find somebody to encourage. You may quote this if you so wish, "In the world you will suffer but do not grieve over it, cheer up instead for I, your friend, has gone through it all and conquered suffering."

> There is truth and life in such statements:
> Be led by actions not by feelings.
> You may feel angry but do not be angry.
> You may feel wrong but do not do wrong.

Prosperity is not a miracle. What is miraculous in something that occurs as expected? Prosperity was promised to us by God and it is ours by right. We just have to press our claim on it. I will say what I said before: We can overcome poverty and prosperity is for us all. I have removed the bold characters because it is no longer bold to say so. It is just true. The concept is the same as withdrawing money from your bank account using an Automated Teller Machine (ATM) card. As long as the money is in the bank, and you enter the right pin number in the machine, money will pour out. In our case prosperity is in the account. We have the pin number. All we need is to key in the number and enter.

We can make money, move from poverty to prosperity and do not fall back if we can determine what kind of money we are talking about. Another exercise: Sit and imagine two men came to you to borrow some money. A said, "Can you lend me US 10?" and B said, "Can you lend me some money?" whom would you give?

Once upon a time, a very strong army invaded a small country. The capital fell sooner than expected. The invading battalion was so ahead of its field commanders that when the city fell it did not know which flag to host. It did not know either whether to stay on, attack another city or return home that the mission had been accomplished. History judged the war badly. The invading army lost the war because it had no exit strategy.

This idea came to mind when President George Walker Bush visited Tanzania on a state visit that was drawn to define his legacy. He arrived at Tanzania's Mwalimu Julius Nyerere International Airport with all the pompous of the most powerful man in the world. He came with three huge aeroplanes with hundreds of bodyguards. Roads were closed and his entourage moved with sirens to warn the world that a war machine was passing. He distributed money wherever he went to the tune of US700 million dollars towards fighting poverty, ignorance and disease.

To this man President Kikwete of Tanzania said, "Mr. President many people have mixed views about your legacy". He was speaking for many people who questioned and wondered how come that such a powerful man could not defeat Iraq or the rag-tag Taliban army of Afghanistan.

The answer was clear. He went to war without defining his exit strategy. He had no goal.

If you want to move from poverty to prosperity and make no return, choose your exit strategy now. Choose your exit strategy before you plan your upward journey. Choose your exit strategy before you plan your attack.

Do you want to make money just to pay your bills?
Do you want to make money enough for your family to go on holiday?
Do you want to make money so that you have a roof on your head after your retirement?
Do you want to make money so that you may retire young and retire rich?
Do you want to make money so that you may get a decent funeral?
What is your purpose in getting rich?

The Bible says, "When you pray you do not get what you are praying for because you have bad motives." This is not a condemnation or judgment against you. "My people perish because of lack of knowledge". It is not because of health. It is not because of lack of accommodation or employment that they perish, it is because of lack of knowledge. It is not because of lack of money that they perish…..repeat after me…."My people perish …My people perish because of lack of knowledge…... because of lack of knowledge. My people perish because of lack of knowledge". You need to know very well what 'those forces to which you have no control over are. Pack them and forget about them. Have nothing to do with them. Do not think about them. Do not meditate about them. Any living thing that is not fed starves to death.

Growing rich is like building a house. In building a house the most important thing is not laying the foundation but finishing the house. The foundation may be huge and deep, the walls may be tall and strong but if you die without putting a roof to your house you will have built yourself a magnificent Wall of Shame.

Tick what you want.

( ) Make at least one dollar a day.
( ) Make at least ten dollars a day.
( ) Make at least a hundred dollars a day.
( ) Make five hundred dollars a day.
( ) Make one thousand dollars a day

In the space below write why you made the choice you made
_____
_____
_____
_____
_____
_____

You could have made the choice based on your own experience. Suppose God said, "Go into the world and multiply and I am sending you in the world of wolves and I knew you even before you were created in your mother's stomach and you are my son and I am your father and you shall have no other father but me and I am sending you in the world of wolves to be my ambassador", how much money would he send you off with?

Suppose God said, "Everything in the world is mine and I give it to you", how much money would he give you?

Now make an exit strategy? State how much money you need, when and what for.

It may appear difficult to overcome your history if your life walks on dictates of your feelings. We fear to appear greedy or unrealistic. We do not want to ask too much. We fear to be denied and therefore we either choose not to ask or we ask a little. This way we limit our exit strategy. We tie up our hands with strings of our history. The obstacle of all ages is how to change our history. We are not saying: Can we change our history? We are saying: How can we change our history?

Jesus answered this question two thousand years ago. He said, "Ask and it shall be given to you." He added, "And whatever you may ask in my name I will ask my father and he will grant it to you." I like the phrase 'whatever' and that certainly includes asking for millions of dollars. I hold this to be true because Jesus opened his manifesto (Luke 4:18) I have come to preach good news to the poor. He could not have said 'whatever' when there were some exceptions.

If we were asking man, prince, government minister how much money we needed, when and what for we would be tied down by the denials we are used to. Let us quote Matthew 7:8 and pin Jesus down with his own words, "For everyone who asks will receive." Let us follow the official procedure he outlined in the paragraph above. Let us fill in every comma and full stop and see who then will deny us our right to receive whatever we may ask.

We have the authority on our side. If God is for us who can be against us? Let us stamp our claim on our prosperity today. Let us decide to be poor, middle-income earners, rich, millionaires or billionaires ourselves. Let us not be tied down by our history. Let us exercise our democratic right of choice. Let us do this by jumping out of our box. Let us not lock ourselves in the mold other people have built for us. To hell with procrusteanistism (conformity).

Let us build our own image. We may be poor but we reject stealing, lies, idle talk, murmuring, bad company, misjudging others, being false witnesses, working in jobs that demean our birth rights. We build our own box not based on self righteousness but on the teachings of Jesus. We then do not treat others as they treat us but as we want to be treated. By this the world may know that we are Jesus' disciples. We are then not looked at as the poor lot but inheritors of the Kingdom of God. Citizens of the Kingdom do not live by edifying themselves but edifying their King. In return when they ask him anything he listens.

Think of it. Is prosperity genetic?

No!

Why then do we blame our poverty on the sins of our ancestors? Why do we tie down our prosperity on actions of our past? Why do we blame our problems on our bosses, jobs, environment and even the devil?

We can change our unstable behaviour, poor attitudes, lack of productivity, physical disabilities, lack of will to live and yet not willing to die, by jumping out of our history box. Yes we can. Yes we can. Yes we can. We can break away from our history.

Now check your answers out. "If you were told that all your life is going to be destroyed but you were given one piece of it to choose to be preserved what would you choose?" You wouldn't choose any of your physical organs. You would choose your soul. You would choose the power to believe in the Almighty Living God.

"If you were told that the road to prosperity begins at the mark you identified above, how would you answer the question of all ages: Where do I start from?" How can you answer the obstacle of all ages: How can I change my history?

Start by looking at your past. Get a big piece of paper. Mark one half ACHIEVEMENTS and mark the other OBSTACLES. Think of your history in the past one hour. Write down in the two columns what you have done, thought or said. Did you think of reading a book? That was an achievement. Did you read it? That was an achievement. What was your achievement? Your thoughts and your actions went together.

Did you think of reading a book? That was an achievement. Did you read it? No. No? There must have been an obstacle? You have any excuse? That is the obstacle. You did not have time? Someone visited? You had something more important to do? You postponed the action. Your thoughts and actions did not go together. There was an obstacle. Put your case under the obstacle column.

Take any other event of your life in the past one hour. Is your life full of excuses? Do you keep on doing wrong things and blame them on someone else? Are you no longer responsible for your own life? Are you an imbecile?

Now extend your period to two hours. How have you messed yourself up? Have you neglected yourself? Have you opened yourself to the devil? I will give you the devils program and see how you can change your history. Read this extract from an email of unknown origin. (Read even if you're busy)

SATAN MEETS DEMONS

Satan called a worldwide convention of demons. In his opening address he said, "We can't keep Christians from going to church. We can't keep them from reading their Bibles and knowing the truth. We can't even keep them from forming an intimate relationship with their Saviour. Once they gain that connection with Jesus, our power over them is broken.

"So let them go to their churches; let them have their covered dish dinners, but steal their time, so they don't have time to develop a relationship with Jesus Christ. This is what I want you to do. Distract them from gaining hold of their Saviour and maintaining that vital connection throughout their day!

"How shall we do this?" his demons shouted.

"Keep them busy in the non-essentials of life and invent innumerable schemes to occupy their minds. Tempt them to spend, spend, spend, and borrow, borrow, borrow. Persuade the wives to go to work for long hours and the husbands to work 6-7 days each week, 10-12 hours a day, so they can afford their empty lifestyles. Keep them from spending time with their children. As their families fragment, soon, their homes will offer no escape from the pressures of work!

"Over-stimulate their minds so that they cannot hear that still, small voice. Entice them to play the radio or cassette player whenever they drive. Keep the TV, VCR, CDs and their PCs going constantly in their home and see to it that every store and restaurant in the world plays non-biblical music constantly. This will jam their minds and break that union with Christ."

"Fill the coffee tables with magazines and newspapers. Pound their minds with the news 24 hours a day. Invade their driving moments with billboards. Flood their mailboxes with junk mail, mail order catalogs, sweepstakes, and every kind of newsletter and promotionals offering free products, services and false hopes.

"Keep skinny, beautiful models on the magazines and TV so their husbands will believe that outward beauty is what's important, and they'll become dissatisfied with their wives. Keep the wives too tired to love their husbands at night. Give them headaches too! If they don't give their husbands the love they need, the husbands will begin to look elsewhere. That will fragment their families quickly!

"Give them Santa Claus to distract them from teaching their children the real meaning of Christmas. Give them an Easter bunny so they won't talk about his resurrection and power over sin and death.

'Move into their recreation. Let it be excessive. Have them return from their recreation exhausted. Keep them too busy to go out in nature and reflect on God's creation. Send them to amusement parks, sporting events, plays, concerts, and movies instead. Keep them busy, busy and busy!

"And when they meet for spiritual fellowship, involve them in gossip and small talk so that they leave with troubled consciences. Crowd their lives with so many good causes leaving them with no time to seek power from Jesus. Soon they will be working in their own strength, sacrificing their health and family for the good of the cause. It will work!"

"It will work!"

It was quite a plan! The demons went eagerly to their assignments causing Christians everywhere to get busier and more rushed, going here and there. Having little time for their God or their families, having no time to tell others about the power of Jesus to change lives; the Christian world almost fell apart only to be rescued by God himself taking charge.

I guess the question is, "Has the devil been successful in his schemes?" You be the judge.

You can change your own history by taking charge of it. Blame no body for your past. Do not blame yourself either. This is what we call forgiveness. It is not that you were not wronged. It is that your sins have been wiped away. Your history report shows nothing. It is not that those events did not occur. You are your own witness. They did occur but by relegating them to the past they are denied the chance to affect your future. You can indeed change your history by forgiving it. Do not accuse yourself of your past short comings. Bear no witness to yourself. Any case without witness is bound to collapse even with strong evidence and exhibits presented. Not to forgive yourself is like keeping poison in your mouth in the hope that you will not swallow it.

One of the things Tanzania and Tanzanians are known for is their culture of burying the hatchet and constructing new relationships quickly. Tanzania and Tanzanians are tolerant in their basic principles of religion, a policy which was initiated by the father of the nation Mwalimu Julius Kambarage Nyerere. The Vatican invited President Kikwete as a Chief Guest in Nepal, Italy on October 21, 2007 for as the Papacy envoy put it, "his stance on implementation of policies that encouraged Tanzanians to live in unity, respect and tolerance in spite of their religious beliefs".

Tanzania Government takes credit in this. In 1999 the American Embassy in Dar Es Salaam was attacked and bombed by what was internationally known as a circle of some Moslem terrorists. In this incidence and in many others the police did not link crime to Islam. Even in circumstances where the police registry showed that there were more Moslems in prison than people of other faiths, there is no evidence that police hunted down people of a particular belief. This thinking has left men of different religion to live and work together as equal citizens.

Tanzania takes pride in its own history. It is the only country in Africa or one of the very few that has not fought inter tribal wars since independence. All countries surrounding her have been tearing themselves to pieces but in Tanzania the sheep and the lion, the calf and the cub are lying together. This is one country where Moslems and Christians are living together sharing everything from homes to churches without conflict. Conversions from one religion to another are done and there are no clashes thereafter. Remember this book is written in 'Jerusalem'.

How did Tanzanians get rid of their tribal differences? How did the Tanzanians change their history?

President Nyerere had a goal of building a unified state. How would he do that? He knew that what human beings like best about themselves are their names and he planted a seed of change here. At the time of independence Tanzania (then Tanganyika and Zanzibar) had areas known as predominantly Christian or Moslem or Native. Moslems were known by names of Arabic origin, Christians had names of English origin and Natives had names of African origin. A name like Abed bin Ismail would tell you that the person is a Moslem, Happy Charlie and Jane are Christians and Popo is a Native-Faith Believer.

A new culture was born in Tanzania. Boys were named after their father's first names not surnames and girls took to their mother's first names. Godfrey Mathews was a son of some man whose first name was Mathews. Amina Florence was a daughter of Florence. This way one cannot tell from which tribe Godfrey or Amina came. One could neither tell whether Barrack Hussein was a Christian or a Moslem.

The naming wiped out cultural identity and with everybody encouraged to speak Swahili in public instead of tribal languages tribal differences were greatly wiped out. The Tanzanian experience shows that one can do something about one's own history. You do not deny your own existence but you frame it wisely.

There is really no danger in changing your name. Abram changed to Abraham and from some miserable name came a Father of all Nations. Sarai changed to Sarah and a fruit was born from a barren seed. Saul changed into Paul and a terrorist became a liberator. The only trouble we see in Tanzania is that boys and girls call each other brothers and sisters. You must keep a keen eye when your brother-in-law or sister-in-law visits!

Your history should not tie you down. Paul told Jews to forget they were children of Abraham, Isaac and Jacob and do as Jesus told them to do. In your case forgive your past. Remove those negative fears from your thinking. Do not lock yourself up in your past mistakes. Love tells us not to keep a record of wrongs. If you cannot love yourself, who can love you for you? You have to focus your thinking on issues that give you courage.

As you know, if you have read this book this far, this is the time for starting over and setting out to truly change your life once and for all. If you want to restart your life with a splash of inspiration, or if you know someone wishing for a second chance in life or love and you want to be of help, then I highly recommend that you read "A good thing about life" on Page 34 again.

A good thing about life is that you can change your thinking without changing your records by reading only the positive side of your life page. You keep a record of achievements not a record of wrongs. Now get your paper on which you wrote your Obstacles and Achievements. Tear off the sections you named obstacles and light a fire and burn it. I do not want you to keep it. Burn it. Let it go in flames before your own eyes. Smell the burning as the obstacles turn to ash and get your eyes choked with the smoke of your failures. What you are left with is the list of your achievements. Meditate upon your achievements. Praise and worship them. You may never before have ever appreciated yourself. Today you have overcome your history. This however is just a means to the end. Satan wanted to break relationship between Jesus and believers. He discussed many ways of doing this but the aim was one.

You have read this book this far. What is your goal? What shall you do to those forces to which you have no control?

CHAPTER TEN

CLIMB

Abed is a good example of a man born in poverty grew up in poverty but managed to shake off this curse and prospered. He challenges those who say one cannot start a business without money. He likens them to those who say one cannot start a family without a girlfriend (or a boyfriend). They cry, "No one loves me!"

He does not want to discuss his childhood and I am writing this hoping he will not read this page. Rich people tend to scheme through books instead of reading from cover to cover. This explains why most millionaires are not university graduates. Sincerely speaking this is merely a theory based on certain evidence or observations but lacks scientific proof. A great number of millionaires however are school drop outs. Look at the rich men you listed in Chapter Four. How many of them ever finished High school? This is not about the rich men beating our education system; it is about the education system failing us out.

Suppose he does read this page, I wish to add it here for this purpose that all names in this book have been changed to hide the true identity of the people being talked about. In the event the names or circumstances fit the description of a known person, take that as a coincidence and the views held as of the reader not of the author. All inconveniences are highly regretted and as for me for the offence of labeling Abed, I plead not guilty.

This is the story of Abed's childhood (and I repeat this story is not accurate. Errors and omissions expected as the story gets over-simplified). Please and I beg you: Do not believe it. In reality remember Abed kept changing his names according to circumstances. Some circles knew him as Charlie, others called him Ismail and we meet him here as Abed and what I present here is when he acted as Abed.

Abed was born Abed Ismail in a village on the Tanzania-Mozambique border. His family was so poor that when the tax collectors came from Tanzania, the parents run across and hid in Mozambique and when the collectors came from Mozambique the parents returned to Tanzania. As fate would have it the colonizers of Tanzania were British and those of Mozambique were Portuguese and the two never seemed ever to coordinate their efforts. Their summers and winters differed according to London and Lisbon and so were their holidays. Financial years in Mozambique and Tanzania were far apart. Tax collection was timed to come at the end of the financial years in Europe and this meant different months in the two neighboring colonies. Abed's life as a child knew nothing but constant moving.

He was born at a time when those who fought to overthrow the government in Mozambique were greeted in Tanzania as heroes and freedom fighters yet in Mozambique they were regarded as rebels and vandals. He says he used to hear Radio Tanzania describing his village as a 'Liberated Homeland' and yet in Mozambique they referred to the same place as a 'Camp for Internally Displaced People.' His father was both a hero and a felony. Secret: Abed holds two passports of Tanzania and of Mozambique. This confused identity could easily grow him into a divorcee, drunkard, addict, criminal and a beggar. He challenged this prediction and grew prosperous.

Abed spent his childhood running from the police, running from drought or running from forces he was too young to know. All he says is that he grew up crisscrossing the border. He is one of the few thousands if not millions of unsuccessful school leavers who tried to be socially and morally accepted on this earth with the help of religious Non Government Organizations (NGO or charities for short). I say this because many religions of the world according to Abed are born out of man's need to fill a kind of hunger that creeps in when man fails to balance his needs with the needs of the world.

One of Abed's earlier teachers described him as a boy with a difference. "He was not a youth who could do anything to survive—such never succeed—he was a young man with a vision and a direction. He often asked what the Bible said about their next meal, school fees or a good shelter. He asked this not because he had a good Christian upbringing but as a child who had to be a good Muslim at home and a good Christian at school. What however he is most remembered for was this quotation he must have made at an early age of sixteen. He said, 'Any government that's worth its name –whether on earth or in heaven—has to reach out to its people and give them a solution to their problems or risk civil disobedience.'

The well-known character he left in his school was his eloquence of speech. He attended one class taught of course by one overseas missionary lady. Each student was asked to stand up and talk about one's home condition. We take the story when it is Abed's turn.

"I live in a typical African village. We are very poor but I thank God every day that he gave us the trees we live in. My grandfather lives in his own tree. My father has his own tree too and soon I will have my own family tree. I may look poor to you today but before I go to bed every night I pray and thank God, Teacher, for your coming to help us. I may not be where I want to be but I am not where I used to be. I give thanks based on where I came from not where I am."

The teacher asked all the relevant questions about how to use a toilet and how to cook the food up in a tree. Abed had answers to all these questions. One issue was significant. Abed was answering questions he did not understand. He was like most poor people trying to get rich without knowing what prosperity is all about. The teacher too behaved like those international organizations that design poverty relief programmes without calling for participation of the poor. They expect the poor to follow by filling in the blanks and in the end grow up rich. Usually such donors retire before the solution to poverty is found.

Abed's story was a correction of junk. He never had a pit latrine because God had given them a big garden. It sounds like poor people who excuse their poverty on "because God gave us a colour."

Abed's home hardly cooked their food. "Flesh tastes better fresh."

Does this sound familiar? Have you heard people say that they never work so hard because they have fine weather?

Or they do not need a medical checkup because flu is a seasonal disease; it comes and goes? I have heard people equate malaria to resurrection. It puts you down for three days!

The remarkable thing is not the truth about this story. The idea that Africans lived in trees like monkeys had been told so many times that even missionaries came to take it as true and used it in their home churches for fund raising. When you hear something and tell it to yourself a number of times you reach a certain point when you come to believe it and feel it and think it and do it. In fact Abed told this story so many times that in the end to save himself from further embarrassment he eventually built himself a tree house.

Do you constantly call yourself poor and yet you expect to escape from poverty? Wake up. Those who keep on saying, "I'm broke" are broke indeed. You will never succeed if you keep on telling your mind, "I cannot pass this one!"

At sixteen Abed left school and joined an organization called PRC (Poverty Relief Charity). His widely published lies earned him some sort of scholarship. He was deployed in a program that suggested him to join either business or agricultural sectors. There was a choice to be made. One course meant a career designed for black people and the other for men of colour like Indians, Arabs and Mulattoes.

Abed chose not to be tied down to traditions and be fitted into a particular box. He went for a business course. He was sent to Hongkong PRC and then to Japan PRC—two places where he learnt to work for a living. PRC's system of assistance is based on a theory that those who do not want to work should not eat either. Similar to many other international Aid Agencies, PRC call loans grants. They give AID with strings attached. You have to believe and confess in words and in deeds that there is only one God–the owner of heaven and earth; you cannot be saved unless you are baptized. They praise themselves for giving interest free loans in US dollars but when it comes to paying back no matter the inflation rate you have to pay back the same amount in US dollars. They offer free scholarships but you have to work for the sponsor free too.

In Hong Kong Abed went to an evening school but during day time he was employed to look after a dog. He had to feed the dog, walk the dog, talk to the dog and find out what the dog wanted.

Abed used to call his master "Boss" because that fitted the way his master behaved. He wanted to call him H.E but only presidents are ironically called His Excellency. Whenever his boss saw him, the master saw the dog in him not the Abed in him. Never in a single day did his master ever ask Abed how he had spent the day but how the dog had spent the day.

Abed says most fathers do not like dogs in their homes because their wives and children show more love and care to the dogs than they ever show to the father or to the husband of the house. This rivalry thing is another story. We take the tale from Abed himself. "I reached a point when all I could do was to bark to my master other than talk to him. I made up my mind and I did it.

"He returned from office one afternoon and I ran to the gate, went down on my knees with my hands stretched, fingers on the ground and I started, "Bar, bar, bar, wolf, wolf, wolf." I knew he was coming from a bar and he was a wolf in human body.

"That is when my master knew I existed. The more I wanted him to treat me like his dog the more he wanted to treat me human. 'Every action has got an equal and opposite reaction'...... Newton's law of Emotion.

'Have you ever felt that sometimes some animals are more human than human beings themselves? This is what I used to feel when I would compare my master to the dog. My master would make you hate rich men. He used to behave as though he had no master himself—either on earth or in heaven. I got the impression that all rich men are mean, greedy and inconsiderate. There was nothing good to admire of them.

"I learnt something different in college. You cannot grow rich if you do not admire the life of the rich. You cannot become what you hate. You cannot be a robber if you hate to steal. You have to change your thinking if you want to see the money".

Abed has made up his point. Let us leave him here.

Abed questioned himself what was in the dog and lacking in him that made the dog more acceptable to people than he could be. He says the dog taught him to wear a smile every day. Jasper –the dog– was the only animal in the house that never worked for a living. The chicken laid eggs and the cows gave milk but Jasper had nothing to do the whole day except making and treating you as a friend.

Every day Jasper sat still waiting for his master to wake up, see him off the door and welcome him back home. He would sit in front of the doorway or lay down in a couch but as soon as he would hear the master's voice, he would spring off whatever he was doing, racing breathlessly to greet with joy, bark with joy and wag his tail with joy to the master. There is nothing he left reserved. He would wag his tail and when the master stopped as he often did to pat him, Jasper would almost jump out of his skin to show how much he loved the master. In front of Boss, Jasper showed how human he had become by standing on two legs. Jasper was one animal that gave you a real feeling of love. You felt right away that he did not want to sell you anything or marry you. He only wanted to be your friend. That is why dogs are described as the best of friends on earth. On a scale of friendliness marked 1 to 10, Jasper earned 10 and Boss earned 0.

This teaches us something about masters. All masters of any kind (God inclusive) love to be praised. We live to give God glory. The Almighty Father in Heaven feels greatly insulted when we fail to glorify his name. We were created for his own glory. Imagine if God does something good for you and you stand up and call it works of your hand or of your brain. God calls this blasphemy. It is just the same as if you said the spirit of your ancestors helped you through your hard times. It is not hard work that brings riches. It is blessings. Give glory to God and collect your bounty.

Jasper went through life happy Abed observed. He drove the best cars, slept in the best couches, lived in houses he never built, ate the best meat without going out hunting. How did he do all this? He made himself relevant and credible at all times. Jasper was always where he was expected to be and doing what he was expected to do and did this without ceasing or complaining. Abed resolved to behave likewise and the results were positive.

We shall see Abed's life in Japan later on. The point here is that as Jasper could leave the bush and live in sky scrapers of Hong Kong, so can you change from life of extreme poverty to extreme prosperity. Mark my words: Accountability and Caring. If you want to see the money I show you two things: a heart that is accountable and a heart that treats others as it would want others to treat it. Once you engrave these two virtues in your character you are then ready for the real thing.

Turn to yourself and check how many times you have been criticized by friends and foes alike for failing to keep to your words. A man who does not keep time for instance wastes his own time and angers others. Can he make friends? No! Which one is easier to make money with –friends or with enemies? If there were two camps, one is made up of friends and one is made up of your enemies and you were given five minutes of your life to visit one of these camps which one would you go to?

My point is that if you want to make money, work for it. If you want to put money in your pockets check first to see that there are no holes in your pockets. If there are any, sew those holes up. The demand of all ages is: Show me the money. It is wrong to think that you cannot grow rich because you cannot see the money to start your business with. There is a lot of money around you. I am eager to show you the money but you have to open your eyes first. See. There is a lot of money in drugs. There is a lot of money in gambling. There is a lot of money in child trafficking. There is a lot of money in the bank. There is a lot of money in robbery. Your choice is how to get it.

Turn to yourself and check how many times you have been criticized by friends and foes alike for failing to keep to your words. If you want to see the money I show you two things: Accountability and Caring. My point is that if you want to put money in your pockets check first to see that there are no holes in your pockets. If there are any sew those holes up. I have repeated this paragraph as a matter of emphasis.

Now write down three things in your life that you want changed. Write them down in order of importance. Ask God to sew your heart up. Close your eyes and pray that this burden may be carried away from you. When you wake up you will see the money.

If this does not work out for you try this alternative prescription. The people in Tanzania teach their children to take care of their teeth. At six or so years when a child picks out a tooth, he is told to put it under his pillow. The story says when he wakes up in the morning he finds that a rat has taken away the tooth and replaced it with money. Rats are known to steal but they never take children teeth without paying for them. If rats can be so accountable and so caring why shouldn't you? Do an act of love to your otherwise enemy.

The third prescription is taken from Malachi 3:10 "Bring the whole tithe into the storehouse, that there may be food in my (God's) house. Test me in this," says the LORD Almighty, "and see if I will not throw open the floodgates of heaven and pour out so much blessing that you will not have room enough for it. I will prevent pests from devouring your crops, and the vines in your fields will not cast their fruit," says the LORD Almighty. "Then all the nations will call you blessed, for yours will be a Delightful land," says the LORD Almighty"

As the story turns Abed took this prescription and his harvest was as described in Luke 6. He planted coffee. At harvest time he filled bags, shook them, pulled them and filled them more and the more he filled them the more money they fetched. There are no secrets to prosperity. The more wisdom you put in the search for prosperity, the more you get out of wisdom.

Do you remember Jane my secretary? She argued that this Malachi 3 is a Bible reference used by pastors to steal their flock's money. In her view God never needed any money and Jesus never needed it either. Just eight months of his wages were about enough to feed 5000 people with bread. You cannot buy a blessing by giving so that you may get ten folds your seeds she argued.

Imagine her situation. She had lost her job. She could not pay her rent. She could not find enough money to go to town looking for other opportunities. What was her 10% to give to a church? If the church could carry 10% of her burden perhaps she could tithe.

She was right as far as human wisdom goes. God however calls her thinking robbery. The key to prosperity is revealed in Deuteronomy 6:5. I told you there is no secret on the road to prosperity. The trick is getting acquaintance with the giver, live in peace with the giver and listen to the giver. Let me qualify the last key. Listening is doing what you are told. In here no reference to money is made.

Abed and Jane often argued about this teaching. If God told you in Malachi 3 to give, listen to the whole instruction. If you want to see the floodgates of heaven opened give into his ministry. Of course if you give money so that the pastor may buy a new car or have a kilo of meat on his table, for sure you have received your reward not in heaven but in that pastor's handshake or letter of thanks. God rewards the motive not the outward appearance. In Jane's terminology man rewards outside appearance but God sees the socks and the underwear.

The purpose of this chapter is to show you where the money is. If you are still in the mud, this shows you the direction you have to swim to. If you are at the ladder, it shows you the goal to climb to. The money is in your hands. The money is in your heart. The money is in your thoughts. The money is in your feelings. The money is in your actions. The money is in your belief. If you cannot believe me, change your thinking. You are not looking for money but prosperity.

Prosperity is not born by preferences but by principles. Have peace with God and you will see that there is money all around you. You will have more money than you will ever need. You will have more money than you will be able to spend in your life time. You will leave enough money to your children and children's children when your time is up.

We have a lot of opportunities to make money but more often than not we do not use our chances. We have a built-in mechanism which tells us: Reject that idea because there is something wrong with it. Reject that idea because you will not be credited with it. Reject that idea because it is hard or impossible. Reject that idea because your mind is already made up otherwise. Reject that idea because it might not be in line with the law. Reject that idea because there are no resources to put into it. Reject that idea because it might offend some people. Reject that idea because it is not your style of doing things. Reject that idea because you might be criticized for it. (10)Reject that idea because it might not succeed.

You cannot see the money all around you if you are a dummy. You are a person, an individual, not a people. You are uniquely wired with a set of temperaments designed to make you interact with the world and to overcome the world. If Latvin had lived to please me she would never have accomplished her mission. Abed succeeded because he understood his circumstances and worked through them. Jasper lived the life of a king because he knew who his master was. Jane failed because she kept on grumbling. If your mission is to move from poverty to prosperity control what your eyes see. Limit the silly justifications you make. Purify your thinking. Streamline your action and climb up.

Can you start a family without a girlfriend or from nothing? Yes, you can.

CHAPTER ELEVEN

Accountability

You may not like what I have just said above. Many people do not want promises leaning on closing eyes or bending knees. There are so many rich men and women around us whose accountability has been questioned, tested and proven defective. They keep on making and making more and more money. It appears therefore prosperity has nothing to do with accountability.

Remember I started writing this book from Kipepeo Beach. I now tell you that I have visited this beach so many times that I am sometimes mistaken as one of the workers there. I do not sleep at the beach. At the beginning I used to go back to Liiban Hotel for a rest. Then I met up again with Abed who introduced me to another hotel called The Promised Land. He was working there as a security guard.

I want to leave life at the beach and tell you some surprising story. I know you may not believe it but all the same I will tell you what happened. Anyway you bought the book; you paid for this story.

A thief introduced himself to me that he was a thief by profession and he wanted me to be his customer. You may skip the next few paragraphs if you think this is ridiculous. This is true and the thief was my friend Abed.

It was about midnight and I heard a tap on my hotel door. I woke up, opened the door half way, hinging it on my other leg and asked, "Who is that?" He answered or he must have answered something like, "Room Service" or "Security Personnel." I am not sure of what he said. Perhaps I was half awake and half careless.

He then told me he was a thief by profession and yet he had been hired as a guard to improve the security of the hotel. He knew his job was conflicting with his life style. He did not change his history. He found a way of living with it. He needed rehabilitation. He took the job anyway because he had children and a wife to feed. He did not hide his troubled past of course from the guy who hired him. He had just been released from prison. The job was full of temptations.

He worked but no single day passed without him thinking of quitting. He always put the thought off because jobless he would surely return to jail but with a job he had a mean chance of living free. He sought my advice because he needed to talk to somebody. He had learnt in college that you can avoid frustration by talking your troubles over with any trusted friend. (Of course College lessons like pride are only remembered after a fall).

He then disclosed to me that after that fateful taxi ride he was picked up by the police. He pleaded not guilty but the judge did not listen. It was difficult to argue his case innocent in front of a judge who thought the society was rotten and it was his duty to clean it up. Whatever he said the judge was bent on locking him up. He kept on asking: If you are innocent why did they bring you before me? The system of justice in Tanzania for the accused to Abed was clear: You are guilty as accused unless proven otherwise.

He was locked up. Bail was denied to him because he had lost a case in a previous conviction where he was accused of dealing in fake American dollars. The judge even joked about it that he feared Abed could pay his bail with fake money. Removing him from society was the only way of protecting the society.

In prison he behaved so well that his sentence was reduced to three month and one year of rehabilitation.

When we met he told me that in the four months he had worked in this hotel he had found that many guests go to sleep with their doors unlocked. "I sometimes find couples dead asleep with their things open. Just last week I found my neighbor with a school girl. I picked the man's clothes, the girl's school uniform and bag and took them to the neighbor's wife. The man has never been here again and I think that is the last time he ever committed adultery".

It appears Abed kind of believed that by stealing he had discovered his god-given ministry. He would improve the security of this place, fight adultery and turn this Hotel eventually into a real holiday place. He said progress is not marked by where we are but where we are coming from. The world was crooked. He alone had however discovered the way to live in it without fear or tear. His rule was, "Learn and Obey."

"That is what happens always". I agreed with him. In the back of my mind I knew that before Jesus returns there would be many tribulations on earth. The devil leads the earth into tribulations. I guess what this says is that the devil wants us to keep us in poverty as much as God wants us to prosper. We were talking of the same things but on completely different platforms. You realize he was talking and I was not listening. What he was actually saying was that alongside the crucified Jesus were two thieves—A Good thief and a Bad thief. The Good thief worshipped Jesus but the Bad Thief rebuked him. In the end one went to Heaven another went to hell. Abed could have been one of the two and now he had decided to complete the ministry of the Good Thief.

I now confess that I admire the young men and women who are reading this book today. Taking responsibility for not listening to a man who is talking creates a guilty feeling. I have learnt to be accountable for my mistakes. The denial of all ages is accountability. You cannot prosper if you cannot confess your failures to one another. When you confess your weakness you create a desire to overcome it. The group around you will empathize with you and try to keep you standing instead of letting you down sinking.

Of course there is a kind of confession that is common among failures or the poor. They confess and praise themselves of things they should be ashamed. They are proud when they cheat some unsuspecting passenger; they pride in how they laid a school girl; they praise themselves for the way they fooled the police. These are not things to be proud of.

Confess in how God has been so good to you. Take responsibility for your mistakes even if this means hanging you on a cross. Accountability has a reward. You will never decay in hell.

I do not want to go into the biblical argument now but what the thief said serves the purpose for those who want to defeat poverty once for all. The principle is controlling fear and putting faith in God. There are signs that one is approaching victory. When attacks against sewing your heart become more fierce and your life sees battle after battle know that the time for your salvation has come.. When you find yourself in relentless struggles, realize you have entered the devils stronghold and a break-through is eminent. If you keep getting money by one hand and losing it by two, you work from pay-cheque to pay-cheque, you borrow in order to pay a debt, realize these are the hard times. It is the time for change.

Have you ever lost something perhaps a key or money? What is the first thing you do before you say "Oh, dear, it has gone?"

You close your eyes and slap your face!

What do you do if you have lost prosperity?

You close your eyes and slap your face!

I guess the idea of slapping your face is to shake up your brain– to refocus your direction– and to start all over again from the point you got lost. Shake your head. Close your eyes. Shut your eyes to your past failures. Shut your eyes to your accidents of birth. Close your eyes to your threats. Close your eyes to everything that is not Godly. Close your eyes to your selfish interests and start all over again. I repeat: Control what your eyes see.

Imagine you are thirsty. You have got clean water in a bottle. Would you drink that water if it is poured in a dirty glass? Or if clean water is poured in a dirty glass would that clean the glass? If we mere human beings cannot pour clean water in a dirty glass how can we expect our father in heaven to pour prosperity in dirty minds?

The thief told me he wanted me to be his customer on condition that I slept leaving my doors open. When you leave your door open to the devil, he comes in.

Open yourself to adultery, it will come in.
Open yourself to divorce, it will come in.
Open yourself to prostitution, it will come in.
Open yourself to doubt, it will come in.
Open yourself to poverty, it will come in.

Shut all avenues that take your revenue and focus on prosperity and everything else shall be added unto ye.

Suppose a thief broke into your apartment and gave you a choice, either to stand locked up in your bathroom naked and wipes out everything in your house or sleep with you and touch nothing of your property; what will you choose? (He could use a condom!) I asked someone while writing this and she asked, "Would he use a condom?" Our life is determined not by the options we have but by the decisions we take.

Abed told me on another visit how he became a thief.

When the war for independence ended and Mozambique became finally free his father put down his gun and became some Portuguese man's driver. His father was sent on the usual errands of picking up this or that. On one such occasion he picked up his girlfriend on his way to work. He was on a night shift. He went off the high way and packed off road. A policeman, who might not have been aware that the war was over, spied his way to the car. Suddenly he noticed that the car was not moving but something in the car was moving.

He walked to the car and with a hand on his revolver said, "I want to see your driving license".

"It is in the trouser, Sir."

He fumbled to look for the trouser but he could not find it quick enough. The policeman dragged him out and made him stand legs stretched, hands on the back and head on the bonnet of the car. He pointed his revolver onto him and declared, "You are a dead man now." The only excuse for this rage was perhaps the policeman thought my father was pointing a gun at him!

"He was half naked, my father!

"Without saying a word, my father turned, kicked the policeman in a surprise martial art attack. He got his gun and showered him with bullets. He shot him and kept shooting even when he knew the policeman was surely dead.

"My father radioed his master. "I have killed an intruder"

"My father was sentenced to a firing squad. As he was being led to the gallows, he said, "This is what I get for being a man".

"I grew up to be a dead man's son. I programmed myself that way. When I went to the missionary school I learnt that our destiny as men was preplanned by God. Our task is to read God's blue print and follow it. In my latter life I forgot the last part of the sentence. I did not fulfill my task and came to believe that if my father had been George W. Bush and my mother Barbra Bush and I grew up in the White House I would have been elected the President of America twice and I would have attacked Iraq whether or not the United Nations supported me or not.

"If my father had been a cock and my mother a chicken and I a female I would lay eggs like any other hen. If I had been born by a cow, I would allow you to milk me and I would not complain. If I were Sir Elton John I would have divorced a woman and married a man.

"Those who put their trust in fate teach that our life follows a predetermined path. You can bleach your skin but cannot turn its colour. I practiced this religion whose foundation is grounded in half truth. I was born an orphan and no kindness would ever fill that gap. Now I know that kindness is the language the deaf hear and the blind see. In those old days, if I stole it was no big deal as long as I was not caught. If you caught me my peers would not laugh me off if I stole for survival or from a rich man or woman. Everyone wants to eat, anyway. If you locked me up that would be touching my body but not killing my spirit. We should be scared of those who can kill both the body and the spirit. Those who can kill only one of these should only be feared by cowards".

Do you think criminals have a mind of their own? Or do you think the thief who loved me had life of his own? Read on. In 1930s America had a gangster called Crowley. Police hunted him down and what did they find on him? A note written in blood, "Beneath my skin is a weary heart, but a kind one – that would do nobody any harm".

I have personally worked in detention centers. I have found no detainee who cannot explain why he is behind bars. Most of them (if not all of them) deny their crime maintaining their innocence. They blame their arrest on police mistakes or betrayal by enemies they mistook for friends. What is common with most criminals is that they never admit their folly. This is not a blanket criticism but any prisoner who shows a sense of responsibility or accountability is subject to parole (where parole exists).

Abed finished his two year contract in Hongkong PRC and went to Japan. There he worked under the supervision of Mr. Kato in a metal milling factory.

I promised you meeting Abed again in Japan. Here he returns and let him speak.

"Mr. Kato could not speak English and I could not speak Japanese. Time and time again he would pick my product, looked at it with admiration and said "Aligato" It did not matter how I milled, every product was "aligatous". Sometimes he would pick some of my finished products and put them back in the mill but with a smile – no blame – and "Aligato". Mr. Kato was thankful at all times. I learnt from him that it is foolish to scold. Most supervisors, parents and Governments spend much of their time scolding, criticizing and condemning. None of these build up the soul. They rake the mind. The Japanese industry is growing from day to day because the Japanese realized early that a dog rewarded for good behavior will learn much faster and remember better than one that is punished for wrong doing.

"Criticism defeats its own purpose because it puts a person on the defensive and usually makes one to justify oneself and by the time one would like to improve on the performance all the energy would be already spent out on feeding anger, restoring a sense of dignity, developing self confidence or resisting resentment. Surely as for criticism no one likes it - not even criminals. If no one wants to take it why should we give it?

"At one time Mr. Kato picked a piece I had produced. He looked at it and laughed. He told me. "You are very diligent. You have done this perfectly badly. You have broken all the rules and your product is perfectly bad. I am sure if you could do it again and keep all the rules you would produce a product 100% good. Be diligently good not diligently bad. That is an advice not a criticism. Tell it first to yourself and then to your children and children's children."

"After two years of stay in Japan I returned first to Mozambique and then to Tanzania. My first desire was to see my mother whom I had not seen for four years. Then I moved to Tanzania to set up a business practice. I wanted to set up an import and export business but I did not have the seed money. I searched myself and found that I had something that made me unique. I could use that element to make money.

I had knowledge. I could easily sell that. I had learnt that the fact that you cannot do everything should not prevent you from doing what you can. God said, "My people perish because of lack of knowledge." I was computer literate. I had been to Tokyo, Komaguchi and Yokohama. I knew how these port cities operate. I had been to Dar Es Salaam and Maputo. I knew what kind of goods was needed in this East African region. I knew the market. My aim was not to beat my fellow competitors out of business. I wanted to bring integrity in the business. We had learnt that knowledge without integrity was dangerous and dreadful. I had learnt that integrity without knowledge is weak and useless. My exit strategy was to retire young and retire rich. I had to set up business where I would earn US$ 1000 a day in profit. I had to reach this target within five years. I agreed with my heart upon this. So I setup a forwarding and logistics company. I decided in handling goods from the Far East especially from Hongkong, China and Japan.

"I talked to a number of people about my business plans. There were those who wrote me off right away because they believed that one cannot start a business without money. There were those who could not go in business with me because I had had no previous experience in business. There were those who feared losing money that they could not dare invest in any business. I said you are either with me or against me. I created two camps in my mind. There was one for people who were ready to prosper and those who had chosen poverty. Those whose decision was based on negative feelings and fear were bound to fail and live in poverty. Those who looked ahead with faith and hope were bound to grow from poverty to prosperity. I knew the camp I needed to grow with."

I ask you again. If there were two camps, one is made up of friends and one is made up of your enemies and you were given five minutes of your life to visit one of these camps which one would you go to?

Abed remembered the words of Jesus quoted in John 10:10. It says that the devil comes to steal, kill and destroy but Jesus comes that we may prosper. Whoever needs true prosperity as we saw in chapter five has to cling to the words that support life.

Out of his support group he formed a Task Force. This committee sat regularly to map out the way forward. He impressed upon the committee that prosperity was for them all. He preached that prosperity is power to overcome misery. Prosperity like political power only comes when it is shared out with the masses. If you want to prosper and to prosper absolutely you have to make sure that those below you prosper and as they do they propel you to the top.

Prosperity is an accountability issue. This truth Abed learnt from his father. In the war of liberation his father was once captured. A priest visited him in the prison and urged him to pray for his captors. The argument was that if they prospered he too would prosper. He needed prosperity? He did. Result? He was released from prison.

Everyman is responsible for his own life. Look at this: Luke 4:18 … 19."The Spirit of the Lord is on me, because he has anointed me to preach good news to the poor. He has sent me to proclaim freedom for the prisoners and recovery of sight for the blind, to release the oppressed, to proclaim the year of the Lord's favor."

We are told that Jesus read this text to the church and sat down explaining that this is all they could expect of him. They could measure his performance by this manifesto. He would be accountable for everything in this manifesto. "I have come to set captives free…..to preach good news to the poor……to release the oppressed".

What a wonderful thing reading is! You can also learn how to succeed at whatever you wish to accomplish. Not only can it be immensely entertaining, but you can actually discover the tools to use in overcoming your obstacles. This chapter shows you how to overcome conflicting thoughts.

The road to prosperity demands that you forget the self and strive to serve others. Look at the biggest known corporations. They employ the greatest number of people. They look into the welfare of many families. A good company is the one that serves the interests of its workers and its customers. Isn't this true of the guys you wrote down in Chapter one? Look at your list. Revise it if some of the people on your list do not meet this criterion. That is about them. As for you if you want to make money and move from poverty o prosperity you have to forget the self and carry other peoples' cross. The word "I" is one of the most spoken words in any language. Stop using I, I and me first. Use we, we and us. The cooperative nature of 'We' surpasses the selfish life of "I." As you do this the world would like to move with you. The road to prosperity is not to be walked on alone. Were you thinking of forming a sole proprietorship? Isn't two heads better than one? Can't one cover the other when the cold breeze blows?

Take a stand. There are so many rich men and women around us whose accountability has been questioned, tested and proven defective. They keep on making and making more and more money. Prosperity therefore has nothing to do with accountability. Is the statement true or false?

Solomon gave the answer in Ecclesiastes 7:12. I quote him because he is thought to be the cleverest person that has ever lived. 'Wisdom is a defense, and money is a defense but the excellence of wisdom is, that wisdom gives life to them that have it".

Look at Solomon's words and replace 'wisdom' with 'accountability'

Abed explains his experience this way. He returned from Japan with all elements of a successful man. He had a beautiful car and a beautiful girlfriend. He had a sweet life style and everything on the outside looked so good for him. However his wealth brew away like dew. He blamed his failures on activities of others and never took personal responsibility himself. For instance he did not keep records of his daily expenses and when his girlfriend walked out on him that he could not take her to the saloon she wanted, he blamed it on her extravagance –a habit himself bred.

As Abed's business enterprise was cracking and breaking down he shifted away from the very principles on which he had built it. Something that had been started in good spirit was then being maintained by personal strength. He sold fake dollars and drugs to finance his trade. He went into commitments which he signed knowing he could not fulfill. He wanted money to overcome his problems on the spot and forgot his future completely. He lied and cheated. In the end he was a thief by definition.

He lost sight of God and he blamed his failures on a God who had become deaf. In fact it was Abed himself who declared that his faith in those "religious ideals" was over and broke away from God. He particularly made up his mind to annoy God by not praying to him, not consulting him and breaking his rules. He got angry at himself but put the blame on others. He might have come close to committing suicide but surely God does not want sinners to die.

This turns now into a serious warning that if you have to move from poverty to prosperity and maintain your balance up there, you have to be fully accountable to your activities.

In my stay in Tanzania I experienced a political saga unveil in my eyes. President Kikwete's beloved Prime Minister was caught up in a corrupt deal in which he had authorized illegally a company to supply electricity to the country in a time of emergency. There was drought in the country. Rivers dried up and the country that relied on hydroelectricity for its industries suffered terrible power shortages. To save the situation from becoming worse the Prime Minister allowed an American company to supply new turbines and to generate electricity. The company failed to deliver. The Parliament accused the Prime Minister of irresponsibility and by the end of it all, the Prime Minister was forced to resign and his cabinet dissolved.

Of course the Prime Minister was hurt politically and financially. If he were on a road to prosperity irresponsibility made him take the Prosperity-to-Poverty lane. According to him he resigned to account for his mistakes. When he did the mood in the country changed. Those who were shouting, "Crucify him, Crucify him' were silenced. Accountability may not stop us from making mistakes but may reduce the pain the mistakes would breed. The mistake of all ages is behaving unaccountable.

When we deny our part in our mistakes; we blame our weaknesses on others; we bear false witness; we commit untold crimes. There and then we walk from prosperity to poverty. This is a lane we should never take. Latvin, Abed and many others are just but examples. Prosperity and accountability are closely related and cannot be separated.

CHAPTER TWELVE

THOUGHTS

The desire to grow rich is not difficult to form on any one's mind. That has been the desire of all ages since time immemorial. We have always wanted to make money and grow from poverty to prosperity with no possibility of falling back. (That is the title of this book). The greatest difficulty of all ages has been the question of how to resolve conflicting thoughts and here is the answer.

You cannot go anywhere unless you start. I wrote about this in the Face to Face with Grief. As I said it in the preface I wanted to write the book. I was always ready to start but I did not start writing because I always felt I would start, "Tomorrow". My wife Letty got me up, handed a pen and paper and ordered, "Start now." That is when I started writing that book. So I said of her, "This book could not have been completed nor started nor written without the driving force of my dear wife Letty A. Gamiao Kawuma.

To succeed you need Hardwork, Encouragement and Justice. This is what Abed got and made a lot of money. You could do it too and grow from poverty to prosperity.

Call a task force and this could be as small a team as yourself alone, your wife and you, your children and you or your partner and you. Declare that the days of procrastination have come to an end. The time for action is on hand. Take the first step. Begin your day with prayer and do not ask for anything else but wisdom. Learn it from Solomon. When he took the throne of his father David, he did not pray for power or honor or wealth but all these were added to him when he asked for wisdom. Of him it is said that no king of his time and of these days and time after ever came to or will ever come to Solomon's prosperity. He dressed like a butterfly and his bed and dishes were made of pure gold. If you do think that was only the figurative language of the Bible, question what exit strategy you did choose. Did you choose to earn one dollar a day or are you blinded by disbelief?

Get an ordinary size piece of paper. Hold it horizontally and fold it in half and fold that half again. Get your envelope-looking paper and hold it such that the shorter side is the top. Fold off the top something like a centimeter wide piece. Use your thumb to iron the ages of the paper well. Unfold the paper and with a pen trace through all lines of the fold. You have now four equal portions Title your columns: Where I am, Where I am Going to be, What to do and When.

Do not fill in these gaps right away. Get another piece of paper and write your exit strategy in as few words as possible. If you cannot write your dream you cannot turn your dream into reality. Take it from me. I could not write a book by thinking about it. Ideas came and went but the real task began when I put a pen on paper. You cannot achieve your business plan if you cannot write it down. You need to think all through your operation before you mount on it but the real task begins when the pen is on paper. A great leader is the one who leads events not the one who follows them. You do not want to be a follower in your own business. You do not want to be a follower of your own life. You do not want to be a follower of your own prosperity. You want to lead your life. Think before you act but once the thinking starts mark your ground. Raise your flag and claim your territory. Your pen is your flag. When the thinking process is all over and your writing can show the boundaries of your thinking that is when you start implementing your thoughts. That is when you put your thoughts into words. Thereafter your words become actions. Every important piece of art has a signature to it. Write your business plan and if it is good enough put your signature to it. Do not sign or commit yourself into what you cannot do. Many people have gone to prison for this. Do not risk your life for what you cannot do. If you work on a business plan you have not written you will be like a squatter. Your complaint will be your only defense, "It is not fair. I came here first!" but you will surely be removed by a newcomer with a land title.

Your exit strategy is your vision. A man without vision is blind. If a blind man leads another blind man won't both of them fall in a ditch? Do not pattern with a blind man (unless his mind can see)! Find someone to share your vision with. If you cannot believe your own strategy do not expect others to follow. Agree with your heart on the strategy you are building. Are you sure you can retire young and retire rich? Are you sure you are not too old to start a new project? Are you sure you cannot start business when you have no money at all? Are you sure you can grow from poverty to prosperity? Are you sure you are ready to change your life style? Are you sure God is looking at your business plan? Are you sure you are not struggling alone? Are you sure you are not fooling yourself?

Then take your mind to Germany and look at the World soccer match. Look at the goal. Build your goal posts and decide what is going to be called a 'Score' and a 'No goal'. What is your goal? Is buying a car a goal? Is building a house a goal? Is taking your children to college a goal? What is a goal? Go back and read Chapter Five. In this chapter you will find the real gist of prosperity. Read this chapter as often as you can. Pick your goal.

Now that you have a vision and a goal, go and fill in the columns on your first paper. This is a tough exercise. I recommend taking a fifteen-minute break before you continue your work

Think seriously of who you are. You are a son of your father. That is a fact. You have authority over who you are. You have a right to call him Father and him to call you my son. You have a right to say this is my land because it is my father's land. You have a natural right of sonship. You are your inheritance.

Develop this picture further. At the beginning of life God created the world out of nothing. He used no material to build the earth. His word was sufficient. He said: let the Earth be and the earth was created. He then said to Adam: Take authority over that. Jesus too said: By authority invested in me by my father, I extend this authority to you mankind that if you talk to mountains to move they will obey. Whatever you may ask in my name I will say 'Yes'. I have paraphrased these facts but you can check them up in Genesis chapter One and in the Gospels of Luke ......, Matthew and Mark 11:22-23......

Now see yourself in this new light. You are not a broke brat. You are a son of God. Add this to your profile of who you are. Like your father you can build prosperity out of nothing.

You can simply say: Let there be prosperity and prosperity will be. Your word is sufficient. If you say you have no money or you are broke that is what you will be. You were given the authority to say something and it occurs. You are what you call yourself. You certainly tie yourself in poverty by pronouncing yourself poor. You certainly tie yourself in poverty by thinking that being poor is the same as being disabled. You have the authority to move money. You can say to it "Come here" and it comes. You can say go there and it goes. You can say enter this pocket and it enters. By mere word Jesus ordered the evil spirit to run into pigs and drown itself (both the Koran and the Bible document this story) you too have the authority to command doubts to go and drown. You have the authority to be rich. You have the authority to mint money. You have the authority to move from poverty to prosperity. It is sometimes hard to believe but take courage and believe. And if you do believe order your mouth never to say again such obscene words like I have no money. Say instead money is here soon. You have the money only that you have not seen it yet. Why do you believe you have eyes and yet you have never seen them? Believe Money is soon coming in. Believe money is already in your own pockets though you have not checked your pockets yet. At first it has to be an idea, then a thought, then a word and then action. All this happens in a splash as it were in the creation of the universe if you claim the spirit of your father in heaven.

If you had not added yourself as a child of God in your profile better do so now. Next add those things you possess which help to define you e.g. I'm a believer in the lordship of Jesus Christ. I am a college graduate. I have a degree in Business Administration from Japan PRC. I'm computer literate. I have been to Tokyo, Kamaguchi and Yokohama. I know how these port cities operate. I have been to Dar Es Salaam and Maputo. I know what kind of goods is needed in this East African region. I know the market. I know what I'm doing.

You need stamina to start making money. You need to know your background. You need to know your strength and where it comes from. Count all the money you have. Count that which you can get from your brothers and sisters. Count that money in your uncles' pockets. Count all the money from members of your task force. Add it all and see how much you have. If it is not enough for your venture extend your hunting field. There is a story in the Bible in Luke ….. when Jesus needed to feed five thousand people and he did not have even a single fish or a toast of bread. He asked his team what they had. They answered that they had had nothing. All they could see was a small boy with five fish and a loaf of bread. Jesus added this boy to his task force. He got the fish and prayed and gave thanks. The Koran dedicated a whole book called the Surah V of Table Laid to this event. Prosperity is for us all. Get into gear. Gather all your possessions, bless them and give thanks. At the end of the day, the leftovers were more than one fish and five loaves. I told you before that when your spirit is low and you cannot find anything to thank God for the day find someone else to whom you could say a word of encouragement. I say it again here that if you find that your resources are not enough; find someone who can agree with you that prosperity is for us all. Invite him to your dream team. Isn't two heads better than one? Can't one cover the other when the cold breeze blows?

You may take a short break if you so wish. Read chapter three again. Read your vision and goal statements. Out of this decide where you are going.

You are not just kicking your life haphazardly. You have set up a goal. You have setup the rule that if you get the ball in the wrong way, for instance if you are offside, even if you kick the ball into the opponent's net that score will not be counted. God set up the rule: Like a partridge that hatches eggs it did not lay are those who gain riches by unjust means. When their lives are half gone, their riches will desert them, and in the end they will prove to be fools.

A fool or not a fool that is a choice you have to make. In the beginning you had a choice to be born or not to be born. You have had a choice to be poor or to be rich. You have had a choice to make money or to lose money. You have had a choice to determine your life paths or to follow others. The truth about choices, even if you are given only one choice, you have no right to choose a wrong choice. Even if you are given two choices, between life and death, you have no right to choose the wrong choice. Whether you are given three, four or five choices, you have no right to make a wrong choice. Be very careful as you choose.

Traveling in Tanzania by public transport is an easy thing to do. You do not need to know much of where you are passing but you need to know your destination. Each town has its own colour code. For instance Ubungo is red and Kariako is dirty green. A van from Ubungo to Kariako would have a red and green stripe. Buguruni is brown. A van from Ubungo to Buguruni has a red and brown stripe. The Promised Land Hotel is in Buguruni. When I had to move from Ubungo to the Promised Land I could only use buses with red and brown stripes. Kipepeo Beach had no colour code. That meant there was no public bus going to Kipepeo Beach. To go to Kipepeo I had to use a bus to a place called Ferry Port (Kivukoni) and take a ferry from there. I repeat: You do not need to know much of where you are passing but you need to know your destination.

Learn something more about traveling in Tanzania. You do not need to know many Swahili words but one word 'Shusha' is essential. It is a word everyone in a bus must say when getting off the bus. It works like this. When you enter a bus you say nothing and you are asked nothing. The bus conductor rattles coins against each other in your face to show you what he wants from you. He hardly says a word except making that crick sound in your ear. The bus conductor calls out the name of the stage a number of times as the bus reaches the stage. You will hear Buguruni, Buguruni, Buguruni, Buguruni maybe ten times. Whoever is going to Buguruni then answers, 'Shusha' and is let out. The stage to the Promised Land is called Malapa. If you were going to the Promised Land you would wait for the conductor to call out Malapa, Malapa, Malapa, Malapa. You answer: 'Shusha' and then you are let off.

To make money is like traveling on a road to prosperity. You need to know where you are going. You do not need to make your prayer in many words. You need only to determine where you are going and tell your conductor, "This is the kind of prosperity I need. Dear God let me 'shusha' here.

Now read through your goals. Determine your bus stages. Building a house could be one such stage. Paying off your debts could be another of your stages. Read through chapter five and underline all stages in the chapter. Looking at your ladder picture might enhance your understanding.

There was a time I was traveling from Ubungo to the Promised Land. I took the right bus but when I heard Buguruni, Buguruni, Buguruni I said 'shusha'. I went off the bus and I could not find the hotel. Then I was told I had got off the bus too early. I did not miss my mark. I simply did not reach my destination. I did not have the joy I was promised. We are meant to enjoy this life abundantly. In other words we are meant to have joy that overflows our heart. We have to have a life that goes beyond riches. We cannot have that unless we reach our destination. That day I got off the bus at Buguruni my spirit sank.

My heart was hurt. I felt disturbed and panicked. I knew I was close to the hotel. I decided to walk. I tried this and this shortcut but I could not see the hotel. I stopped and asked passersby. Some said "Right ahead" others said "It was too far off. I better took a taxi." Others warned me of pickpockets on the way. This could have been a useful guideline but the most unnecessary to a lost man. I stopped and asked a police man and all he could say was that he was not a traffic officer. He said I could try over there or there but he was pointing in different directions. I tell you young men and women reading this book. Never drop off your life paths too early.

Here is another assignment for you. Fill in the stages you are going to pass in the column <u>Where I am Going to Be.</u> Remember if you get off the bus at any of these stages you would have missed your destination. You will be like me getting off at Buguruni instead of getting off at Malapa.

Many people of Tanzania have the common characteristic of the poor people the world over. They have no sense of time. At the best they are always late at the worst they never turn up to their appointments. Those who have lived abroad blame the delay on long traffic jams on the roads and the 'Stay-homes' explain failure to turn up that they had had to bury someone who had died of Aids the previous night.

Both circumstances are possible excuses. They can neither be confirmed nor denied. Those who give such reasons for the sake of getting out of trouble are in danger of keeping in poverty and being written off as liars. Our attitude in this book is that there is no excuse for being poor. We are children of God, created in his own image with permission to go in the world and multiply. God did not send us in the world to suffer. He told us to overflow suffering with joy. There is no comfort for those who live in poverty. We have to find ways of making money and making it in such abundance that we have reason to give glory to God. We do not need to make money just for the sake of it. We need to enjoy making money. We do not want to work for money. That is enslavement not prosperity. We want money to work for us. That is what prosperity is all about. We do not even need to sacrifice ourselves that our children may prosper. We need to prosper ourselves. Our children will build on this foundation. We need therefore to put the sense of time in our journey to prosperity.

Go back to your folder. Check the time your master plan gave you. Did you want to see prosperity in 3, 5 or 10 years? Can you afford the wait? What are you planning on? Are you thinking of prosperity for your children or for yourself? Take this view in mind and start timing yourself.

When you ride a bus from Liiban hotel to the Promised Land, you will go through a number of stages: Mnazi Moja, Congo, Kariako, Market, Karume, Ilala, Amana, Malapa. In your traveling you may expect at least a minute of stopping over at each stage. You may also consider that there are usually traffic jams around Kariako stage. You may spend fifteen minutes or so without moving at all. The trip therefore from Liiban to the Promised Land may take you between 30-45 minutes on ordinary days and perhaps longer if you travel during what is ironically called 'Rush Hours.'

It is sometimes faster to take a longer route to save time. You could come from Mnazi Moja, take the bus to Posta (this is in a direction opposite to where you are going) and then from there perhaps go to Kivukoni and then take a bus to Buguruni and then to Malapa. In terms of distance alone Kivukoni to Buguruni is longer than Mnazi Moja to Malapa. What is important to you is how long it takes to reach Malapa. The distance may be longer but the time may be shorter. Adding prayer, consultations, writing business plans may seem to be making your journey longer but no it saves time. It took the children of Israel a matter of days to leave the land of slavery but took 40 years to rich the land of milk and honey. It is taking them even longer to find the milk!

Does it matter to you how long it takes to prosper? Are you satisfied on being on the journey for the rest of your life? I said in the opening pages of this book that I sincerely envy the young men and women who are reading this book today. If I knew what I am telling you now before I got grey haired; if I knew the art of living when my body was strong enough to go on falling in love with the best girl in town, if somebody had told me what is in this book or if when I was told I had the guts to listen I would have grown richer than I am today and I would have done it long ago. I would have had many days to enjoy prosperity and I would not have struggled so much to make a living. I now know that what is good for grand parents is not necessarily good for grand children. I know if I were given the chance to live my life again, I would never spend a bit of my life in sorrow. Wisdom has taught me what to do. When thoughts are against me, I change the thoughts. I do not have to allow all sorts of thoughts in my mind. If they are for me, I let them to go along with me. If the thoughts are confusing me I dismiss them. I choose what to think. From page one I told you to believe my story. That is what could win for me. On page 95 I begged you not to believe. Why did I do this? We have the power to control our thoughts. I think this is true for all people who do want success in life.

Thoughts are ideas conceived in the mind. We do not walk by sight, smell, hearing, tasting or feeling. Thinking allows beings to model the world and to represent it according to their objectives, plans, desires and ends. We are human beings not plants!

Go back to your folder and decide when you need to reach each stage you indicated in your flow chart. Do not allow yourself to change your exit strategy. The temptation is to say that it does not matter whether you exit at 40 or 50 years of age. It matters a lot. If you feel you are pressurizing yourself; or if you feel like doubting your timing, check your heart up. Is God still part of your plan? Have you shut him out in this planning stage and expect to turn to him on your knees in the end and say, "Dear God, I know I did not consult you when I was planning all this but since you are a good and merciful father, please approve my deal'? Is this what you are going to do to your partner? Try it one day on your Task Force! Take all the decisions alone and when you are stuck call the Task Force up and ask them to pull you out of trouble? If you ever find it easy I give you my email address (cares@kayiwa.com) write to me I will send you a gift.

I say this because what we usually do is to lock God out of our planning stages. We lock him out of our meetings. We limit his hands by allowing him to operate at our own level. We assume God can give us one dollar a day but giving us US$1000 a day in profit is too much for him. We trust our doubts and doubt our beliefs. I am reminding you that it is not us as human beings who asked for prosperity. It is not us as human beings who asked God to create us. It is not us as children who chose our parents. It is not us but God who did all this. We can only show our appreciation by going to him and say, 'Daddy can I go out today?'

If you know at what time to reach each stage of your journey you are almost ready to start your journey. Now fill in the last column of your chart. What do I have to do to achieve that? What obstacles are there on the journey?

You do not have to carry a spare tyre in the bus from Liiban to the Promised Land though there is a possibility of having a puncture on the way. The thinking pattern at this stage is very important. Do not labour with what you are not supposed to do. In the buses 'Do not Smoke' signs are written right on the doors. You must not worry yourself with what might happen to you if you lit up in a public bus. The emphasis in this book is that we should not be concerned with what we should not do but with what we should do. Spend your energy on what needs to be done. Speak out your possibilities and work on them. Make up your mind and do what you are supposed to do.

Read through your plan four or five times. Revise it if you really need to. Put your signature to it. What you have accomplished today is your master plan. Check to see that it is an excerpt of what you read at the time you cried out that message: "I know it is going to be tough but I will try it anyway". I admit the difficulty of all ages: Taking the First Step. A word of encouragement is here. Most of these successful men and women you see around have gone through the same steps. Warning: You cannot go to Step 2 unless you pass Stage 1. Shortcuts to prosperity are called bribery, fraud, corruption, theft. They are suggestive but very dangerous. Avoid them as much as you avoid invitations of an enticing prostitute.

Get on your marks, get set and go. Do not look back until you have won the crown! Lot's wife according to Genesis 19:6 was given the same instruction but she looked back and turned into a pillar of shame.

There is no prosperity for those who fear to take the first step. Suppose God told you, "Go into the world and prosper", what would you do? Would you remain skeptical and say, "Show me the money!" Would you rise up and walk? Would you continue in your slumber? Or would you say, "I will not believe it was the voice of God until my bills are paid. I will not believe until I have a new house or a new dress. I will not believe until my children are out of college. I will not believe until I have got a job. I will not believe until I am healed. I will not believe until my problem is solved! I will not believe until...."

Now take that first step. Rise up and walk. Go with one mind. Throw out all opposing thoughts. Throw out all thoughts that come to discourage you. Throw out all fear-breeding thoughts. Keep only those thoughts which are on your side. This is your life. You have to guide it by taking charge of your thoughts. As much as exercise and routine discipline can improve your physical body, exercising your thinking and setting up strict guidelines for the flow of your thoughts can and does improve your mind.

Your mind houses your thoughts and it is your responsibility to keep your house knit and tidy. The solution is in dismissing all opposing thoughts and limiting entry and invitation to only encouraging remarks.

The desire to grow rich is not difficult to form on any one's mind. That has been the desire of all ages since time immemorial. We have always wanted to make money and grow from poverty to prosperity with no return. (That is the title of this book). The greatest difficulty of all ages has been the question of resolving conflicting thoughts and here is the answer. Prune out the weed.

CHAPTER THIRTEEN

Doubt

When I ended the previous chapter with 'Here is the answer' I did not mean 'This is the end of the story' I meant go back to the Master Planner and say,
"Dear God,

Hallowed be thy Name
Your Kingdom come on earth as it is in heaven
Forgive us as our trespasses as we forgive those who trespass against us
For yours is the kingdom..........Amen.

Growing faith into children is perhaps the best gift we can give as parents. Trusting God for things we can do ourselves is perhaps the best gift we can give to the father. We often give God the hard part of our lives and yet he deserves the whole of it. We need God on Monday, Tuesday, Wednesday, Thursday, Friday, Saturday, and of course on Sunday. Seven days without God make one weak. Who needs a week of Sinday, Mournday, Tearsday, Wasteday, Thirstday, Fightday and Shatterday? We need God while making our business plans. We need him while implementing our plans and we need him even after we have turned from poverty to prosperity or else we fall back again into poverty. I sometimes wonder how God feels when he sees us on our knees, fasting and praying when we are stuck into trouble, beating our chests and shouting, 'Where are you God I need you' and yet we were the same people who chose to shut him out of our plans! Thank God. He is all loving and full of mercy!

In the same previous chapter I mentioned something I did not spend time on. I said: To succeed you need hard work, encouragement and justice. This is true because every plan is a force in itself. Newton said: Every action has got an equal and opposite reaction. Remember Abed quoted the same principle sometime in the previous pages. (I get it. See page 99). Paul however cried out when it came to implementing plans. He said I do what I am not supposed to do and I do not do what I am supposed to do. Was he talking for everybody?

In psychology we are told that when two or more people come together they form a group. The group so formed however has a life of its own and its thoughts are more powerful than all the thoughts of the individual members put together. When individual members try to control the group or the group tries to impose itself on its creators then a source of conflict is planted.

James 4 says: You kill and fight when you cannot get what you want............The greatest wickedness of all times is doubt. There is no business plan you can make with God that the devil will not oppose. If you ever make a plan and see that there is no opposing force to it suspect that you are either doing things in your own strength or you are hand-in-hand with the devil. It is so dim-witted to say but it is as true as said that human beings as we are cannot do anything on our own.

There is a letter Abed claims to have received from a grave. I had earlier headed this chapter a Letter from the Grave but on editorial advice I changed it. I had chosen this strange title because the message itself came in a dream and the main character in the story had died almost a year before Abed was born. Isn't strange to you that death is not the end of everything? People die and go but they never leave.

The story begins when Abed had just returned home from a business meeting. It was in those days when he would go by the Christian name Charlie. He felt tired and fell on a couch and napped off. There and then he got this strange dream.

Before you understand any dream you need to know the background of it. The event happened a few years after Abed had returned from Japan. His business was running well but his home was in pieces. Abed was spending all his time with his business friends and hardly remembered that he had a wife and children to love. The dear wife used to spend sleepless nights waiting for him or searching for him in pubs and street corners. In the dream he told her that he had found a new girlfriend and he wanted to live with her. He wanted an immediate and unconditional divorce because he wanted to get married in a church. The wife needed to leave and if she did not Abed for one would leave.

In reality Abed had only seen his father in a black and white picture his mother had kept. In the dream the father had come to pay a visit because he had seen things that did not please him. He was so scared he said the world was going to ruin because we had forgotten the great teaching of the prophets. This isn't surprising because his father had converted to Christianity in prison. He had seen how great criminals had turned into saints on baptism. He had seen the blind regain their vision. He had seen the lame walk. He too prayed for his captors and he was released. He knew that one could turn from a negative personality to a positive one by merely confessing ones sins.

"I wish to return to the good-old days. These days self criticism is dead. People only criticize others and hardly do they criticize those who deserve to blame. Everything is going the wrong way around. You love doing favors to yourselves. You say, "I did not intend to do that." "Forgive me on the basis of my intentions". When it comes to condemning others, you say, "Who can forgive such behavior" You animals of small brain, why do you judge yourselves on your intentions and judge others on their actions? Be consistent."

Abed did not see his father coming in but he saw him go. He walked towards Kipepeo Beach. He walked towards the sand and he kept on going. He reached the water front and he kept on going. He entered the water. He did not sink. He kept on walking. He walked on the water! He walked. He walked and walked until he vanished but he did not swim nor did he sink. Abed was left thinking about what happened. He woke up trembling. He did not doubt whom he had seen. He did not doubt the meaning of the message. He knew exactly what his father was referring to. He shook.

Abed called his mother in Mozambique and told her this strange dream. His mother confirmed that death is not the end of everything. When we die according to her we only change our piece of dressing but the soul lives on. She mentioned men like Elvis Presley, Coban, and Bob Marley who have continued to work and even pay taxes long after their death. Some of them are even earning more money now than when they were living.

She said walking on water was not strange either. Jesus walked on water and he said whatever he did if we had faith even as small as a mustard seed we could do too. She blamed all our failures on a simple source: Doubt. 'By definition', she said, 'doubt makes us undecided and the indecision and lack of clear purpose lead us to failure.'

Peter too tried to walk on water. He succeeded on the first attempt. Why? He first asked, "Is that you Lord?" In God he trusted. He only sank when he lost that faith. He looked at the size of the waves. He lost sight of Jesus and in that short period of loss he saw his own humanity. It was inadequate. He doubted his ability to walk on water. He believed his ability to sink. He did what he believed in.

It is like building a business. The business will never sink unless we lose faith in it. Abed's father did not sink because his foundation was the truth. When you keep the truth you will pass through all dangers and you will never sink. You will walk on like a human being and walk on to your destiny. Keep focused on how to make money and do not doubt the plan you made with God as a participant– not as a witness– and you will succeed in all that you will do. The good old days said, "Seek you first the kingdom of God and the rest shall follow".

He told her he wanted to fulfill whatever his father would ever have wanted him to do.

He decided that the only way he would ever understand his father's will was by going back and study his father's words. He asked his mother to turn over all the documents of his father to him.

Abed wanted to scavenge through, study them all and discover the mind of his father. Abed had learnt long time ago that the only way you can find God's mind was by reading the Bible. He was convinced that regular Sunday church attendance was good but not enough to replace reading the Bible by oneself. Church attendance turns you into a Christian as going to a garage turns you into a mechanic! Satan hates Bible study. Satan's advice is always, "You are not learned enough to understand the Bible for yourself. Jesus only spoke in parables and the Old Testament is as outdated as the name suggests". The weakness of all ages is the longing to doubt what you believe and do what you doubt.

In the letter box was found this mail and Abed tells us the story.

"I confess the handwriting was genuinely my father's but the papers the letter was written on were newer than all the papers in the box. To the best the document could be a forgery or something just written in a week's time. The first page was missing and we do not clearly know to whom it was addressed. I will read directly from the pages we found.

"Criticism is dangerous because it puts the victim on the defensive and usually challenges one to the task of defending oneself beyond all reasonable doubt. It neglects justice and relies on the power of defense to establish righteousness. Criticism wounds a person's dignity, destroys one's worth and hurts the desire to go on living or to go on doing well. Refrain from criticism (except self criticism) and you will be on the road to prosperity. By criticizing –learn it from me–we do not correct situations we only develop resentment. Why would you take such a course? Condemn not and you will not be condemned. Judge not and you will not be judged.

"You will appreciate my saying that your words did not edify the spirit but carried with them the venom of anger and you spewed them out with the necessary accuracy to hit and hurt your victim. You aimed well and hit your target but in doing so you defeated the purpose of peaceful coexistence. You broke the covenant you made. Do not expect such a sin to go unpunished. You had a rare and golden opportunity to settle the matter but like a fool you brew it up. Not many people are offered chance for reconciliation on a silver plate. You had everything in your grasp but who bewitched you?

"There are many words in your mouth. You do not have to use them all. If you were not sure whether what you were going to say was right or wrong, why didn't you keep safe, and keep quiet? You abused. You condemned. You cursed. You blamed and yet you thought I would lay quiet in my sleep? You did wake me up. I did not want to interfere in your affairs but what would my love be if I did not come to intervene. I don't want to leave your life unguided. Give me a peaceful rest.

"There are other things I want to talk you about. Before you ever get tempted to criticize, condemn or blame try to figure out why the other person did whatever he did. Figure out if it were you in his position and time would you have acted differently or the same. If you would have had the choice of doing the same or differently and by luck you chose to do the same would you deserve sympathy, kindness or tolerance? These are virtues worth living for. Remember all those who have prospered before you sought wisdom before anything else. In all things seek understanding and the rest shall be added unto you.

"Under the sun there is only one way you can compel another person to do what you want. Make him or her feel like doing it. The same tricks you use to take a child to bed works to take a woman down. In the past I am sorry I addressed you as a child and you missed the point. Now I see you as a grown up man who should be able to understand the mechanics of a human race. Wake up. Get rich today. If you can start today, why do you have to wait until tomorrow? I want you to enjoy your own prosperity in your own time. If you start working on my words right away, you will equally prosper right away.

"You can recall how many have blundered through life by trying to force others to love them. They have miserably failed. You at one time did such a thing you know how futile your effort was and now you can count how many people have suffered the same way. The principle is that if you want people to do what you want, get them interested in what you want them to do. Human beings are selfish by nature. Everyone loves oneself more than one loves others. Everyone is interested in oneself more than one is interested in others. Everyone is interested in what one is doing more than one is interested in what others are doing. Follow the argument through if you want them to do what you want. Of course you may use threats, whips or bullets to get your desire addressed but at the end you will have taken the long and wrong way. The desire to be appreciated tops the list of people's craving. "People need people" is a fundamental law of human nature. From this law all other laws like 'Hurting people hurt', 'People of the same degree of happiness hung out together' spring. Yes, health, food, shelter, sex, money, job are all good and desirable cravings but appreciation tops all these. Give it always. Do not worry yourself out. Appreciation is like joy or love. The more you give appreciation the more of it you get. Of it you will never give more that you can bear and will never run the stock down. Give it all. Give it always. Give it persistently. Give it with open mind. Do you know why people who keep antiques in their houses live longer than people who keep modern furniture? The antique lovers appreciate the value of long life and so they live longer. If you doubt what am saying just do some little research. If you find me wrong knock my door after midnight. I will wake up and serve your table.

"The desire to make you appreciated determines the cars you drive, the style you wear and the stories you tell about your children. What has this to do with the great question of prosperity you asked? You can't grow rich unless you appreciate the value of money. Money is such a thing that if you have a lot it keeps on multiplying and attracting more money. When it dies, however, or when you lose it, it poisons and kills even the little money you might be left with. It may not only kill the money in your pocket or bank but it will also cut off roads that bring in more money. We should all have the desire to have it and resist the pressure to lose it.

"If you want to make money, learn to give it away. As a matter of trial and practice give 10% of your first month's earnings to church or to your favorite charity and see what happens. I guarantee you. You will receive more than ten folds in return. The Bible tells you not to give grudgingly but I tell you to give in all circumstances and you will get back the value of your money in all circumstances. If you doubt this teaching principle give 10% of your salary to your wife, give10% to your friend or give 10% to your enemy and see how much that gesture yields! If man corrupt as he is can be delighted by your sacrifice how much more would your father in heaven be if you lived your life the way God wants? Won't he turn you from poverty to prosperity?

"Appreciation can never be over appreciated. Call a waitress in a Hotel or Pub by name. Ask her about her life and telephone number. Ask your employee how the children at home are doing. Tell a traffic officer you are sorry it might be uncomfortable for him to stand in that hot sun or freezing weather for your sake.

These tiny tips will tip love in your favour. Give honest and sincere appreciation and give it all the time. All those who have prospered before you gained so because they appreciated something in their surroundings. They called this, "A deal". The real gist in the matter is to appreciate in your situation what could make you prosper. Cling to those positive moments and focus on them all the time. Surely you can turn life around from extreme misfortune to wonderful prosperity.

"Hurting people physically does not change them. Appreciate others and you will be appreciated. Whatever is appreciated gains value. When you appreciate your wife she gains value. When you demean your wife you break your marriage down. It is also true in business. If you keep complaining in your office you destroy your business. You deserve no promotion and you will never prosper".

'The page abruptly ended there. There is nothing more to add or to take away from this letter. It clearly spells out the way to prosperity. I am very grateful to my father in the grave or to the unknown author of this letter. Taken seriously it spells appreciation as one of the important virtues you want in life. When you talk to customers let them see their benefit, not your benefit. Then they will respond to their own needs. Everyone has a need to prosper but doubt has cast doubt on our power or on our means to get what is ours by right. Customers always want to buy for instance but they have doubt in their mind. A good salesman is one who erodes away this doubt. We need to conquer doubt if we are to prosper. The way forward is always to appreciate others as they appreciate us. We forgive others as we forgive ourselves. We get forgiveness as we forgive others. The desire of all ages is to make money and grow from poverty to prosperity and never to fall again. The message is true whether in family or in business'.

Abed has a story about this topic but we will meet him again in another chapter. Meanwhile go back to your mind and recall those events in your experiences that ended in failure simply because you developed some form of doubt as you were implementing your plans. Search your soul and see how many times you failed when actually you were destined to succeed. If only you gave your project one more thought now you are saying, you would have succeeded. Resolve never again to quit when you are just minutes away from success. The history of many men and women who have prospered has shown that the difference between failure and success is the extra mile after the stage where others have called it quits. Remember what I told you before. To succeed you need aspiration, inspiration and perspiration. In other words you need hard work, encouragement and justice. Now I add: success delayed is not success denied. Do not doubt your prosperity when it looks delayed. Go on. Work on your Master Plan and you will get the prosperity we saw in chapter five. Here is one more thing. Whenever doubt comes to your mind ask yourself this great question: What would Jesus do in this circumstance?

Doubt usually comes in by a way of reminding you of past failures. It blames your present predicament on your past performance. It threatens your future by saying you are bound to fail. Think of it. Can two walk together unless they agree? You say, "No." Here now is the cure to your double minded heart. Disagree with those negative "warnings". Shout out aloud: I provoke my right to disagree. Devil I disagree. I choose to succeed not to fail. Success is the choice I took in the beginning and success is the fruit I have to take in the end.

Have a positive attitude for your future. Have a positive attitude to your success. The fact that the work is difficult does not mean that it cannot be done. It is hard but it can be done. You can turn from poverty to prosperity. You can make enough money to meet your needs. You can make enough money to meet your luxuries. You can make enough money to pay for what you do not need. You can overflow your pockets with money. You can overflow your bank account with money. You can be filled with joy. You can overflow with joy. Just do not doubt what you started in good spirit. Work up your plans towards the end.

Abed found a note in his father's documents. It said, "I have a stubborn will to succeed." Let this be your shield against doubt. When Doubt sends you its arrows pull up this shield. Remember nothing is ever stronger than a shield. The Masais of Tanzania have a saying that the only thing stronger than a spear is a shield. It is the only weapon known to man that ever stands in a way of an attack. Write this shield on a piece of paper and keep it in your money purse. Carry it with you wherever you go. God has a word for us all, "Be strong and courageous, (1 Chronicles 28:20) and do the work. Do not be afraid or discouraged, for the LORD God, my God, is with you. He will not fail you or forsake you until all the work ~~for the service of the temple of the LORD~~ is finished.

CHAPTER FOURTEEN

EXPERIENCE

Suppose God told you.......No.. no.. no..... . Just imagine God told you, "Go into the world and multiply," would you take a second wife? Would you look for another partner? Would you throw your current boyfriend or girl friend out of the window? What would you do?

Suppose God told you, "Come unto me, all ye that labour and are heavy laden, and I will give you rest," would you relax?

Some people have called experience the best teacher—because it tests first and teaches later. I think they are saying this in contrast to the school system which they rate as out of date with the times. What however they are saying of experience is true for all people. Experience's synonym should be Confidence. Experience produces Confidence and Confidence produces Experience. This is confirmed true by all people who have achieved success through trial and error. Trial and Error (T&E) is costly for people who would like to grow from poverty to prosperity. (Perhaps they may not even be able to afford it). T&E is unacceptable to people who have tasted prosperity to think of using again. They cannot imagine taking a path that can easily slid one back to poverty. Life is not a game of cards. You cannot afford to gamble it away!

Games are good but this is not true of all games. Similarly experience could be the best teacher but you do not have to go to jail to learn to avoid crime. Experiencing hardship might train your soul not to grief over losses and may even develop resilience in your heart but it is not a welcome idea as a teaching method. Experiencing negative forces, criticism, discouragement, abuse, anger, sorrow, fear, hatred, sadness, failure and doubt might cultivate in you a feeling of doom. All you will see then will be failure and a failure you will become. Experiencing success after success or success after repeated failures is most likely to drive you into further attempts and better yields. This is why we think of experience as a real mystery. Some people have used their previous pains to get out of poverty but others have lost the drive to invest in money-making projects. The losers have not only remained poor but as time passes by the world seems to bypass them and they eventually become poor and poorer. What then shall we say?

I have experienced many events in Tanzania which have changed my perspective of life. Writing this book is a good example. As I embarked on the task of showing that one can grow money and change from poverty to prosperity I have examined many cases which have built up my story. My belief that you are what you think has grown and got refined. In Face to Face With Grief I emphasized the importance of your brain but I have refined that idea to what you read in the first pages that you can turn your life around from surviving to thriving by simply changing your thinking. I am standing on that ground to add an afterthought. It is not what you feel that matters. It is what you believe. I said this before but as you read it again it develops a deeper meaning than the one you got when you just opened this book. If I repeat a number of times this statement you will reach a point when you will just remember it automatically. Check what I have just said.

"It is not what you feel that matters. It is what you believe".
Now repeat it to yourself five times. What does it say?
"It is not what you feel that matters. It is what you believe".
Repeat it three times and then two times and then once. I promise you will see the power of persistence by doing this simple exercise.

Abed told me how he avoided capture by the police for almost three months yet the police was looking for him every day and there was even a price tag on whoever would turn him in. He said after stealing one had to avoid bad company and by definition that is keeping in company with fellow thieves. Police is trained to identify criminals by studying the company people keep. Every day crime is reported, the first people to be suspected are the gangs, migrants and minorities. Do not keep in company of thieves, drunkards, drug users, (including smokers). We are always identified by the company we keep. By interpretation if you keep company with the poor, the miserable, the complainers, the lost, who will ever come to your rescue? Abed came to a great discovery while in prison. 'You do not plan jailbreak with fellow prisoners'. All successful jailbreaks are those planned by free men!

Keep among the rich, the good, the wise and you will always be free and you will grow to be as prosperous as them. The other advice Abed gave was that never steal from the same place or from the same person more than once. Tricks are like miracles. They only succeed once. Who but a professional thief would be a better teacher at stealing and avoiding arrest?

I had an experience with my secretary Jane who could never write a sentence grammatically correct in English – that is not condemnation nor criticism – that was what she was at the time she was hired. Jane has typed through part of this manuscript and has confessed to the truth in this paragraph. The only reason that could justify keeping her my secretary was the very reason she was appointed to the post.

She was Abed's "niece." She needed a job and I did not need a secretary but I wanted to do Abed a favour. Whichever way you look at it everything worked together for the good of us all.

I drafted all my letters, typed them, and mailed them. All she did was to read them and I gave her strict instructions not to edit them nor disclose their content but beneath my skin I was confident even if she read them she would never have understood them.

She picked my phones wherever I would be out office or busy on another line but she could hardly remember who called or she gave me the right numbers but wrong names. Such was she as a secretary. I do not mean to hurt anybody. This is not what she is today. She may not be so good still but she is better than what she used to be.

Do you expect someone who could not pick simple verbal instructions to understand a written word? I could add a bet. Even if the letters had been translated for her into her native Swahili she would still misinterpret them. I speak however on her side now. You and I agree that having read this book this far, you may not be as prosperous as you want to be but you are not as you were before you started reading this book. Her story, naivety, is making a strong contribution to your life.

Show me your experience and I will show you mine. There is one thing to add for keeping such a lousy worker on job. When visitors came to my office and saw I had a secretary they believed I was a busy, successful entrepreneur and they valued my time more.

Look at it this way. All the clothes you wear are not for covering nakedness. Not all secretaries are there to keep secrets. A secretary may be part of the office furniture but that does not make her salary a luxurious waste of money

Anyway, how did she change?

"Alligato go zai maste." I thanked her for everything. When she greeted me, I answered "Fine, thank you" "Thank you", when she picked up my pin or pen, "Thank you." Thank you, thank you and thank you.

One of the most important principles in overcoming poverty lies in the hands of the poor. **Do not criticize, condemn or blame.** I write this in bold italics to emphasize its importance. Encourage them. Support them. When you do so they do the same to themselves and in turn they will do this to you. Do you see how the prosperity machine works?

This book, "The Desire of All Ages: How to Make Money and move from Poverty to Prosperity with no falling back", is a practical guide to changing one's life from poverty to prosperity. I know there is a great wall between poverty and prosperity. In fact this is what I see. I see a picture of the world. In this world there is an economic ladder on which is tied the fruits of prosperity. Everyone is trying to climb this ladder. Some people run in teams called countries and some people run on their individual merit. The entire human race is competing. Developed countries are right at the top of the ladder and developing countries are right down on the base. The division is so big that one can see the ladder as covered in different colors. Not every person however is on the ladder. The people in extreme poverty are stuck away in the mad far from the ladder. To these even to live is an act of courage. The hardest part of their struggle is getting to the first step. We know the reason why this is so. The first step does not lie in the lifting of the leg but in the thinking process.

As you read the past paragraph you realized I said it before. Experience is based on familiarity. Many poverty eradication programs have failed to deliver because the donors have suffocated the receivers with their generosity. We are not making a kind of criticism here but giving a learned observation. Where donors have come out with a program to follow and the poor have been given a set of rules to obey and carrots to eat in order to get aid, those schemes have failed. Success has only been achieved where the poor have participated in the poverty eradication planning stage. We can mention for instance that countries that have been forgiven debts in order to encourage transparency and good governance have had those governments plunge their countries deeper into debt.

I'm writing this section of the book from a town some 20km west of Dar es Salaam. I'm in Bagamoyo. The name itself means "Lay out your heart". This was next to Kilwa in the south as one of East Africa's biggest slave trading post. Slaves from the hinterland were first packed, counted, weighed and sorted here before being sent to Zanzibar and further on to Middle East, Europe and America. Those slaves on whose shoulders America and Europe's economy were built were filtered and weighed through this port. There is nothing of the old glory Bagamoyo can show except its museum of pain. You can see sculptures of slaves carrying ivory tasks bigger than their own body weight. You have but to be reminded of Golgotha. The slaves did not build Bagamoyo because they were only brought here and carried away. They were used as part of the money generating machine but their brain power was not part of the asset. Even where they went, few are known to have grown prosperous. The failure can be blamed on concentrating on developing physical power instead of mental strength.

If you turn your attention to the ladder you see that in front of the failing lot are those people who are at the bottom rungs. They do not sink because they have some ray of hope. Though their development is sometimes uneven and slow, they are generally making some progress. The greatest challenge of our time is that the poorest of the poor get lifted to the bottom of the ladder so that they may too start their upward movement. There is so much confusion in this world. There are people who keep on shaking the ladder to stop others from going further up. My mind says, 'These must be stopped'. This is not a crab race. Have you ever seen crabs trying to climb a wall? They always fail to climb over it not because they do not have strong hands or legs. Each crab is pulling the other down! Should the human race be this way? No. Humans being guardians of civilization as they are, the strong should be lifting the weak to the ladder. Look however at what is happening!

There is a common factor in the politics of the world's least developed countries. All their leaders preach a rhetorical condemnation of their people's poverty on the countries colonial past. By such criticism not only have they failed to make any lasting changes but they have suffered serious resentment and ridicule in the international community. Blaming our poverty on our forefathers or colonial leaders has not and will not put extra dollars in our coffers. It only serves to worsen the situation condemned. We can get out of poverty if we practice the attitude of freeing ourselves from the scourge of criticism. We should neither take it nor give it. I repeat, do not criticize, condemn or blame. If ever you wake up with a wrong temper and you want to blame your poverty on yourself or on somebody else remember Bob Marley's song: <u>Emancipate yourselves from Mental Slavery.</u>

Let me talk about my experience in Tanzania. As I went on interviewing different people on how to change from poverty to prosperity I asked for a physical sign that a doctor can take as a symptom that a poor man is starting a journey to recovery. I desperately wanted a sign. A patient in coma is thought to be recovering when the body makes a voluntary response to a physical action. All I was asking for was a sign as simple I mean as a twinkle of an eye when the patient name is called. Movement of fingers could be another. Is there any way we could see economic recovery?

Economic recovery comes in a quick succession of phases. First it is an idea. In the lifecycle of a butterfly this is when two adult flies fall into love and lay an egg. The idea grows into a desire. The egg grows into a larva. This is a wobbling sort of creature. It has life of its own. It does not look like the mother nor the father. It is fragile and it can even be disastrous. The larva eats a lot and changes fast. The desire through a process similar to metamorphosis changes into hope as the larva changes into a pupa. Hope is a resting stage. Outwardly that is what it looks like. The internal chemistry of the pupa is changing. The pupa is developing legs, wings and muscles. It looks dead outside but inside it is getting ready to fly. The proper butterfly engine is built at this stage. All defects are checked at this time. One thing is clear though. If you open up the cocoon at this stage the butterfly dies.

Similarly to change from poverty to prosperity you will have to develop an idea. When the butterflies are falling in love they do not care a damn whether the baby will be black or white. They have a desire to fulfill. Mr. & Mrs. Butterfly, when you fall in love you are not done yet until the egg is laid. Lay the egg. The Project Aim is your desire. That written statement is your egg. Lay it down. The egg will hatch itself. Butterflies do not incubate their eggs. They do not sit there and wait. All parent butterflies do is to lay eggs in an environment good enough for eggs to survive and the larvae to grow. Good planning does the entire trick. The caterpillars hatch out and live on by hide and seek. They eat and strengthen their muscles. When they have taken in enough they build a factory around themselves. Outsiders think they are dead at the worst or sleeping at the best.

Lay the desire. It will keep on acquiring new data until it's strong enough to survive on its own. Then it will turn into hope. Do not allow doubt to lead you to premature birth or to give you a still born. Go up to the Promised Land. Remember how I suffered so much by getting off the bus at Buguruni instead of Malapa. This is not an experience you would like to go through. Keep your hope to the end. It is only when the butterfly crawls out of the cocoon that its prosperity can be compared to that of King Solomon. (Page 117: He (Solomon) dressed like a butterfly..........)

Every butterfly comes up with a smile. It slowly emerged that a smile was agreed upon as a sign on the face of a person changing from poverty to prosperity. Who can keep a burning candle covered? Who can hide happiness of the heart? Do you see the significance of a smile?

We read that Abed told me that a dog taught him to smile. I found it funny, strange but true. Of course a dog could have made him smile because by looking after him (it) Abed made a lot of money. The amount of money Abed managed to send home in a month while working for free in Hongkong was more than what he could ever earn if he worked at home (either in Tanzania or Mozambique) no matter what job he would do, for a year. This however was not the main issue. The issue is that Abed learnt to change his perception of life.

Some weekend I went to visit a Moslem friend who owns a mansion near Mbezi Beach. Dar Es Salaam as a city is full of beaches and Mbezi is one of them. A dog greeted me at a home of a devout Moslem man. I grew up thinking that what separates Moslems from Christians was the keeping of dogs, eating of pork and drinking of alcohol. A dog is thought to be called so because it is a mathematical inverse of god. I thought to be smelt by a dog or to touch a dog is like associating with evil. In this country it is agreed the spirit of Satan moves in dogs. Those who say a dog is man's greatest friend might have to relearn their lessons if they came to Tanzania. This was not the kind of dog that teaches you to smile but to control your fear.

I went to visit this friend and when lunch was over I proposed visiting the beach nearby as I had become accustomed to spending my afternoons cooling at beaches. Again out of the ordinary my host told his son to take the dog out for a walk. Usually the dog walks within the confines of the compound but I went to the beach with the dog. On the way I was almost stoned. The dog was on a lead. It could neither attack nor bite other people. It did not look a threat to anybody. It was however under a constant danger of being attacked and beaten by people. All hostile words of insult followed me all the way and at the beach I could not be allowed to swim because I had touched a dog.

Now you understand how culture had taught Abed to have nothing to do with dogs. You did not have to be circumcised to keep away from dogs but you had to obey the demands of the neighborhood. Let me nip the story in the bud. Culture or traditions might be keeping you in poverty because it might be barring you from associating with certain groups of people. Look around you. Some of the restrictions you might have placed around you might be blocking your passage to prosperity.

Yes it was a dog that taught Abed to smile. I praise the revelation he observed in making that statement. You remember how he sold his own soul to buy his life in Hong Kong. You understand how it takes courage to adopt new ways of living. Prosperity does not come easily. To succeed you need aspiration, inspiration and perspiration. It might cost you throwing out your old self, your old customs (and costumes), your old beliefs to adopt new and modern ways of doing things.

Abraham the prophet was told to leave his imperial homeland to go search for a new home and by doing so with faith in God he would prosper. He did and his sheep at one time could not fit into one valley. Can you imagine that after reading this book you could make so much money that it could not fit into one bank or one bank account? You cannot prosper simply by forcing people to get interested in you. You can however prosper by seeking and finding genuine friends to walk with, sleep with, eat with. Unhappy people hate happy people. They always try to upset them. Hurting people hurt. The company you keep is very important onto your road to prosperity. Keep in company of fools and you will genuinely be one of them. Keep in company with the poor and you will certainly be. Keep yourself among the rich and wise and you will prosper. Have nothing to do with failures, agitators, complainers, criticizers, doubters, self-seekers, blamers because to such poverty belongs.

The first step in building genuine friendship is in understanding yourself. Look at a group photograph. Pick yourself out and see how you are different from others. Define yourself. Find your interests and then find someone else who could have similar interests. Talk to that person in a language clearly that expresses your interests as his or hers. You will never fail to develop a relationship this way. This is the same technique used in selecting your Task Force.

If this teaching fails, check again. Your 'common interests' may not be common. If your interests are genuine, this is bound to develop into a true, long lasting relationship. The Bible is an authority on this. Study the example of Nicodemus. I quote John 3: *Now there was a man of the Pharisees named Nicodemus, a member of the Jewish ruling council. He came to Jesus at night and said, "Rabbi, we know you are a teacher who has come from God. For no one could perform the miraculous signs you are doing if God were not with him."*

In reply Jesus declared, "I tell you the truth, no one can see the kingdom of God unless he is born again."

"How can a man be born when he is old?" Nicodemus asked. "Surely he cannot enter a second time into his mother's womb to be born!"

Jesus answered, "I tell you the truth, no one can enter the kingdom of God unless he is born of water and the Spirit. Flesh gives birth to flesh, but the Spirit gives birth to spirit. You should not be surprised at my saying, 'You must be born again.' The wind blows wherever it pleases. You hear its sound, but you cannot tell where it comes from or where it is going. So it is with everyone born of the Spirit."

"How can this be?" Nicodemus asked.

"You are Israel's teacher," said Jesus, "and do you not understand these things? I tell you the truth, we speak of what we know, and we testify to what we have seen, but still you people do not accept our testimony. I have spoken to you of earthly things and you do not believe; how then will you believe if I speak of heavenly things? No one has ever gone into heaven except the one who came from heaven—the Son of Man. Just as Moses lifted up the snake in the desert, so the Son of Man must be lifted up, that everyone who believes in him may have eternal life.

"For God so loved the world that he gave his one and only Son, that whoever believes in him shall not perish but have eternal life. For God did not send his Son into the world to condemn the world, but to save the world through him. Whoever believes in him is not condemned, but whoever does not believe stands condemned already because he has not believed in the name of God's one and only Son. This is the verdict: Light has come into the world, but men loved darkness instead of light because their deeds were evil. Everyone who does evil hates the light, and will not come into the light for fear that his deeds will be exposed. But whoever lives by the truth comes into the light, so that it may be seen plainly that what he has done has been done through God.

The story shows three important steps:-
    -the need for developing the relationship….. "we know you are a teacher who has come from God.
    -Discuss the problem that obstruct the development…. *"How can this be?"*
    -Solve the problem. ……..born of water and the Spirit.
Question: How can I prosper?
Need: Be born again.
Problem: Mistrust
Solution: Believe.

The world hates flattery. Do not use it. Be genuine in whatever you do or say. Let your tears be tears and let your laughter be laughter. True friends will always be around you. This is another step to prosperity. Now that you have the first step, go on and master your living. You are on the step to prosperity. These tips have been developed by experience and of course they are not a one man's discovery. It is the experience of many people put together. They are new words of old age. They are words of wisdom. Of them I said: I sincerely envy the young men and women who are reading this book today. If I knew what I am telling you now before I got grey haired; if I knew the art of living when my body was strong enough to go on falling in love with the best girl in town, if somebody had told me what is in this book or if when I was told I had the guts to listen I would have grown richer than I am today and I would have done it long ago. I would have had many days to enjoy prosperity and I would not have struggled so much to make a living. I now know that what is good for grand parents is not necessarily good for grand children. I know if I were given the chance to live my life again, I would never spend a bit of my life in sorrow. I now know that my actions should have been led by my beliefs not by my feelings. To lose your partner simply because love has lost its zeal should never be a guiding factor in deciding to sign for divorce or to commit abortion. The desire of all ages is one: Make Money and the purpose of this book is to show you how we have got it wrong all along.

The only thing I can add here is that it is never too late to prosper.

Experience

The men and women at Mbezi Beach like those of Butterfly Beach were good at displaying the relationship between faith and action. I noticed here too that those who were genuinely interested in beers, drunk more beers and got more drunk with the beers. Those who did not like drinking beer much, drunk fewer bottles and got drunk less. Love prosperity with all your heart, mind and body and you will prosper. This of course does not neglect the part of God's blessings in your prosperity business. That counts too but more as a reward than a mere chance of living. The results are of course different if you made God a member of your task force and not a private observer.

Living in this country and doing this research in particular has taught me the value of being genuinely interested in people. Before I could hardly speak a word in Swahili, I had fewer friends and described Dar es Salaam as hostile. The more I described it as such the hotter it became, the more humid it became, the more I noticed water and electricity shortage, the more I saw violence and theft in the streets, the more I saw a rotten city and the more I lost friends. You cannot prosper when you look at life with a negative eye. My negativity was soon destroying me. I had to change things around.

I started learning Kiswahili. More and more people became interested in me. I realized I was surrounded not by enemies but by friends. These people introduced me to their compatriots and I was able to conclude some money generating projects with these people. This worked out well for me as it worked out for the Prince of Windsor. Check in history. The Prince of Windsor wanted to visit South America. He studied Spanish for the purpose and when he went down to the America he was delighted to hear every one chanting, "Our King, our King long live the King" He spoke in Spanish and that made history. Take another case Pope John Paul II was famous for spreading Catholicism in the twentieth century. The credit that went with him to the grave was the number of languages he could speak. Learning the local language, even if it means only greeting or saying 'Susha' is a great step towards building a relationship. Where there is no relationship there is no prosperity.

People in Tanzania today have the common characteristics of poor people the world over. I am saying this again. Poor people never keep time or they never fulfill their assignment. They never say "NO" to any proposal even if deep in their mind they know the issue is unacceptable. They never commit themselves to anything. They have a form of politeness that forbids them from delivering bad news. They would choose to tell a lie than to tell a hurting truth. If you find yourself with this sort of mindset you are bound to be poor. If you want to keep yourself in poverty this is a sure deal. Just keep this kind of behavior. As a way of qualifying this statement let me say that, the people of Tanzania are going nowhere unless they change this attitude.

I might be sounding very negative here. This is not what I am meant to do and I do not want to sound like apologizing. I want to make sure you do not overlook this tip. I want my warning to be strong enough to overcome all your reasons and excuses. I am calling for a change of attitude and this requires editing your brain registry.

The vehicle to prosperity does not follow a one way street. The buses are marked Kariako-Ubungo. This means when you stand on one side of the road the bus will take you from Kariako to Ubungo but when you stand on the opposite side of the same street, the bus will take you from Ubungo to Kariako.

Watch which side of the street you are standing on. You may go from poverty to prosperity by the same bus that can take you from prosperity to poverty. You need faith to believe in God and you need faith to be an atheist.

You must learn from my experience. Use the experience of others to drive you forward. Records of those who failed to prosper should teach us what not to do but should not discourage you or dissuade you from attempting to prosper. Experience can lead you to recovery and success but if misinterpreted can lead you to fear and automatically to failure. Experience is a mystery but learn from it. I am speaking from experience and this is the bit of advice you most likely would like to throw away. I did not but hopefully you will be a little bit smarter than I was.

CHAPTER FIFTEEN

Failure

There is a day I woke up with three appointments already set. I was going to meet someone at 8.00 a.m. At 9.30 a.m. I sent him this message "Did we say we would start at 8.00? Do not blame delay on the phone".

You realize the man was late. You may be able to guess from what was said above (your experience) that this man was from Tanzania. This chapter is how to handle disappointments.

My friend used to have a problem with his phone. It broke down as often as he used it. This phone had another bad habit. It had a mouth of present-day politicians. It could switch off in the middle of a conversation and give a lying official message, "The called party is busy at the moment, please call back later". It was doing this to a friend that was close to what I would call my Program Manager. I made up my mind that even if I did not love him as a person I would give him a working tool. The truth in the rule: 'It is better to give than to receive' explains that when you give workers tools you get better output.

This friend named Hosef had no office and no place could he call home. He used to run small errands as he would be called here and there. This is very common of many busy poor people. (A similar description was used at one time to describe Abed's life style). In addition when sent out as a messenger he would come back with a smile on his face and a "Mission Accomplished" message. He never recognized failure. He would choose to lie other than appearing less successful. To him exaggeration was not a form of dishonesty but a way of cheering others up. This was so common of him that you would have to ask several questions before you would take in his answer. The more you handled him this way, the more disillusioned of him you would become. However do not count this on Hosef as an individual. One thing Tanzanians do not hesitate to do is warning you against trusting other fellow countrymen. I remember I was told by one such man on arrival at Ubungo. "Do not trust any Tanzanian. I am telling you this because I am a Tanzanian and I know Tanzanians. There is no Tanzanian who can tell the truth. Tanzania is called Brainland. This is so because we see with our brains not with our eyes".

Hosef was not only late but could not be contacted. His life line was cut off. You can calculate that he was therefore bound to lose some form of daily income and I was getting hurt too. If I were out to invest in him this could be called off. I would stand firm and tell him to blame nobody else but himself for letting me down. Isn't it this way it happens that developed countries refuse to invest in Africa and blame it on Africa? Knowing that such conduct deserves criticism I resolved no matter how bad Hosef had been in the past to bless him with a working phone. I confess I did not think of buying him a new phone but I proposed repairing his set.

Hosef outwardly was poor and slave-like but inside that head was rich and defiant. He said the reason why Africa is kept in poverty is because of using industries with out-of-date technology. She imports second hand vehicles in dangerous mechanical conditions. She clings to tried and failed socialist principles. She has developed a culture of relying on survival on outside assistance and lives on misguided advice. Hosef told me that every worker deserves his pay but he had decided to work for me pay or no pay. This way he could never fail to serve me and I would never fail to find some work for him. He called it something like part of his education course. He said he was learning something from me every day. No relationship develops without giving. By giving me his service he was developing that relationship essential to his growth towards prosperity. Where there is service there is prosperity.

I sat down and thought of the challenges that came from this scholar who had never been to school. My head started seeing reason in his words though I never reached the convenience of believing a person I despised. I came to understand why he had not turned up until 10.20 am. I saw the reason why he had not stopped by a public phone and called me to say he would be late. If I were him and he were me how would we do things differently? Suppose someone had given him some job in the same time I was expecting him and that meant immediate payment would he deny that job in hope that I might give him a bigger stipend? What if I had waited and left off in disgust would he earn anything that day? Suppose it were me with $0.20 or Tshs 200 to board a taxi and that was just enough for taking me to work would I leave my home with no guarantee for the return fare? Suppose I borrowed the fare only to realize I was leaving my wife and children with no food for lunch would I insist on using the money on transport or would I buy food?

This art of putting yourself in the shoes of another creates a positive image in your thinking and sets off the power to see life positively. This is an essential element in moving your life from poverty to prosperity. Employ this power and you will make the money you needed for so long. By understanding why others fail you will choose sympathy, forgiveness and mercy for them. When it would come to pray: Our Father who art in heaven, forgive us our sin as we forgive those who wrong us…… you will not be guilty conscious. Once your relationship is good before you, men and God, who then can be against you? You need a clean mind to start your journey to prosperity. What I am asking you to do here is at least not as outrageous as "If your enemy is hungry feed him, if he is thirsty give him water ….(Romans 12:10 check). Yet that too is a good principle for people who want to end up rich. We do not employ that. We are friends, aren't we?

The tragedy of all ages is failure including failing to be friends. Take any scheme; there are more people who fail than those who succeed. There are earnestly many men and women who try and fail. The purpose of this book is that once you have read up to this far you should never be any more one of such people. Choose success to failure. Life always presents you with choices and how you lead your life is not determined by the options you are given but by the choices you take.

In the course of writing this book I have had the privilege of sitting down with a number of people classified as 'failures'.

I have confronted them with one question, "What happened to you?" The answers have yielded important information on why people fail to move from poverty to prosperity however much they try. It also explains why even those who have tasted prosperity reach a certain moment in their life when their empires crumple before their own eyes. Listening to the stories was like watching a horror film. At every bit you know that something more terrible than what you have seen so far is bound to happen. Failure is life's greatest tragedy. I sincerely envy the young men and women who are reading this book today. If I knew what I am telling you now before I got grey haired……………………………..

I developed a list of excuses my interviewees came up with. Check yourself against the list and see where you stand. This is of course a summary of many encounters' work. A point may have been missed out. Email me at cares@kayiwa.com if you found a serious omission. My analysis came with many reasons including not having enough time in a day. I asked some of my contacts who had that feeling and I ask you too: If you were God how many hours would you have given a day?

In the table that follows, by inserting numbers 1-30 rank the reasons that could have led you fail to move from poverty to prosperity. Mark with 0 those which do not apply to your circumstances.

As you come to any one of these terms like money or betrayal your brain may go into a dictionary mode. There is something that tells you to define the term and even to question whether you really understand what you are talking about. Do not be bothered by the fear that what money means to you might be different from what it means to somebody else. You may be thinking money is the answer to all problems and yet your neighbor may be thinking it is the source of all evil. I held my interviews in bars, beaches, buses, churches, mosques and one word meant different things to different people. Take the word Race for instance. What does it mean to you? Pick a dictionary and see for yourself what it might mean to someone else. I am trying to emphasize that getting different results does not necessarily mean failure. Pick courage and do the exercise.

CONDITION	score	CONDITION	score	CONDITION	score
Money		Childhood		Associates	
Betrayal		Time		Beliefs	
Planning		Misfortune		Stupidity	
Heredity		Perseverance		Intolerance	
Ambition		Negativity		Unfriendliness	
Skills		Greed		Corruption	
Discipline		Indecision		Dishonesty	
Health		Job		Selfishness	
Emotions		Immorality		Craziness	
Marriage		Race		Environment	

Now hide your mark sheet. Copy this table and ask someone else whom you think knows you well and ask him to rank excuses for your own failure. You may do the same for him or her. Compare your notes in the end. Do not be shocked if your partner appears to have been too aggressive against you and yet over sympathetic to oneself. Somewhere between the two extremes the true you lie.

There are certain specific questions I want to ask you. If you find some of these too confidential lock yourself up in the privacy of your room before you read the next section. I want to come right to your heart. I want to touch you and feel you as you confront your failures. There is no kidding about it. The operation might be painful. It might be more painful than what you expect to get at a dentist. I want you to prepare your mind. The other advice I can give is that you should pray for your own soul.

Let us go into the room.

Do you have a life goal? What is it? When did you set it and what have you done towards meeting it?

Have you to the best of your judgment put in the best effort towards meeting your goal? If you said 'Yes' to whom should the glory go and if 'No' who deserves the blame and why?

As you setup your life goal you realized there were certain faculties you lacked to fulfill your ambition. How did you decide to fill this gap and how has your progress been?

Man is not an island and there is no way you could have imagined reaching your goal without coming into contact with other people. How has your relationship with others been? Have you been cooperative, harmonious or struggling all the way through?

A tree is seen by its own fruits. A man rich or poor is seen by his own decisions. Poor people are slow at taking decisions and quick at changing them. Rich people are quick at taking decisions and are slow at changing them. What is your state?

Have you been driven by a spirit of procrastination (delay and postponements) or have you lacked perseverance in your work?

Winners do not quit and quitters never win. Where are you towards meeting your goal? Have you reached that point called "the Decision Summit" where failures surrender and winners overcome?

There are two important types of personality. The negative personality sees danger in every move, is overcautious and is slow to invest in any income generating venture. Stupid like worms it destroys the very stomach it lives in. The positive personality says with God nothing is impossible. It sees chances of survival through its eyes called faith, hope, belief and undeserved blessing (grace). How has your efficiency been affected by the personality you have chosen to follow?

Leaders devise the way forward and followers implement the idea. Leaders are richer than followers. Which life have you chosen to live? Is your decision based on guesswork, well informed thinking or on accidents?

(10) The truth hurts. How have you been hurt by your own consciousness as you were striving to reach your goal? Have you indulged in sex, dietary, alcohol, fashion or life styles you are ashamed of? If you have answered 'Yes' to any of these what concrete steps have you taken to save your soul?

(11) If you were given a chance to live your life again what activities of your life would you change and when?

Get out of the room.

Perhaps he had nobody to lend him the money. He borrowed the money and he chose to buy food instead.

It is amazing that the same principles that bring prosperity are the same principles that bring poverty. I say it again: You need faith to believe in God and you need faith to be an atheist. In order to succeed in any venture you need to start with an idea. The idea may be as a small as a mustard seed. You plant this seed in the head. Then it germinates and grows into a huge tree.

In many parts of Tanzania are seen different types of trees. In between the Butterfly Beach and the Paradise Beach lie many baobab trees. They look gorgeous and gigantic. Their stems are more than two meters in diameter. These trees have stood more than five hundred years. I asked Abed how these trees managed to survive that long. He said they ran their roots deep in the ground. Trees that know this secret live long. Grass does not survive seasons because its roots are not deep in the soil. Those which simply grow where water is found die as soon as the soil is dry. If you were to choose would you live the life of a tree or of grass?

Prosperity requires that the idea is placed deep in the head. You have to keep it growing. As the idea sinks deeper the tree grows taller, gorgeous and elegant. The tree grows more leaves which fall on the ground and fertilize the soil. The roots go deeper; the tree grows stronger, grows more leaves, gets more fertilizers and grows taller. The whole process repeats itself.

This is similar to our beliefs. When we believe in something and give the idea thought after thought, the belief grows stronger and the results come more readily. Apply the same idea in the opposite direction. The more you think negatively of your situation the more prone to failure you are likely to become. Get rid of your negative thinking. Sensitivity to failure makes you prone to fail. Fear of the unknown, fear of failure, fear of losing will all weaken your motive towards investment. Encourage yourself. Be cooperative with others. You will become more gorgeous, elegant and prosperous.

I once accompanied Hosef to his home town Morogoro.

Morogoro is a small town at the foot of the mountain from which it takes its name. It is about 4 hours drive from Ubungo. I estimate the distance to be about 250 km. The road is tarmacked, bit too narrow for the heavy traffic it holds and is full of unexpected bends.

You realize the way I described the road to Morogoro is not a warning that you should drive with care. It is designed to stop you from visiting Morogoro. Personalities are nothing but masks. The way we express ourselves is not usually the way we are. If you need to succeed in life, start by taking the mask covering your face off. Clean your tongue and be yourself.

Fruit kiosks are set up all the way from Dar Es Salaam to Morogoro. You see a lot of fruits on sale notably mangoes, oranges, water melons, bananas, apples and berries. Hawkers run to the windows of vehicles in a mad rush to sell fruits or juices to passengers when the traffic stops. The system is so disorganized that more often than not juice is poured on passenger clothes or fruits are thrown to passengers as salesmen compete for buyers. Would you still want to go to Morogoro? If you want to travel clean it is better to keep your windows closed as you come to these stops. Traffic officers are suspected to be running many of these kiosks. They add to the confusion by stopping traffic arbitrary in order to draw customers to their fruit stores. I drew this to Hosef's attention. He however responded by explaining to me that Morogoro is the "Mango capital" of Tanzania. You can have mangoes for breakfast, lunch, tea-time and dinner. "Would you still want to go to Morogoro? Opportunities to eat fruits come to us but unfortunate incidences may spoil our life. So it is with chances to grow prosperous". This needed further explanation but I am here only to quote what Hosef said.

We walked around the Mango Town. Houseflies and mangoes were lying everywhere. The trees were strong, tall and full of fruits. Hosef explained to me that mangoes come in a particular season. The trees I was looking at today were planted many years ago. Perhaps those people who planted them were long gone but we are eating the fruits of their idea. Generations after generation have kept these trees by pruning off the branches that bear no fruits. For mangoes the tradition is that as the trees enter a flowering season, the owner inspects them very early in the morning and prunes off those branches with few flowers. Interestingly a tree with fewer branches bears more fruits than a tree with many branches. It is just like in business. Specialized entities yield profits better than general practices. Another analogy is here. The more the tree is pruned the more fruits it bears but either way whether the tree bears fruits or does not bear fruits it would be pruned anyway. If it is not worth pruning, it is then worth cutting down.

This idea of pruning is good to recognize as we ride to prosperity. We do not have to uproot the tree. We do not have to kill our master plan. We have however to keep updating it and pruning off bad ideas that might reduce our efficiency. Pride, greed, procrastination, doubt, arrogance, disbelief, (mention four others). If you want to keep your dream from turning to dust, read this paragraph again.

You want fruits? Prune your life.

The reason why we brought God in our Task Force is because he has that power to prune us when we are overgrowing. Every member of the Task Force has his own unique quality. What makes you special? If you were to join any one taskforce, which quality would you contribute to the team? Knowing what you are is an essential quality in the walk towards prosperity.

You are always more than one quality. Morogoro is not only good for producing mangoes. This belt covering Mt. Morogoro, Mt. Moshi, and Mt. Kirimanjaro is an area full of minerals and precious stones. Talk of rubies, sapphires, tanzanites, tantalites, cobalt, copper, gold and you are talking about the local stones of this area. When you study this area you realize surely prosperity must be a gift from God.

On the contrary, the people who live in this mineral rich belt are some of the world's poorest people. They have eyes but cannot see. They have ears but cannot hear. They have the potential to grow rich but they have not planted the idea in their heads. Even in circumstances where the government and a few individuals have tried to exploit some of these minerals the praise is dismissible. The level of investment made is not deep enough. There are no road structures going deep into the mines. The people have to carry the heavy stones on their backs down to the trading centers and the traders pay peanuts to the diggers and carriers. Did you want me to call this exploitation? Where there is receiving without giving can there be prosperity? One of the laws of prosperity says those who sew a little, a little they will reap. In its absolute terms: Nothing for nothing.

Hosef wanted me to see the source of these minerals and suggested we visited the mines.

We left Morogoro Hotel at 4.30am and armed with a torch, a mobile phone and a stick we set off to the mountains. By two o'clock in the afternoon we had reached one of our resting posts for lunch. The journey resumed at 4.00pm. I was told we would be at our destination by six. By three o'clock anyway I had doubted the logic of my trip more than three times. I was not going up to buy stones. Was the desire for adventure worth such a fit? My legs were paining and at this time of day we stood little chance of seeing any mining activity.

We walked on and I thought how stupid I had been in joining this team. We reached a point and I swore not to go ahead with the journey. I would rather go back to the world I was accustomed to other than seeking adventure into this unknown. Do you know how many foreigners had ever been kidnapped on such trips? Hadn't you heard or hadn't you read newspapers of ……

There were attempts to encourage me to go on up to the end. It was so difficult however to trust the advice from people whom I felt had ill advised me in the beginning. I reached a point when I had to choose either to quit or to walk on. I saw a stone and named it the Decision Summit. I said to myself that was going to be the furthest I could go. I reached there knelt down and cried out to the Lord for help.

My team were thrown into total confusion. They did not expect me to pray at this time. In a Muslim country it is quite ordinary for one to stop and pray in public no matter the place but this is done when the official time of crying to the Lord has come. I was collapsing of exhaustion others thought. Some opted to go back with me but others said surrender would lend the whole day's exercise worthless. The story in my head was different. It was self condemnation. How stupid I could have been! Had I prayed at the beginning of the trip I would have expected victory not rescue. Many people do not want promises leaning on closing eyes or bending knees. Many people do not want promises leaning on closing eyes or bending knees. What about you? The answer reveals your hidden strength or clear weakness.

Hosef was clear. Who can expect something out of nothing? He whisked us to follow him. He said he would not tolerate defiance. It was him who thought out the expedition and it was him to lead us. He allowed us one bottle of water and ordered us to leave everything else including the phones at the campsite. He said there was no telephone network where we were going and it was useless burdening ourselves with unnecessary luggage. The journey had been started in good spirit and had to end up that way. How stupid could we be that we had walked fifteen or so kilometers and failed to finish one or two kilometers left? "Who bewitched you?" he asked.

As I look back I see the character that is demanded of everybody who wants to reach prosperity. Trials, tribulations, temporary defeats, disagreements, confusion shall never put our mission out of focus. We set out at the beginning to grow from poverty to prosperity in a fixed time frame and nothing aught make our mind changed. Take it from me. Your victory lies at that moment when you feel like quitting. When everything else seems tough and you feel like you cannot go an extra mile take courage and do what all brave men and women do. Move an extra mile. On the other hand when you realize that these words of encouragement were coming from Hosef, you learn not to despise anybody. To know it was I of all people discouraged mean none is immune to discouragement but take courage and persevere.

Revisit your plan from time to time and plant it deep in your head. Keep watering your thoughts with new possibilities. Let your plan grow. Prune out all those branches which might reduce the efficiency but walk ahead to prosperity. There is no room for failures. Failure is a painful tragedy. Guard against it and remember with failure it is not the first time you fail that matters but it the last one. You can fail as many times as you can but count every fall as pruning and rise up again and walk.

Hosef's marriage life is another example. His third marriage ended in a divorce because his wife was caught red-handed with his houseboy. His fourth wife was not a harlot but also left him with such shock that you would think he would never marry again. She died. Her body stayed in the Morogoro Hospital mortuary for two days. On the third day Hosef and the relatives went to the hospital to collect the body. On pulling it out the guard found it warm and run away screaming, "She is alive. She is alive. She is alive". He left the mortuary open and everyone shaking.

Yes, the body was taken out re-examined, returned to the intensive care unit and after a week Hosef's wife returned home alive. The incident was widely covered in local newspapers and Hosef keeps these papers to this day.

The lady became a church preacher and she went to many places telling people what she saw during her Death days and arguing them to repent. She said death was so scary that she would never die again.

She preached for four years.

The last day Hosef saw her in the house was after a powerful town crusade. She took an afternoon nap in his bed. He left her there and went out to do some of his work. When he came back she was not in the house. There was nothing strange. She did not call him to say where she was. In the morning out of the ordinary she was not back. That evening she did not come back. The next morning Hosef reported her to Morogoro Central Police as a missing person. File CD/ 14011/2004/03/28/58810 has the details. She has never been seen again.

Suppose you were divorced once or twice or let us say you have ever been divorced or you are contemplating divorce,… and …..a beautiful woman or this awesome guy comes along and says, "This is me to dry your tears" what would you do? Wouldn't you marry him or her?

I asked Hosef, "Suppose a beautiful woman comes along and say, "This is me to dry your tears" what would you do? Wouldn't you marry her?"

"I would marry her."

I said, "Hosef, one woman almost made you crazy and another one almost made you take your own life. You have just been divorced not once and not twice. Would you consider marrying again?"

"Marriages are not made to last long based on the status a man or a woman holds in the church or in the community. It does not matter how many pastors attended the wedding or reception and from which countries they came. With death out of consideration, the length of a marriage relationship depends on how much warmth, romance and love between the two spouses. If there is a vacuum in a matrimonial relationship, even a houseboy can fill it! I would marry her."

Did I say I had three appointments for the day? I tell it to you in passing. Hosef turned up late. The second appointment was an interview with the "thief who loved me". Did he turn up? Of course he did not. The third person I was expecting did not turn up either. I did not allow these disappointments to ruin my day. The way to live is to forget those discouraging moments in life and ride ahead towards success. Expecting hardships might strengthen your planning but should never allow you to change your life course. By birthright you were authorized to move from poverty to prosperity. Nothing can ever be as tragic as failing to grow rich. The tragedy of all ages is failure. Guard against it. You must succeed as a matter of choice.

CHAPTER SIXTEEN

Decision

I have said it throughout the book that life is determined not by the options you have but by the decisions that you take. You were given these options:

( ) Make at least one dollar a day.
( ) Make at least ten dollars a day.
( ) Make at least a hundred dollars a day.
( ) Make five hundred dollars a day.
( ) Make one thousand dollars a day

Note that it is the decision that you ticked that rules your life in the end. If you chose to earn at least ten dollars a day do not complain if you find some other people coming by and growing pass by you. When it comes to sleeping in hotels you will choose to be a bag packer, budget traveler, sleeping in a room without attached bathroom, preferring a hostel to a hotel.

I talked to a guy in City Garden. The City Garden is one of the so called "Must Visit restaurants" in the heart of Dar Es Salaam. He told me twenty years ago he built a business and was able to send his brothers to school. I quote his words. "These days' people do not believe that the LandMark Hotel at Ubungo belongs to my younger brother. I sent him to school and gave him the money to start the hotel business. He is far gone that I cannot meet him without a written appointment. Last time I reminded him of this he answered that he would give me my school fees back!"

What makes a difference between these two brothers is the level of prosperity each one of them chose to make. The elder brother chose to make enough money to support his family and that is what he grew up to. The younger brother had a bigger vision and now he owns this three star hotel, which is the pride of the town. Interestingly at one time the elder brother built a very big empire that was bigger than his own vision. As expected the empire collapsed back to the level of his vision. You cannot grow tall beyond where your head can reach.

I will quote myself again here. "Our feelings are determined by what we believe. …... We are what we think. Our thoughts follow our belief pattern. If you think you are doomed to fail, your fear will certainly get you to what you fear most. If however you are determined to succeed and you work towards success, nothing, absolutely nothing will deny you your success. Tribulations, temptations and trials will come but hope and courage will standby you up to the battle's end. Believe right now that success delayed is not success denied… You see our action should follow our feelings. Our feelings should follow our thoughts. Our thoughts should follow our beliefs. We are what we think. We think what we believe. We feel what we believe. We do what we feel. If we are to prosper…. let me start all over again. If we have to change from poverty to prosperity we have to change our beliefs, we have to change our thinking, we have to change our feelings and we have to change our actions."

An analysis of men and women, who bothered to fill in the table in chapter fifteen above, revealed that indecision or failure to take a decision in time topped the list of why people failed in their ventures. Fewer people were guilty of taking wrong decisions than those who were guilty of postponing decisions or postponing decision indefinitely (abstain). History has it that people who have had the opportunity to amass wealth had the habit of reaching decisions promptly and the courage to stick to those decisions.

The information in this chapter combined with bits of information from other pages will help you develop the capacity to take quick decisions.

This statement tells you two things. You have to read this chapter critically but you will not find everything you need here. You cannot close the book here. You will not get the whole benefit of the treatment. To get the full dose you have to read some more chapters. Just as looking at this one statement reveals a lot of what is before us, a mere look at the forces around us shows us the passage to success.

We may look surrounded by debts and poverty but if we look carefully we may see that we are beaten but not crashed. We are hard pressed but not overcome. We are destined to victory. There is a way you can look at a man and say, "He looks like a doctor". You look at another and say, "He looks like a priest". "He looks like an engineer". A successful man has his own characteristics. He smiles. He looks relaxed. He dresses smartly. He is satisfied. Even if he loses a relative or a deal he does not change. A failure has ones' own characteristics. He is always complaining, criticizing and blaming either himself or others.

Look for those physical signs and you will discover where you are on the road to prosperity. I went to one of the stinking slums of Magomeni (a suburb of Dar es Salaam) and a man said, "We are not asking for safe and piped drinking water. We are asking for water!" In the midst of your troubles always thank God because life could have been worse.

God has not given us a spirit of fear and failure but of victory and of a sound mind. When you sneeze you say you are catching a cold. You can look at the clouds and say it is going to rain or to shine. You can similarly look at the time you take to make up your mind and decide whether you are destined to succeed or to fail. In the olden days the guideline was "Slow but Sure". The new motto for those who seek prosperity is, "Fast and Accurate". Procrastination will kill you and will kill you in poverty. If you have any decision to make, do it, do it quickly and stick to it.

Taking a decision is like falling asleep. If you want to sleep well close your eyes and switch off your brain quickly. If you take a decision quirkily you will reap failure. Grow a habit of recognizing how many minutes it takes you to take a decision. For every other occasion you take a decision strive to make the time shorter. Teach yourself to take snap decisions. Mr. Kato had a habit of looking at a milled product and deciding all at once to mint it again without debating what other alternatives (so called options) were available. Do not be a party to those who boast, "We took long to reach this decision. We weighed all possibilities.......... (and all other outdated nonsense). Such a speech signifies failure and those who sit on a board that makes such statements call for retirement.

I do not apologize for being harsh here. There is no room in the kingdom for those who cannot choose what they want. When you go for a party and you want a high seat, you do not take this decision when you are in the party. You decide this when you are dressing up. Better you decide this when you are shopping for what to wear. The way you hold your bag (bag pack or a brief case); the way you make your handshake (strong or weak and fuzzy); the way you fix your gaze (eye-to-eye or down on the ground) determines where your seat will be. Jesus says if you want a high seat, you have to choose between humility and arrogance and you have to do this before you take your seat.

Realize at least two characteristics essential in taking decisions.

Our statistics revealed that the majority of people who failed to grow rich or to make sufficient money to meet their basic needs had one weakness in common. They all loved gossiping. They knew the latest scandals and gossips in town but they could not tell the source of their stories. They all spoke in passive voice, "Some people say... It is said... I hear... It is rumored..." Their only evidence: "There is no smoke without fire!" I tell these people off. There is nobody called, "They." That person who goes on saying without being seen; that person who speaks without being heard; that person does not exist. Do not fear what They may say.

Those who hide behind They are life failures. Spot them out and run away from them. Blessed are you who do not sit in the council of these evil doers. Run away hurting people hurt. Spot them out by their characteristic lack of looking for details. Look at the way they read newspapers. They only read headlines, assume they knew the whole story and move to the next page. If you are the kind of person who only looks at the pictures in the newspapers, you are seriously warned. You are off the road to prosperity. You are standing on the right highway but on the wrong side of the road.

You cannot take a winning decision when you are ill informed. Winning decisions are fast and accurate decisions. In all your attempts to get knowledge seek the fastest way and the most accurate way. Those who beg and borrow money are those who want neighbors to do their thinking for them. They always value the opinion of others because they lack one of their own. You cannot take a decision quickly if your decision has to wait for other peoples' opinion. Listen to what I say (how does this sound?). Take your decision based on your own opinion. Everybody is entitled to his own opinion. If you wait to assess all other peoples' opinion you will slumber into procrastination and you will die before you take that important decision. You will die in poverty! Hear me out again. If you delay in taking a decision, you will certainly be insulted by a remark, "I knew he would say that!" A good decision delayed is as worthless as an opinion taken on an empty basis. In everything seek knowledge but the key word is fast and accurate knowledge.

Let me qualify what I am saying. Look at the desire to grow rich. Whose desire is it that you grow rich? Is it your neighbors' desire? Whose opinion do you need? Can you allow your wife to sleep in your neighbor's house? Why then should you keep your desire away from you?

Keep your own counsel. Take no one in your own confidence except yourself. If you need any exception (Psalm 1:1 says, "Blessed is the man who does not walk in the counsel of the wicked or stand in the way of sinners or sit in the seat of mockers". Do not give any part of your territory to others until you know where you stand. Examine your opinion and do not accept "I don't know" for an answer. When you are absolutely sure of what you want, how and when summon your Task Force. Remember the work of the taskforce is not to brain-storm the issue. You have such important guests like God with you. You cannot go for a lousy business agenda. This time you come together and brief each other of your duties and responsibilities. What you expect out of such a meeting is encouragement and empowerment to move forward. That is why it is necessary to choose your seat before your dressing. That is why it is necessary to choose your task force before you plunge into business. That is why it is necessary to determine your exit strategy before you go to war.

I booked myself into the Landmark Hotel. I was going to take a bus trip to Mbeya—the southern tip city of Tanzania close to the country's borders with Malawi, Mozambique, Zambia and Congo. The first bus was leaving Ubungo at 5.00 am and passengers had to be seated an hour before departure. There was no easy way of catching the bus other than sleeping on it or in the LandMark.

That is not the only reason I chose the Landmark Hotel. I desired to talk to the owner of the hotel. I asked for an appointment and I got it. This is what he told me of his elder brother, "The trouble with my brother is that he talks too much".

If I wrote a newspaper column of our conversation I would have titled it: The Trouble with My Brother." This is what I would have said in the order the discussion went:

–"People with little knowledge tend to speak too much. They expose all that they know and eventually empty themselves of their own dignity. No one blames you for what you see or what you hear or even of what you eat or drink. These are things which go inside you, which are shot at you and you cannot be blamed for being a victim of attack. However this is not true of what you speak. Words come from you and you are not obliged to say anything but whatever you say may be taken as evidence against you.

–"The trouble with my brother like the whole lot like him, 'He talks too much and does too little listening'. When I tell him point blank that you cannot take a decision with your mouth open he says that I am arrogant and disrespectful of old age. We are not bound to respect old age but the wisdom of old age. If you have a brain, use it. The wisdom of old age says: Keep your eyes open, keep your ears open but keep your mouth like your money purse. You do not keep it always open, do you?

–"The Bible says when your enemy is hungry feed him. When he is thirsty give him water to drink. When he is sick take him to hospital (and when he is recovered kill him). I am not sure of the truth of the last part. There is always a danger in speaking too much. The biggest danger is perhaps in mentioning your plans prematurely or to the wrong audiences. Watch out for those who seem to enjoy your utterance yet all they want from you are plans to beat you out of the business competition. Every person you associate with is either directly or indirectly competing with you for the limited supply of opportunities.

–"Conflicts always arise when there is scarcity of resources or when the cake to be shared is too small for all the competitors. You see this clearly when you stand in the LandMark and look down the window to the bus stage. When the queue of passengers is long the struggle to enter the bus is rougher. When there are many buses but fewer passengers even the line disappears.

–"Talking about your plans carelessly will hurt you. One such passenger pointed to a bus loading passengers outside the park and announced that the bus was loading and she was going to run to the bus. Many passengers overheard her. They run to the bus and as for her she did not run to the bus. She stayed stuck in the long queue. It is not that she did not want to break the law. She simply could not make up her mind quick enough. Your business plan is your secret. Do not share it with those who will rake it apart. Other people may put into action your plans ahead of you.

–"The trouble with my brother is that he does not realize that it takes twice as much effort to disagree with somebody as it takes to agree. He thinks there is wisdom in arguments. When I take snap decisions, I save a lot of time and mental energy and increase my opportunities to make money. The desire of all ages is to make money but the demand of all ages is the right to decide and to decide rightly. To me faith without actions is dead. I do not want to tell but to show the world what I am doing.

–"I decided long ago not to be in anyone's shadow. I take my own decisions and even if it is in a group meeting I try to be the first always to decide. A leader who cannot decide is not worth the title. I run this company because I always seek to be the first one to know what the company needs, what the customers need and what I need. I strive always to be the first one to know the right thing.

–"We were told when we were young that we were God's children and we had to live a Godly life. I did not understand that until I learnt that the adjective godly meant like God. My decisions are always simple. There is only one question to all problems. What would God do in this situation? Snap decisions save a lot of money. If our education system taught us not how to follow decisions and obey contracts but how to make decisions and contracts each one of us would be making more money than one needed and would be growing from poverty to prosperity without a possibility of returning. My brother must have been spoilt at school.

–"I find this indecision in many "Book Worms" who come to my office applying "for any job." I decided to be seen only on written appointments. I read through their chits and I say if he cannot articulate his idea in writing then he has not thought enough of what he wants. There is therefore no basis for discussion with a person who does not know what one is talking about. Such meetings only end up in another meeting. What a waste of time! If you cannot write your dream down you cannot see that dream come true. Life is like implementing your business plan. If you have no written business plan think nothing of growing rich.

–"I want an employee who has dedicated his life to be a subordinate. He will follow my path. When I grow high up the ladder I grow with him. I give him what is called 'Promotion'. He works harder and he promotes me too. We easily work as a team.

–"I run my company the way I run my family. One makes the suggestions and another one decides but the two subordinate each other. The husband is the head of the family but does not rule his body, the wife does. And the wife does not rule her body but the husband does. This two partisan system demands the courage to keep ones decision. There are always conflicts and arguments. I have therefore to take my decisions knowing that I am doing something that I am not going to change. I do not stubbornly keep decisions made but I make sure I take the right decisions.

–"You think I have no brain? That is up to you but I do not have to see my brain in my hands to believe I have one. In fact I believe I have eyes yet I have never seen my own eyes. To the best I have used mirrors to see my eyes but what I see is a distorted view of myself. When I touch my left eye the mirror touches its right eye but I have to reverse what I see and rely on my imagination. I can sign a postdated cheque and I swear such can never bounce. My decisions are taken with confidence.

–"I never say, "I am broke. I have no money." Instead I keep on saying, "I will never be broke in m my life". This commitment has put money always in my wallet. When I take financial decisions I rightly assume that God shall provide the necessary funds. He cannot give me an idea without giving me the provisions to implement it. I have a living God as my business partner.

–"The trouble with my brother is that he spends so much time worrying about his fortunes than he spends on enjoying his life. He spends more time mourning his glorious past than he spends on planning his future. He worried about me when I was a child. Now that I am grown up and his fears have not been realized he should sit down and relax.

–"I am a decision maker. I take a decision and that marks the end of my assignment. My subordinates implement what has been decided. I do not busy myself with details of implementing the decision. I maintain the office of the boss. I have the characteristic of a leader. I dress like a leader. I stand straight like a leader. I laugh with a deep voice like a leader. Even when walking I walk in front of the line. I decided to be a leader not a subordinate. I decided not to work for a dollar a day. I will retire young and retire rich and I will continue making money even after death. I want my brother to count my success as his success. I want him to see me as a fruit of his labor but he thinks I am his outspent energy. Then he mourns about the sacrifices he made for me.

–"Let me tell you one more thing. If I had to relive my life again I would still take the same decisions.

We parted company and I went to my room to write this article. I wanted to pick out the important points but in the end I decided that the reader will benefit better by reading the whole excerpt. It is up to you to judge me on this decision.

The journey to Mbeya was full of adventures right from the start. You would thank God that you chose to stay at the LandMark the moment you stepped out of the hotel. Two worlds meet you at the doorstep. LandMark guests are collected at 4.45 am and decently led to their respective buses. Of course not every guest goes to Mbeya! Some go to Mount Kirimanjaro, Serengeti National Park, Tanga Port, Bagamoyo and Fort Jesus.

For the rest of the world there are so many Abeds and Ismails and Happy Charlies outside jostling passengers going to different buses. If you were carrying two bags you would be lucky if they ended up on the same bus. These 'helpers' are so reckless that they would never listen to a passenger. They would put you on a bus, issue you with a ticket and pull money out of your own purse without even asking you where you are going.

As soon as you land in Ubungo you are bombarded with at least ten safari companies and the boys here don't give up. They follow you everywhere! They ease drop on your conversations, finding out where you want to go, and then tell you they have a safari at "a good price". You don't book before hand, as it's cheaper to saddle on with other groups, or get a discount price for an out of queue bus.

There is no way one can describe a situation like this. It is like a bomb has just gone off and everyone is shouting: "Run, Run. Run."

Yes, it is like another crab race. How can you achieve what you want if you cannot stick to your own destination? How can you take a decision when you do not respect your own opinion? How can you take a decision with your mouth open? The way to handle these useless helpers is to neglect their pleas. Do not talk to them. There is no prosperity in disorganized societies! Looking outside the bus window before taking off I realized poverty is rough and brutal but prosperity is sweet and decent. In the midst of all this chaos there is only one option to choose from. Stay a night at the LandMark.

Some people told me there are more pick pockets than passengers in the park but I was not able to assess the truth. One thing for sure you had to fear anybody or anything that walks on two legs. I saw one passenger with a t-shirt who might have thought of what to wear while shopping. It read: "Two legs are bad four legs are better."

At exactly 5.00 am our bus pulled out of the park. There was a feeling of relaxation as the journey started. This should be the same feeling one should get when one is pulling out of poverty. It is a definite point of saying the journey has started and I am on my way to prosperity. Those who have no written plans think riches must come over-night. They want to see fruits of their labor immediately. It is said they fail in the beginning. They forget it is a long journey from poverty to prosperity.

Hours came and hours went. The bus went on and there was no Mbeya in sight. The vegetation started changing from dull green to dark green but there was no Mbeya in sight. I looked at the right and the left and life looked the same. I turned my attention from outside the bus and looked inside. There were very few people looking out but the majorities were now sleeping. The bus was running on. Perhaps the only person wide awake was the driver who seemed to be munching some green leaves (Mairungi or a weak form of marijuana) to keep him awake. He drove on and on and on.

In this picture I saw what it means to prosper. It is always tough and rough to begin a journey but thereafter life goes on smoothly. You do not have to struggle to prosper. All you have to do is to take the right decision in the beginning and stick to it. Laboring to be rich is a waste of energy otherwise most wheelbarrow pushers would be very rich now. What can be added here is that decisions must be put into practice once they come to your mind. Thoughts that come to mind but not acted upon become ideas and if left for long they starve to death. Follow your thoughts with feelings. See this pattern belief>thoughts>feelings>and then action. You are always bombarded with feelings, thoughts and decisions. In order not to be knocked down, force them to enter your head following that pattern.

I remember what one of the three people with appointments who let me down told me at one time. He wanted to start an Internet Café. What discouraged him is that whenever he would like to start one, find suitable premises, negotiate the right rent, by the time everything would be ok, he would find that a few days before that somebody else had started the same business in the same location. It happened to him so many times. He complained people were stealing his plans.

I have squeezed this idea here because if I think about it and do not write it down immediately I may never write it at all. Decisions must be taken immediately they are thought of.

We passed Chalinze, Iringa and some other small trading centers. There were people who looked at us angrily as our bus passed without stopping. I knew what they hated most was the loss of a chance to sell to us meat, cassava, maize, bananas, fruits and juices. Some knew the driver in person and wanted free rides. The driver was aware that if he served everyone's interest he would never reach his destination or he would never reach Mbeya in time.

We cruised passed many places without stopping because there is a law in Tanzania forbidding driving big vehicles like buses and lorries after sunset. I was told later on that that law is seemingly ignored by those buses which are not classified as "Tourist Coaches." Those buses at Ubungo served by the Abeds stop at every kiosk on the road.

Dar es salaam to Mbeya ordinarily is a twelve hour drive. The driver aimed at being in Mbeya by 5.00pm but not later than 7.00pm. There were moments when he sped up almost dangerously and then there were times when he drove below average speed. Some sections of the road were more dangerous than others. There were hills and valleys. There were straight patches and sharp bends. There were populated areas and there were empty grasslands. The route had predetermined stopping areas. The driver knew where to stop and let passengers ease themselves. He knew where to stop to let the passengers have lunch. He knew where to stop to let the bus engine cool down. All this was predetermined before he took on the journey.

This is a reminder to those who want to embark on the journey to prosperity. You must make a written master plan. You must follow it through. Do not change your plan to please those who were not part of it in the beginning. Some people particularly relatives may want you to pick them up on your way. In the middle of a business investment some cousin may ask for school fees. Some auntie may pay you a courtesy call with some good advice from your forefathers. Be aware there is wisdom in a counsel of advisors but blessed are those who do not sit in a council of fools. Relatives may come with the best of intentions but not at the best of times. They may derail you instead. You cannot please everybody.

At a time I was writing this book I received numerous requests from one such cousin. I picked up courage to 'text' him back, "There is time for everything. There is time to laugh and there is time to cry; time to sleep and time to work. You have the right to demand part of my attention but not the whole of it. You cannot complain when you page me and I do not respond. The right to call is yours but the right to answer is mine. You may have a right to ask for favors but the right to grant them is mine. For this space in time I will not help you by putting money in your pockets but I will help you by telling you not to look to man for your financial survival. Money is like a wild game. It cannot be caught by simply shooting it down as it passes by. You need a license to do that. You will be put behind bars for taking money which you have not worked for. The school of thought for those who preached that you can grow rich easily without providing any service is closed. Prosperity cannot come out of nothing. You have to give some service. Money cannot be produced by the Great Bang theory. You need at least an element of faith to begin with. You cannot make money by printing it. Some governments have tried it this way and instead blew up inflation. You do not get something out of nothing. To make money you must choose between either chasing it and trapping it. One needs careful planning another needs strong effort. Check your resources and choose today which route to take."

If this driver were driving from poverty to prosperity he would have made it in time. He knew that there was a time to make profits and there was time to suffer losses. There was time to take high risk investments and there was time not to buy stocks. There was a time to press breaks when going downhill and there was a time to engage a low or high gear. The road could be smooth or rough. The analogy here is that high risk ventures yield bigger profits. It is true also to say that where you expect big profits expect big losses if the tide turns.

We drove on and on. At a time when it appeared nothing but going towards our destination was happening, the bus skidded across the road, made a screaming sound, swayed left and right, woke up everybody and there we were off the road, close to tipping down the valley with a punch in the wheel. Our journey came to an abrupt end.

It was perhaps a nail or some unrecognized stone that had punched our tire. Yes some people said this and others said that. It was either a mechanical error or a manual error. It was soothing to believe blaming or criticizing others could not help us in any way. What we needed was fixing the problem.

This bus company had calculated that such an accident could happen. There was a spare tire on the bus. There was a jack and other necessary tools. There was even a mechanic on the crew. The moment we got off the bus repair work started. In my mind I was happy the bus company was such an organized lot.

I was feeling relaxed that way when the mechanic ordered the job of changing the tire to stop immediately. He had realized that we were in a more dangerous situation than we all thought. If we continued lifting the bus we would run the risk of throwing it down the valley. We had to wait for a crane to pull us out of this predicament.

All questions were asked. For how long were we to wait? How sure were we that the crane would come? Why did we have a punch in such a remote place? Even if everything else was done would we ever be able to reach Mbeya before sunset? Who set such rules anyway? What was happening to the people who were waiting for us?

The more we worried the more we asked ourselves. The more we asked ourselves the more we worried. As Christians we knew that Jesus had told us in Matthew chapter 6 (verse 26) not to worry for what to eat or to wear that our master in heaven knew all our needs. We knew how to read this and how to tell it to others but when we were the victims of circumstances we could not apply this principle to ourselves. We hurt ourselves. Knowing what to do and not do it hurts.

Did God really know where we were? If God could rescue us why did he not prevent the accident all together? Would a loving father let his children go to prison only to show love by bailing them out? The only answer I could get for this was something taught to me back then when I was in a nursery school. I was told that God does not put us in trouble but walks us out of them.

Our life does not depend on what others do but on what decisions we take. Whether we spend the rest of our life in sorrow or in prosperity depends on the way we interpret our circumstances. Buddhism teaches:

1. There is Suffering: Suffering is common to all.
2. Cause of Suffering: We are the cause of our suffering.
3. End of Suffering: Stop doing what causes suffering.
4. Path to end Suffering: Everyone can be enlightened.

Suppose God told you, "Go into the world and multiply", would you take a second wife? Would you look for another partner? What would you do with your boyfriend or girl friend?

What would you do? Would you say, "That must not have been God speaking?" What would you do? Would you consult your pastor or your doctor or your lawyer? Tell me. What would you think?

Suppose God told you, "Go into the world and prosper", what would you do? Would you remain skeptical and say, "Show me the money!" Would you rise up and walk? Would you continue in your slumber? Or would you say, "I will not believe it was the voice of God until my bills are paid. I will not believe until I have a new house or a new dress. I will not believe until my children are out of college. I will not believe until I have got a job. I will not believe until I am healed. I will not believe until my problem is solved! I will not believe until...."

We waited and there was no sign of a crane arriving. We camped around the bus but there was no crane in sight. Everyone on earth or in heaven above who could be blamed was blamed. We went on that way until a few of us came back to our senses. I mean we came to relax. I mean we came to realize that we had taken the pathway to self destruction. We had taken the path of those who end up in poverty. We had to reverse the trend by taking a snap decision. St.Benedict prayed: God help me not to worry about things I cannot change. His prayer was reportedly answered and thereafter anyone who makes this prayer gets answered. Those who have ears to hear, hear this.

I looked up to heaven and thanked God that the accident had not happened in Makumbi Game reserve where we would have been eaten by lions (who in turn would have thanked the Lion King for the feast).There was another thing to thank God for. We had not tipped over into the valley. There was another thing to thank God for. There was no blood shed. There was another thing to thank God for. This accident had happened just after we had just stopped for lunch. There were no empty stomachs on the bus. There was no sound of screaming children. (No body was wetting his trousers!).

It was through this process of counting one's blessings one by one that we came to see how God had been good to us. I believe and I seriously believe that God is pleased when he sees us worship him in all circumstances. He created us to give him glory and when he sees us do so he feels good within his own heart. He becomes proud of his own creation and he becomes quick to answer when we call him, Baba (Father). Who hates to be praised, anyway?

We were on the same bus with another man who was going to the same destination as me. He saw another bus from Mbeya going to Dar es Salaam. He waved it down and wanted to board it and go back to Dar Es Salaam. There was no point for him to continue with the journey. Other passengers wanted refund for their tickets. They were advised to read at the back of their tickets. There it had been written in fainting grey-white letters that tickets once sold could not be refunded. It was a decision that had been taken even before the journey started. To add insult to injury it added, "Tickets are non re routable and valid for that route, date and passenger as specified on the ticket."

What does this teach us?

After another hour of waiting the crane arrived. What we all thought was a huge task was done in a few minutes. You could see ease in the eyes of the fork lifter: For this reason I was created and my company is pleased at what you have gone through. "For God nothing is impossible! When my people turn from me and they fall in the traps of their enemies and pray to me, I will forget their sins and be happy to help them out. They are my people. This is the voice of the Lord".

Imagine you are in the hands of a money lender and he says to you, "When my customer fails to pay my loan in time and he comes to me I will forget surcharging his interest. He is my customer". Next time you are in trouble would you or would you not return to such a money lender? Wouldn't you want such a money lender on your TaskForce?

So we drove on. We reached Ruaha River. The road twisted and turned into endless s s s ss . My mind said a bus that had let us down on a plain and clear road would certainly not survive these zigzags. I literally closed my eyes expecting what to hear next to be a bang as we rolled down the valley. As you realize we survived and reached Mbeya.

What I learnt on this journey is that prosperity is not a destiny but a journey. We reached Mbeya and that was well and good.

The next day I went to meet the mayor of the town because I had carried a message for him from an investment company in China. The message was simple. A Chinese company wanted to open a multi-million dollar super market and a "Made-In-Tanzania" industrial district in Mbeya area. Money and industries would flow into the area the moment the Government of this area could declare this a Free Economic Zone. This would be a job creating project of an unimaginable scale and poverty would be eradicated out of the area in a matter of months. I wanted a Memorandum Of Understanding to be signed there and then.

I presented an argument that whatever China could do; Africa could and could do even better. However the best approach was not for Africa to compete with China but to learn from it and accept it as a development partner. Some matters were straightforward. These were the four golden tips:

1. <u>Investing attracts</u>. China has attracted foreign investors since 1980 by offering them the enticement of cheap labour, a big market, good infrastructure and stability. For stability particularly in light of the 1984 June 4th Uprising at the Square of Heavenly Peace (Tian An Men Square) there was little to show. Beijing however stuck on interpreting it as the signs of the end of a chaotic era.

Africa can offer this as well. The biggest advantage for Africa is the availability of natural resources. Africa can raise the condition that any materials that Chinese companies buy can only leave the continent as half–finished or finished products. This way Chinese factories could be transplanted into Africa.

2. <u>Copy competences</u>. China obliged foreign firms to enter joint ventures with Chinese Partners. This way they were able to copy knowledge and competences. Subsequently, the Chinese partners copied the product, produced it cheaper and pushed the foreign investor from the market.

The last bit has been the black side of investing in China. Africa can assure Chinese that it is aware of this practice but it would not do it to their new partners.

3. <u>Define an industry strategy</u>. China developed itself into an export giant thanks to the efforts of an ambitious state that directed the entrance of big ecosystems of industry sectors. Not only TVs and telephones and electric fans were made, but

almost all the components were produced in China too. Entire production lines of bankrupt Western factories were bought and transferred to China.

4. <u>Recapture immigrants</u>. China's best talents lived in foreign countries. They left China to seek better education and better economic possibilities. Nowadays they are returning to China because China is stable and offers the same or better possibilities.

Africa's best and brightest are scattered in all states of Europe, Canada, USA, Japan, Australia and China. If these could be called back the future of the continent would be more attractive.

These are some changes that require tough choice in the way of thinking and acting of the African elite. Thirty years ago China was also poverty-stricken after a long period of war, repression and hopelessness. China overcame their handicap by opening themselves to the outside world and creating Free Economic Zones. They acted like a people determined to move from poverty to prosperity and they focused their energy to achieving that. They did it. So why should it be impossible for Africa?

The Mayor agreed to my proposal. He called his Council of Advisors and the matter was discussed.

There were fears after fears. China as a new economic giant was out to exploit poor Africa's natural resources. She was investing with impunity. She disregarded human rights violations, factory safety standards and did business with good and evil governments. You cannot trust a man who is a friend of all people. How would you feel if your fiancé kept talking to his ex- girlfriend? What would you feel if he said he would marry you but would not stop seeing the other woman because your marriage has nothing to do with her relationship?

Those who favored dealing with China explained that the best way of taming a lion is not by starving it but feeding it. Someone said the times for wolves and cabs to lie together in the name of common peace and common prosperity (prosperity for all) had come.

We met for another day because the Mayor had the desire but not the right to sign the Memorandum of Understanding. The matter involved the Central Government in Dar Es Salaam and that is where we had to take our proposal. Decisions have a life of their own.

To make the best of decisions, you need to encourage the critical thinking and information sharing skills of your Task Force. The mayor used all his persuasive language but could not have the motion go his way. I admired the way he provided an environment that encouraged staff members input. Information was shared and alternative actions analyzed. The mayor rightly knew that best decisions are those based on the best available information and taken with the most support from the staff and with a high level of consensus.

The consensus came but only in terms of designing an official letter to the Chinese Investor inviting him to visit Tanzania for more discussion. Making decisions the right way is better than making right decisions. Consensus does not mean agreement as to the solution but a commitment to the solution. I got a letter of introduction to Tanzania Investment Authority in Dar Es Salaam copied to the Chinese investor. That was my share of the cake and chose to leave Mbeya.

That night I was given the chance to meditate on how decisions are taken in this part of the world.

Prosperity does not come merely because God anointed you with raw materials at the time of your birth. Your inheritance confers upon you good things but unless you claim it, your birthright is worthless. Taking a decision is like going on a journey. You have to follow the road rules all the way. You may take abrupt and strict-to-the-rule principles as in the LandMark examples. That way you may have quick actions but be warned that a wrong decision might wipe your wealth quickly away. More often than not when you find yourself in quicksand there is none to help but to see you sinking and sinking. This may be the case with that guy I met in City Garden.

Decision taking is a thinking process and if you want good results let the process lie in line with what you believe.

Step 1: Start by examining your own belief and study your interaction with your staff, in terms of seeking their input and sharing information with then. Where do you stand? Do you feel threatened by opposing views, or do you open handedly welcome discussion? On a scale of 1-5 where 5 is 'Intolerant' and 1 is 'Unconcerned' rank yourself on how much you can stand discussion of issues and not feel your leadership is in doubt through healthy questioning of situations and potential resolutions.

<u>Step 2</u>: Next, convey to your staff, particularly the managers and supervisors who report directly to you, what your expectations for decision making will be from now on. You may ask them what to expect out of a meeting. A problem or idea should be brought up by one staff member and discussed by the group. Information from other employees should be shared, and alternative views discussed. You may be a chairman but you could still have the right to exercise your chance to join the discussion in a non binding position but merely as a committee member. More than ever for complex issues or for decisions that might be difficult to reverse even long after you have left office, make sure no answers are taken as "Absolute truth" until all key individuals have participated in the discussion.

<u>Step 3:</u> This step is about building a consensus. Not every action or solution will satisfy everybody. This form of belief is not a license to exclude others but a wake-up call that you have to work harder to reach your goal by touching every committee member. Every opinion counts. Obviously, taking decisions through a step by step procedure might be time consuming. If the house is on fire you do not call a meeting before you call the ambulances in. You too have some brain. Decide when you have to treat the matter as urgent and when group consensus might do better. Generally speaking major directional changes and issues that affect all staff and many people need to move fully through this critical process.

<u>Step 4:</u> Remember, consensus is not about everyone agreeing on one idea, but on endorsing the outcome. The decision reaching process must be understood to be logical and valid. It is a pain to implement a solution that you do not agree with.

Your prosperity will always be determined by what you ticked here:

( ) Make at least one dollar a day.
( ) Make at least ten dollars a day.
( ) Make at least a hundred dollars a day.

( ) Make five hundred dollars a day.
( ) Make one thousand dollars a day

Step 5: Decisions whichever way they were taken are subject to attack and failure. Review them from time to time either to appraise you and your staff or to fix problems. The question to answer when we are loathing with failure is always: Where did we go wrong? Was it because key information was not shared or a particular idea was not considered due to a preconceived solution proposed earlier or the times have changed altogether?

I call upon you to choose between life and death, between poverty and prosperity. What I am asking you is not difficult to decide but if you do not do it yourself somebody else will choose for you. Look again at the revised list you made of men and women you admired. They took the decision to be rich and they followed the way to richness and they reached their destiny. It is your choice to end up bankrupt or wealthy and successful. The path of those who have made it rich has some strange characteristics. For instance, if you are a business manager and at the end of the month your company has not done financially well, whom do you pay first?

Trade Unions and Workers' Rights Organizations will certainly tell you that you should pay workers first and you and the company directors go with nothing. This is legalistically right. Follow it and you are doomed. Ask a judge why and the answer will reveal what is in his heart: "Or close the company down". Surely a man with such feelings must not have been a member of your first Task Force meeting. He is not working in your own interests and the advice he gives deserves to be condemned.

Listen. I tell you today. It is your company. Pay yourself first. Encourage yourself to remain employed and be able to ask yourself while still in employment: Where did we go wrong? Was it because key information was not shared or a particular idea was not considered due to a preconceived solution proposed earlier or the times have changed altogether?

You cannot answer these questions when the workers are reaping fruits of your sweat and yet you the owner return nothing to your wife and children. When you are in trouble remember who covers you up? Isn't it your wife and children? Who should be paid first?

It looks selfish but a man who cannot invest in himself is not a true reflection of the God who made him. When you ask yourself the sole purpose of your existence, would you be satisfied with an absurd answer that you live to lead somebody else's life? The demand of all ages is the right to decide ones' own destiny. The hostile attitude I advocate here means that once you the manager is happily paid you have all the reason to solve the problems of your subordinates. You have the brain to know that a house built without a foundation cannot stand any storm. You have the logic to know that you cannot run a restaurant business when the cooks are on strike. You have the logic to know that you cannot work well when your wife is dragging you to a divorce court. You have however to know that you are the boss and everything rests upon you. You have to do all it takes to avert the strike but you have to protect your household the way Jesus protected his church. Do you remember him sweeping money changers out of 'his fathers' house?' Read John 14:2.

You have to take some tough decisions. If you do so as suggested in the example above you will save your company, your family, yourself and eventually your workers. If you do not obey me someone, some judge or some employee you recruited to serve you, will close the company for you.

Look at what would happen if you paid workers first. At the worst scenario the workers will not be able to meet you because according to your secretary, "You are busy in a meeting". I am sure you would not like to tell your co-workers that you would be off duty as you have to appear in the family court. You will fail to meet your business obligations. In the end the business will collapse, the family will be raked, you will be destroyed and you will have none to blame (not even the devil) because it was your own decision that destroyed you.

Moses confronted his men with this tough talking in Deuteronomy 30 in the quoted verses.

"11 Now what I am commanding you today is not too difficult for you or beyond your reach. 12 It is not up in heaven, so that you have to ask, "Who will ascend into heaven to get it and proclaim it to us so we may obey it?" 13 Nor is it beyond the sea, so that you have to ask, "Who will cross the sea to get it and proclaim it to us so we may obey it?" 14 No, the word is very near you; it is in your mouth and in your heart so you may obey it.

15 See, I set before you today life and prosperity, death and destruction. 16 For I command you today to love the LORD your God, to walk in his ways, and to keep his commands, decrees and laws; then you will live and increase, and the LORD your God will bless you in the land you are entering to possess.

17 But if your heart turns away and you are not obedient, and if you are drawn away to bow down to other gods and worship them, 18 I declare to you this day that you will certainly be destroyed. You will not live long in the land you are crossing the Jordan to enter and possess.

19 This day I call heaven and earth as witnesses against you that I have set before you life and death, blessings and curses. Now choose life, so that you and your children may live 20 and that you may love the LORD your God, listen to his voice, and hold fast to him. For the LORD is your life, and he will give you many years in the land he swore to give to your fathers, Abraham, Isaac and Jacob".

I have said it throughout the book that life is determined not by the options you have but by the decisions that you take. You may be given several options but more often than not, you will have only one choice to make. Take your decision wisely. Life itself is full of options but decisions are limited.

CHAPTER SEVENTEEN

BLESSINGS

I want now to turn to the role of blessings in our journey to prosperity. In the previous chapter I sometimes used the pronoun 'We' without mentioning with whom I was. Throughout this journey I was in the company of Abed. In the writing of that and of some few previous chapters I decided to keep him out of the limelight because this book is not about Abed but how to make money and grow from poverty to prosperity without any possibility of returning to poverty.

When the meeting with the mayor and his council ended we decided to stay for one more night in Mbeya. I am proud to say it was our own decision not something imposed upon us by some super power, weather, sunrise or sunset. You can guess to whom this 'us' refers.

An idea came. Abed wanted to visit his father's grave in Mbeya.

We woke up early before sunrise. Tradition demands that one should not visit a graveyard after sunrise and we could not carry any torch light. We walked through the bush in the dark of the night praying that we did not wake up any lion or some animal that would think us some good game. It is funny when you know that there are no rangers or guns to protect you here and the only thing in your defense is your faith and yet you step out in the middle of the night and step out into the jungle to look for some dead man's grave. We did it and I guess we are still alive!

We knelt down and in the dark of the night I could hear drops of tears falling off Abed's head. More than anything else I heard him mumble, "This is what I get for being a man."

Like you I did not know till then the meaning of these words.

After the war of independence was over it was declared that having engaged in activities aiming at overthrowing the government of Mozambique by any means was heroic and worth of praise. All sentences of treason were reduced to murder, man slaughter or possessing arms without a license. Much more interesting, all prisoners who confessed to these crimes were granted a blanket amnesty and released. Those who did not take this channel were prosecuted. Abed-father's case was commuted to possession of a gun, accidental killing, rape and attempting to steal a car. He turned down the offer. He would rather die for a cause other than live a life of a common criminal.

The judge looked at him in the face. He told him: "A pardon is only a pardon if it is accepted." Do you plead 'Guilty' or 'Not Guilty"?

To the amusement of none and perhaps to those who did not know this man's courage, he answered, "Not Guilty."

He took his own stand. He was his own witness. He narrated everything in truth. There were moments when a lie or silence could have saved his life but he chose to be honest to the oath he had made to the court with the Bible in his right arm. The case dragged on until it came to its end and in the end of it all someone had to be blamed. He was dragged to his gallows as he cited his now famous quote, "This is what I get for being a man."

He was led into a football field with his hands tied behind him and as it was the practice of the day, told to run the moment he would hear a whistle. His executioners went following him from behind.

The whistle blew but he stood still. The executioner instead of running after him jacked backwards a bit and shot him in the head. Abed's father did not immediately coil down but stood for a while and then dropped dead.

The body was wrapped in the new Mozambique national flag and given to his family and the Mozambique Peoples Defense Force who buried him with full military honors. He was carried in Government vehicles across the border to Tanzania to rest in the Cemetery of Our Departed Heroes.

Don't let your ego get in the way—it is not too late to grow rich. This man you are reading about did not do much or achieve much in his life but he planted a seed of doing what he believed in and here we were in the danger of the night seeking his blessings. In life he was not a saint but in death he became one.

We knelt at his grave and prayed that we too may get the courage to forgive our past and live to victory. Wouldn't it be wonderful if by some miracle or some intuition we could reset our lives again knowing what we know now? We would have joy and enjoy it abundantly. Life would be different. We would transform from our poverty driven mentalities to prosperity propelling ones, wouldn't we? It is not easy to reverse our life. Let us have our life the easy way. Let us plan for a prosperous future. Let us clean up our beliefs. It is stupid of course to believe in ourselves. A man cannot be his own witness.

It is stupid to believe in our friends. A girl (Abed's mother) found herself in trouble and her heart was broken. How she wished she could go back and start over, but it was too late. If only we could begin again. These kinds of events occur every day and no one is exempt from them. Jesus said that in life you are bound to suffer but take courage. I have overcome the world. Why don't you believe in such a hero? Think of the things in your life that you would like a chance to change. How sometimes we would desperately like a return to the old good days.

It is stupid to believe in our stocks, which rise and fall, which brokers manipulate and steal, which change value day in and day out. It is wise to believe in God. He has committed himself to rewarding us for trusting him. Why not take the bet? Are we some kind of fish that prefers worms to strawberry? If we were able to live life in reverse we could put off this decision to a later date. Now that we have read this far we have lost the choice to read on or close the book. We had the choice in the beginning of the book but now that option is gone. The offer on table only urges you to use some of your mature knowledge to avoid making the mistakes that keep people in poverty.

That is not all. We all at one time gained knowledge through experience and I suppose like in Morogoro, Buguruni and during that fateful bus ride to Mbeya we all have had our share of mistakes. Without a doubt, there have been many times in my life when things just didn't turn out right. During some of those times I have mentioned, I found myself wishing I could turn back the hands of time or I had not been involved in the first instance.

I believe those times have occurred in all of our lives. Some have made the wrong career choices and wish they could go back to school to be retrained, but now they think they are too old for a fresh start. Some have made a bad business deal and now they are financially ruined. Some people relive the past and recount it in great detail in their mind. We already talked of that LandMark Manager's elder brother. All the negative emotions they felt back years and years ago they feel again and again. Replaying regret steals joy as one battles oneself emotionally for events that are gone forever. Some individuals simply surrender to the past. They decide that they will never rise above the past and resign themselves to be what the past has made them. All these fall in one category. They are called losers.

Those who move on to prosperity defy the past and refuse to be dominated by it. They recognize that while the past is unchangeable, they can do something to change how they deal with their memories. Do any of these situations apply to you? There are basically three things you must do to conquer self destruction.

(1) Treat the past for what it is…Passed. Wallowing in the past will always make you feel discouraged and defeated. Just pick some glorifying moments of the past and move with those. Discard the rest of the stuff. It is breaking your back for nothing.

(2) Leave tomorrow to tomorrow. Tomorrow will worry about itself. Each day has enough trouble of its own. This is not my creation. It is Jesus teaching. He told us to do this 2000 years ago.

(3) Today: Life is too short. God's desire is for us is to enjoy life today. Grab every opportunity to make you happy. Aim at laughing at least 17 times a day. That is what doctors recommend. It calculates to laughing at least once every 30 minutes. Is that too much? If your mood is down do not call someone to listen to your sad movies. Call someone who will not know that you are suffering but can afford to cheer you up. Between life and death, poverty and prosperity, choose life and the rest shall follow.

The difference between a rich man and a poor man is not in the number of hands or legs one has and one doesn't have. It is not either in the amount of money one has in a bank and one doesn't have. It is in the amount of energy or capacity to do work one has and one hasn't. If you have a lot of money, a lot of children , a lot of cars but your heart is broken , your marriage is broken of you it is written in Revelation 3: 17 "You say, 'I am rich; I have acquired wealth and do not need a thing.' But you do not realize that you are wretched, pitiful, poor, blind and naked." A prosperous man lacks nothing. A poor man misses something and that thing is the energy to be successful.

We cannot touch that energy and say here it is or there it is but we know how to detect its presence. "When you see trees waving or when you see water jumping do not say you have seen the wind or the storm. What you have seen are the results of the storm or of the wind. The real wind or the real storm is that energy that empowered the water or the tree to move. Without that energy the water or the tree would have stayed in one place." It is this energy that empowers you to succeed that we call a blessing.

There are many ways of getting it. Abed (also known as Ismail) went to his father's grave and talked to him. There is another interesting story in the Bible about a man called Israel (also known as Jacob) who stole it from his brother. Here is the story.

This is the account of Abraham's son Isaac.

Abraham became the father of Isaac, and Isaac was forty years old when he married Rebekah daughter of Bethuel the Aramean from Paddan Aram and sister of Laban the Aramean.

Isaac prayed to the LORD on behalf of his wife, because she was barren. The LORD answered his prayer, and his wife Rebekah became pregnant. The babies jostled each other within her, and she said, "Why is this happening to me?" So she went to inquire of the LORD.

The LORD said to her,

> "Two nations are in your womb,
> And two peoples from within you will be separated;
> One people will be stronger than the other,
> And the older will serve the younger."

When the time came for her to give birth, there were twin boys in her womb. The first to come out was red, and his whole body was like a hairy garment; so they named him Esau (Hairy). After this, his brother came out, with his hand grasping Esau's heel; so he was named Jacob (Trickster). Isaac was sixty years old when Rebekah gave birth to them.

The boys grew up, and Esau became a skillful hunter, a man of the open country, while Jacob was a quiet man, staying among the tents. Isaac, who had a taste for wild game, loved Esau, but Rebekah loved Jacob.

Once when Jacob was cooking some stew, Esau came in from the open country, famished. He said to Jacob, "Quick, let me have some of that red stew! I'm famished!" (That is why he was also called Edom (Red).)

Jacob replied, "First sell me your birthright."

"Look, I am about to die," Esau said. "What good is the birthright to me?"

But Jacob said, "Swear to me first." So he swore an oath to him, selling his birthright to Jacob.

Then Jacob gave Esau some bread and some lentil stew. He ate and drank, and then got up and left.

So Esau despised his birthright.

Now there was a famine in the land—besides the earlier famine of Abraham's time—and Isaac went to Abimelech king of the Philistines in Gerar. The LORD appeared to Isaac and said, "Do not go down to Egypt; live in the land where I tell you to live. Stay in this land for a while, and I will be with you and will bless[1] you. For to you and your descendants I will give all these lands and will confirm the oath I swore to your father Abraham. I will make your descendants as numerous as the stars in the sky and will give them all these lands, and through your offspring all nations on earth will be blessed,[2] because Abraham obeyed me and kept my requirements, my commands, my decrees and my laws." So Isaac stayed in Gerar.

When the men of that place asked him about his wife, he said, "She is my sister," because he was afraid to say, "She is my wife." He thought, "The men of this place might kill me on account of Rebekah, because she is beautiful."

When Isaac had been there a long time, Abimelech king of the Philistines looked down from a window and saw Isaac caressing his wife Rebekah. So Abimelech summoned Isaac and said, "She is really your wife! Why did you say, 'She is my sister'?"

Isaac answered him, "Because I thought I might lose my life on account of her."

Then Abimelech said, "What is this you have done to us? One of the men might well have slept with your wife, and you would have brought guilt upon us."

So Abimelech gave orders to all the people: "Anyone who molests this man or his wife shall surely be put to death."

Isaac planted crops in that land and the same year reaped a hundredfold, because the LORD blessed[3] him. The man became rich, and his wealth continued to grow until he became very wealthy. He had so many flocks and herds and servants that the Philistines envied him. So all the wells that his father's servants had dug in the time of his father Abraham, the Philistines stopped up, filling them with earth.

Then Abimelech said to Isaac, "Move away from us; you have become too powerful for us."

So Isaac moved away from there and encamped in the Valley of Gerar and settled there. Isaac reopened the wells that had been dug in the time of his father Abraham, which the Philistines had stopped up after Abraham died, and he gave them the same names his father had given them.

Isaac's servants dug in the valley and discovered a well of fresh water there. But the herdsmen of Gerar quarreled with Isaac's herdsmen and said, "The water is ours!" So he named the well Esek (Dispute), because they disputed with him. Then they dug another well, but they quarreled over that one also; so he named it Sitnah (Opposition). He moved on from there and dug another well, and no one quarreled over it. He named it Rehoboth (Room), saying, "Now the LORD has given us room and we will flourish in the land."

From there he went up to Beersheba (Well of Oath). That night the LORD appeared to him and said, "I am the God of your father Abraham. Do not be afraid, for I am with you; I will bless you and will increase the number of your descendants for the sake of my servant Abraham."

Isaac built an altar there and called on the name of the LORD. There he pitched his tent, and there his servants dug a well.

Meanwhile, Abimelech had come to him from Gerar, with Ahuzzath his personal adviser and Phicol the commander of his forces. Isaac asked them, "Why have you come to me, since you were hostile to me and sent me away?"

They answered, "We saw clearly that the LORD was with you; so we said, 'There ought to be a sworn agreement between us'—between us and you. Let us make a treaty with you that you will do us no harm, just as we did not molest you but always treated you well and sent you away in peace. And now you are blessed by the LORD."

Isaac then made a feast for them, and they ate and drank. Early the next morning the men swore an oath to each other. Then Isaac sent them on their way, and they left him in peace.

That day Isaac's servants came and told him about the well they had dug. They said, "We've found water!" He called it Shibah (Oath), and to this day the name of the town has been Beersheba.

When Esau was forty years old, he married Judith daughter of Beeri the Hittite, and also Basemath daughter of Elon the Hittite. They were a source of grief to Isaac and Rebekah.

When Isaac was old and his eyes were so weak that he could no longer see, he called for Esau his older son and said to him, "My son."

"Here I am," he answered.

Isaac said, "I am now an old man and don't know the day of my death. Now then, get your weapons—your quiver and bow—and go out to the open country to hunt some wild game for me. Prepare me the kind of tasty food I like and bring it to me to eat, so that I may give you my blessing before I die."

Now Rebekah was listening as Isaac spoke to his son Esau. When Esau left for the open country to hunt game and bring it back, Rebekah said to her son Jacob, "Look, I overheard your father say to your brother Esau, 'Bring me some game and prepare me some tasty food to eat, so that I may give you my blessing in the presence of the LORD before I die.' Now, my son, listen carefully and do what I tell you: Go out to the flock and bring me two choice young goats, so I can prepare some tasty food for your father, just the way he likes it. Then take it to your father to eat, so that he may give you his blessing before he dies."

Jacob said to Rebekah his mother, "But my brother Esau is a hairy man, and I'm a man with smooth skin. What if my father touches me? I would appear to be tricking him and would bring down a curse on myself rather than a blessing."

His mother said to him, "My son, let the curse fall on me. Just do what I say; go and get them for me."

So he went and got them and brought them to his mother, and she prepared some tasty food, just the way his father liked it. Then Rebekah took the best clothes of Esau her older son, which she had in the house, and put them on her younger son Jacob. She also covered his hands and the smooth part of his neck with the goatskins. Then she handed to her son Jacob the tasty food and the bread she had made.

He went to his father and said, "My father."

"Yes, my son," he answered. "Who is it?"

Jacob said to his father, "I am Esau your firstborn. I have done as you told me. Please sit up and eat some of my game so that you may give me your blessing."

Isaac asked his son, "How did you find it so quickly, my son?"

"The LORD your God gave me success," he replied.

Then Isaac said to Jacob, "Come near so I can touch you, my son, to know whether you really are my son Esau or not."

Jacob went close to his father Isaac, who touched him and said, "The voice is the voice of Jacob, but the hands are the hands of Esau." He did not recognize him, for his hands were hairy like those of his brother Esau; so he blessed him. "Are you really my son Esau?" he asked.

"I am," he replied.

Then he said, "My son, bring me some of your game to eat, so that I may give you my blessing."

Jacob brought it to him and he ate; and he brought some wine and he drank. Then his father Isaac said to him, "Come here, my son, and kiss me."

So he went to him and kissed him. When Isaac caught the smell of his clothes, he blessed him and said,

> "Ah, the smell of my son
> Is like the smell of a field
> That the LORD has blessed.
> May God give you of heaven's dew
> And of earth's richness—

> An abundance of grain and new wine.
> May nations serve you
> And peoples bow down to you.
> Be lord over your brothers,
> And may the sons of your mother bow down to you.
> May those who curse you be cursed
> And those who bless you be blessed."

After Isaac finished blessing him and Jacob had scarcely left his father's presence, his brother Esau came in from hunting. He too prepared some tasty food and brought it to his father. Then he said to him, "My father, sit up and eat some of my game, so that you may give me your blessing."

His father Isaac asked him, "Who are you?"

"I am your son," he answered, "your firstborn, Esau."

Isaac trembled violently and said, "Who was it, then, that hunted game and brought it to me? I ate it just before you came and I blessed him—and indeed he will be blessed!"

When Esau heard his father's words, he burst out with a loud and bitter cry and said to his father, "Bless me—me too, my father!"

But he said, "Your brother came deceitfully and took your blessing."

Esau said, "Isn't he rightly named Jacob (Trickster)? He has deceived me these two times: He took my birthright, and now he's taken my blessing!" Then he asked, "Haven't you reserved any blessing for me?"

Isaac answered Esau, "I have made him lord over you and have made all his relatives his servants, and I have sustained him with grain and new wine. So what can I possibly do for you, my son?"

Esau said to his father, "Do you have only one blessing, my father? Bless me too, my father!" Then Esau wept aloud.

> His father Isaac answered him,
> "Your dwelling will be
> Away from the earth's richness,
> Away from the dew of heaven above.
> You will live by the sword

And you will serve your brother.
But when you grow restless,
You will throw his yoke
From off your neck."

Esau held a grudge against Jacob because of the blessing his father had given him. He said to himself, "The days of mourning for my father are near; then I will kill my brother Jacob."

When Rebekah was told what her older son Esau had said, she sent for her younger son Jacob and said to him, "Your brother Esau is consoling himself with the thought of killing you. Now then, my son, do what I say: Flee at once to my brother Laban in Haran. Stay with him for a while until your brother's fury subsides. When your brother is no longer angry with you and forgets what you did to him, I'll send word for you to come back from there. Why should I lose both of you in one day?"

Then Rebekah said to Isaac, "I'm disgusted with living because of these Hittite women. If Jacob takes a wife from among the women of this land, from Hittite women like these, my life will not be worth living."

This story needs to be read and read again. At the beginning of this book I said there are no hidden secrets on the journey from poverty to prosperity. I swore to you that this book will show you the sure way to prosperity. I am here to deliver.

Go back to the article: "This is the account of Abraham's son Isaac". It is a cynical title for a family of a man of Abraham's standing. Anyway go back to the article and underline every word 'Bless' or its derivatives. You should get at least 13 of them.

Number them 1-13 or to whichever number you get.

For each one of them answer: Who said it; To whom and Why?

Now fill in this table. You may add on more cells as required. Some examples have been done for you.

Blessings

Number	Who said	What was said (Quote)	To whom	Why	Result
Bless[1]	God	Stay in this land for a while, and I will be with you and will bless[1] you.	Isaac	Rewarding father's obedience.	Isaac stayed and prospered in Gerar.
Blessed,[2]	God	I will make your descendants as numerous as the stars in the sky and will give them all these lands, and through your offspring all nations on earth will be blessed,[2]	Isaac	Rewarding association with a blessed man.	Isaac stayed in Gerar "for a while."
Blessed[3]	Author	Isaac planted crops in that land and the same year reaped a hundredfold, because the LORD blessed[3] him.	We (Readers)	Fulfilling the covenant.	The man became rich, and his wealth continued to grow until he became very wealthy.

Just as there are physical laws that govern the physical universe, so are there spiritual laws which govern the spiritual universe (blessing). It is the relationship between the giver and the receiver. One of these laws reads like: A blessing cannot be created nor destroyed. Yes a blessing can be turned into a curse but that is simply turning the direction of the blessing in conventional science. We have seen that with our coffee bean, carrot and egg story.

All blessings come from one source and flow down to different people depending on your relationship with the giver.

God gave a blessing (energy to succeed) to Abraham because Abraham obeyed God and kept His requirements, His commands, His decrees and His laws. Isaac stayed in Gerar because God had told him to stay. He blessed him because he was (one) a son of Abraham and (two) because he had obeyed God.

Like a pardon a blessing is not a blessing when it is rejected. What would have happened had Isaac refused to stay for a while in Gerar? Look at what happened when Esau despised his birthright. Prosperity is our birthright but shortsightedness might make us lose it. Do you remember an occasion when you felt God could not give you so much money? What did you tick? ( ) Make at least one dollar a day; ( ) Make at least ten dollars a day; ( ) Make at least a hundred dollars a day; ( ) Make five hundred dollars a day; ( ) Make one thousand dollars a day. Did you choose something small because that is what God could afford to give you? Did you say in your mind: "Look, I am about to die. What good is the big blessing to me?"

There are many things we do and say to justify our actions. These very actions might bind us in poverty. Listen to how Rebekah explained herself to Esau for sending Jacob away: Then Rebekah said to Isaac, "I'm disgusted with living because of these Hittite women. If Jacob takes a wife from among the women of this land, from Hittite women like these, my life will not be worth living." Was that true?

Lucky Rebekah. Had Esau found this trick out Jacob would have caught up with what he feared most.

Rebekah and Jacob might have got away with it but for how long would this success last. Read Esau's lips: "But when you grow restless, you will throw his yoke from off your neck." Stolen riches cannot last forever. Jeremiah told us in the beginning of this book.

Lead your life like Abraham and you will move from poverty to prosperity without any fear of falling back. You will dig wells. They will be buried (stopped) by envy but in the end they will be dug up again.

You may have experienced rises and falls in your life. You may have excused your failures like Rebekah pretending that Jacob had to go to Laban to avoid marrying Hittite women. You may have blocked your success by thinking that letting your wife out to work might lead other men to steal her. You may have thought that you need money first before you go into any business venture. You may have thought that you need God to call you by name before you pray to him. Whatever has been keeping you from prosperity has been lack of energy to succeed. The world is full of this energy. Jacob was going to miss it hadn't her mother said, "My son, let the curse fall on me. Just do what I say; go and get them for me."

Confidence; the belief that nothing bad will fall upon you; the idea that success is at hand; the comfort that you are not alone; the knowledge that many successful people have ever been in your kind of dilemma will "place your dwelling in the earth's richness and in the dew of heaven above". Of you it was prophesied "Isaiah 65 [21] And they shall build houses, and inhabit them; and they shall plant vineyards, and eat the fruit of them.

[22] They shall not build, and another inhabit; they shall not plant, and another eat: for as the days of a tree shall be the days of my people, and my chosen shall long enjoy the work of their hands.

[23] They shall not labor in vain, nor bring forth for calamity; for they are the seed of the blessed of Jehovah, and their offspring with them'.

No one denies being a child of God. No one should despise his birthright. If you are not aware of what befalls those who despise their birth right go and read the article entitled: <u>This is the account of Abraham's son Isaac.</u>

Now think. If you had to go to the Cemetery of your Fallen Heroes where would you go? Where would you go to claim your birth right? Would you simply walk through life without claiming your blessing?

Comforted by our night of prayers we stayed on in Mbeya and this is what we found.

Mbeya is the capital of southern Tanzania and the first town you will encounter if landing from Zambia, Malawi or Congo. It is a sprawling town that looks like a land between two hills.

The corrugated iron city looks like a river that is about to burst its edges. Mbeya is built in a narrow valley hemmed in by high mountains. It is an incredibly friendly town, and the cool mists and high altitude (1,700m), and the beautiful setting in a bowl of mountains, will make you want to stay. There is trout fishing in the mountains to the south, and for those who would like to go fishing (for fish or for women) like at life of Kipepeo Beach try the Poroto Mountains around Tukuyu.

For its temperature of between -6°C on the highlands and 29°C on the lowlands it is sometimes related to Scotland of Africa and to the Fynbos of South Africa's Western Cape Province. It enjoys abundant and reliable rainfall. It is cool and misty much of the time and sometimes you will need even a sweater to warm you up.

Esau went building wells and giving them his ancestral names. Esau looked at those wells and remembered: Dispute, Oath and Room. Esau looked at his wealth and saw that prosperity is a journey not a destiny. He was up and chased at one time but he was being sought by the very people who sent him away for his blessings. Have you ever thought of taking your old enemy out for dinner? Esau gave them a feast. What was the result of this?

"That day Isaac's servants came and told him about the well they had dug. They said, "We've found water!" He called it Shibah (Oath), and to this day the name of the town has been Beersheba."

Mbeya Town was found as a colonial government station in 1927 for the British had found not water but gold in the Lupa area in Chunya hills to the north.

Sometimes you need a sweater in Mbeya. Sometimes it looks more like Scotland than South Africa. Sometimes a blessing may look like a curse.

> "Your dwelling will be away from the earth's richness, away from the dew of heaven above. You will live by the sword and you will serve your brother".

When you end the story here you think once you are poor and you will always be poor. Does God have only one blessing?

If you struck it rich before and you lost your business in the end does it mean there is no recovery? Does it mean that if your father is dead and buried he is gone forever?

Mbeya has been called the "Scotland of Africa" and with good reason. It is for the same reason Esau dug up his fathers's wells and gave them the same names. With the exception of the lowland areas of Usangu plains, Kyela, Chunya, Kamsamba and Msangano divisions in Mbozi, which are within the Rift Valley Mbeya is mountainous region. It is located about 860km. south west of Dar-es-Salaam, bordering Malawi and Zambia, which are some of the poorest countries in the world. You do not need to be very rich to appear blessed, you just need to be surrounded by poor people and you will stand out.

Sometimes however a blessing may look like a curse. "But when you grow restless, you will throw his yoke from off your neck." Mbeya region is among the blessed ones in Tanzania. It is well-served with road networks from different parts of the country and connected to two main highways linking to Malawi, Zambia, Zimbabwe, Botswana and South Africa. A new international airport is under construction. There is a ferry service on Lake Nyasa linking with Mbamba Bay and Liuli in Ruvuma Region. There is a direct train from Dar es Salaam to Kapiri Mposhi. Mbeya is the best place in Tanzania for hiking and forest walking as encouraged by cool weather. Nature excursions to the scenic part of the country like Lake Ngozi, Rungwe Mountain, Natural Bridge in Kiwira or Flower Garden at Kitulo Plateau and Songwe Bat Caves, Mbozi Meteorite site. Game viewing can be done in Madibila and Rujewa or Lake Rukwa. As Mbeya has grown restless it has produced recommendable lodgings like the Mbeya Hotel, the Holiday Lodge and the Highlands. It has a room for budget travelers or for those who chose to make 10 dollars a day at the Moravian Youth Hostel. South of Mbeya is a signpost off the main road to Zambia saying "The Utengele Country Resort is a charming country hotel with excellent food and a vibrant pub."

The presence of a signpost suggests that to walk to prosperity you need to follow some kind of signposts. If you do not follow this Resort sign post you might think there are no resorts in Mbeya. You might end up thinking that the only thing in Mbeya worth visiting is the Cemetery of our Fallen Heroes. Esau was called Hairy and Israel was no wonder called Jacob. What are the signposts in your name? Do your blessings look like curses? Grow restless and throw this yoke off your neck.

God does not have only one blessing. The blessing of Jacob did not deny Esau a chance of being blessed. Prosperity is for all God's creation. We should not fail to propel each other to prosperity as if by one growing rich one would take all the money and leave us with nothing. The journey to prosperity is not like that race of crabs who fail to climb a wall by pulling each other down. We prosper by praying for our masters such that if they prosper we (the slaves) prosper too.

This is the day for you to claim your blessing. It is your right to prosper. Prosperity does not come by hard work but by way of blessing. The right of all ages: Blessings. Define your blessing. Claim it. Get it.

CHAPTER EIGHTEEN

CURSES

Some people talk about mixed blessings. Some people talk about missed blessings. They are all talking about the same thing. A blessing must be pure otherwise it is a curse. Check it out. If an action is in other words a nuisance, a pest, a blight, a bother, an irritation, an annoyance (you have got it right), that is a curse. A curse sucks out the energy for success. Look at it this way. You have a ball in your hand. When it is full of air it is nice to touch and ready to bounce up and down. This is like you when you have the opportunity to prosper. You behave like a young gazelle.

Look at life the other way round. Imagine a siphon is placed on your ball and the air is let out. You will see the ball collapse in your own eyes. This siphon is a curse. It takes energy for success out of you. The fear of all ages is the fear of a curse. Thousands of years ago Jacob said: "What if my father touches me? I would appear to be tricking him and would bring down a curse on myself rather than a blessing."

The fear of a curse has been with us for thousands of years. For those who accept the theory of evolution, we could put it this way. Fear has been built into our life systems from generations to generations. It denies us our success and imprisons us to life full of fear. There is no success whether in war or in peace for those who move with fear. There is fear of failure, there is fear of death, there is fear of pain, there is fear of fear but the greatest fear of all is the fear of a curse. The fear of a curse is ranked the greatest because in the curse is found all the other evils.

In simple terms a curse is a blessing blocker. The same principles that propel you to success once reversed will lead you to failure. The same principles that propel you to prosperity once reversed will lead you to poverty. Fear will lead you to poverty as much as faith can lead you to prosperity. Fear and faith work on the same principles that having one even to the size of a mustard seed can build or move mountains. Remember: We are what we think. We think what we believe. We feel what we believe. We do what we feel. If we are to prosper….. If we have to change from poverty to prosperity we have to change our beliefs, we have to change our thinking, we have to change our feelings and we have to change our actions.

This is true. A man who believes that God made him a master of the universe or who believes that God has told him to eat some unclean stuff will rise up and do some things beyond our imagination. If it is Solomon he will build a church; if it is Peter he will walk on water. If it is Hosef he will climb Mt. Morogoro. We have to change our feelings and we have to change our actions.

Jane my secretary found a man to marry. They lived together for seven months and Jane could not see any sign of pregnancy. Bit by bit the man started showing that he felt this marriage was not going to work out. Jane visited a number of health clinics, took different prescriptions but nothing was yielding. Finally he was led to a witch doctor at Bagamoyo– a suburb of Dar Es Salaam.

They arrived by appointment at 2 am at the witch doctor's shrine.

The shrine which can sit at least 500 people was fully packed at that time. The parking lot was full of Mercedes Benzes, Prados and all other expensive cars. Looking at this was enough to convince you that you have come to a new life church.

The preaching was led by a soft spoken lady. Different types of curses were mentioned: Businesses of no profit returns, migraines and other headaches, ulcers and stomach ills, shoulder and back pains. The priest called forward those who needed children to come to the altar. Jane felt it was her turn.

Thirty or forty women and a few men were led out to the open grassland. The lights were as bright as day. The priest took off her clothes and stood stuck naked before her audience. She told every luck-seeker to do the same.

She lined up everybody and she bathed all of them one by one. They looked at each other men and women but none realized that they were naked. They were neither shy nor attracted to one another.

Jane was particularly amazed when she went for a counseling session. The priest showed her a mirror and asked, "Whom do you see?"

Usually when you hold a mirror you see yourself but for Jane no matter how she held the mirror the picture in the mirror was of her grandmother. Jane was terrified.

Was Jane told she had hurt her grandmother?

"How did I hurt her? She died many years ago and I was her favorite grand kid".

Jane was given some bowl to hold in her hands and told to close her eyes. Some kind of strong wind brew on her and in a very clear unmistakable voice she heard her grandmother complaining of sleeping outside in the rain. By interpretation Jane had not looked after or visited her grandmother's grave for ages. The truth was that she had not even ever thought about her since her death.

Jane then knew why her stomach was unfruitful.

To have this curse removed she had to be baptized there and then. The Bible says whoever believes and baptized would be saved. Jane had this knowledge from her upbringing.

She was led to the water front and by 4pm she had been baptized and received as a new flock. By obligation she was to attend regular shrine service every Saturday.

Jane for months and months went to Bagamoyo without missing. When her friends were out for disco or other entertainment she was out worshipping her lord. She participated in every kind of ritual but that is beyond the description of this book. I would need another book to account for the sex orgies, bang smoking, naked dancing and all other evils she was subjected to.

In the end of it all here is the good news: The curse was removed.

It is possible to remove a curse.

"How do we do that?"

"We remove the blessing blocker".

In <u>Face to Face with Grief</u> I talked about a sink in my house that got blocked. It was an ordinary day. The sink got blocked, my wife called me in; the children were blamed but despite all that the water could not flow.

As I was writing this book my younger brother, Samuel sent me a text message which said: "Probe + blame = Problem. Take the blame away from the problem and you will see the solution. (Mathematically, Problem - Blame = Probe (search, explore, survey, investigate, look into, check out, query, survey, prod, poke about) and when you do all these you get a clear solution). I use this quotation without permission.

Water did not flow again until I had got down on my knees and unscrewed those smelly pipes and picked out the blockers piece by piece. I had to search, explore, survey, investigate, look into, check out, query, survey, prod, poke about…………….

When the road to prosperity is blocked the traffic cannot flow until the jam is cleared. This is what you see on the streets of Tanzania every day. White dressed traffic officers stand firm in the middle of the road, raining or shining, redirecting traffic. It is amazing they carry neither guns nor spears but by the power invested in their uniforms they command (come or go) and the traffic obeys. Jams however negative they may be obey authority. It is true with water pipes. It is true with traffic. It is true with blood streams. It is true with your thoughts. It is true with your life.

I learnt this when working on the sink I have just talked about. When working on a bathroom sink you do not have to switch off water in the kitchen or the electricity in the sitting room. You do not have to remove the bathroom curtains either. You do not have to remove all the screws in the sink tap either. You have just to target those screws that lead to the blockage. You have to determine your curse and target that curse. Name that curse and go at it.

What is your blessing blocker?

Suppose God told you, "Go into the world and multiply", would you take a second wife? Would you look for another partner? What would you do with your boyfriend or girl friend? What would you do? Would you say, "That must not have been God speaking?" What would you do? Would you consult your pastor or your doctor or your lawyer? Tell me. Would you tip the police? What would you think?

Suppose God told you, "Go into the world and prosper", what would you do? Would you remain skeptical and say, "Show me the money!" Would you rise up and walk? Would you continue in your slumber? Or would you say, "I will not believe it was the voice of God until my bills are paid. I will not believe until I have a new house or a new dress. I will not believe until my children are out of college. I will not believe until I have got a job. I will not believe until I am healed. I will not believe until my problem is solved! I will not believe until...."

Again I ask you: What is your blessing blocker? Is ignorance your blessing blocker? If so seek wisdom. If you did not know that God by the authority he vested in your grandfather Adam, the earth and everything therein is yours, seek knowledge. If you did not know that the blessings of Abraham are for the whole humanity, believe it and prosper. Why do you keep yourself in poverty when you can walk out of it?

What is it that stands between you and the Giver of Opportunities?

What is your blessing blocker?

There are some seven known sins the Bible mentions. Of course all human sins cannot be categorized into seven sets. The so called Cardinal sins are just a few of the blessing blockers. I do not mean there are only seven sins the Bible mentions as can tie you up in poverty. I will distance myself this far. "Nowhere in the Bible' and listen to me carefully, "are the seven Cardinal sins listed." I grew up with the tradition and I take this view as absolute truth that it takes only one sin (where sin is defined as an act in disobedience of God's law) to separate man from a perfect God and thus placing man in a state of need (poverty) and in need of salvation (prosperity).

I have made my statement and the way you walk from poverty to prosperity depends on the way you interpret the relevance of these vices. Culture and religious upbringing has a great influence on your thinking. The speed at which Jane got baptized and the way I am using this word to mean "Bathing in water" is a classic example in point. If your thoughts are harming you, change your thinking.

What is your blessing blocker? Pick one or two from the list and start your journey to prosperity. You may pick all if you are so infected. What is your blessing blocker?

1 Extravagance
2 Greed
3 Corruption
4 Laziness
5 Anger
6 Jealousy
7 Pride

What is your blessing blocker? What is it that stands between you and success? What is your blessing blocker? Why is it that you come so close to success but miss it out in the end? What is your blessing blocker? What is your blessing blocker? What is your blessing blocker? What is your blessing blocker? If you feel this question is far-fetched turn it around and ask, "What is my blessing blocker? What is my blessing blocker? What is my blessing blocker?"

I will keep asking you to name your blessing blocker and until you do so you will not find peace with me. Or you will not find peace in your heart. Or you will not find peace in this chapter. Or you will not find meaning in my words. Or you will not find the answer to your problems but above all these you will not be able to move from poverty to prosperity and if you do you will not stay up for long. Name your blessing blocker.

To take you off the hook, I here assume that you have named your curse or you have identified one or two from the list above. Now you have got the enemy in your hands. What do you do with him? Do you hang him or let him go? Do you sign a peace treaty or treat him with the principle: Once an enemy always an enemy? Can light live together with darkness? Can you mix blessings with curses? To prosper or to lead life successfully you cannot be neither hot nor cold. Watch out if you are lukewarm. You will be spat out of God's mouth. Success demands sharpness, discipline and a clear walk to success.

Slightly out of topic I will mention seven virtues that bring success. I will do it here so that you can easily see the relevance they are with your blessing blockers. In contrast but in the order to the sins they oppose, they are (1)Accountability, (2) Justice, (3) Charity, (4) Hardwork, (5) Encouragement, (6) Caring and (7) Humility.

As I said in the beginning the road from poverty to prosperity has no hidden secrets. Just pluck out of your lifestyle the seven blockers or vices and replace them with the seven virtues. If you do not get rich immediately (and I am using the word "Immediately" with authority) return this book to the author and your money shall be refunded with no questions asked. This is as much a promise as I made at the beginning of this book that you are in for great things in your life if you read and practice what this book advocates.

Prosperity is a journey not a destination. Remove the jams and the money will flow your way.

I once again tell you it does not matter how long you have lived under the curse. It does not matter who put the spell on you. It does not matter what church or religion you identify yourself with. What matters is only one thing. MAN'S GREATEST ENEMY IS HIMSELF and you might be your greatest enemy. The person who keeps you in poverty is you. The mentality that keeps you in poverty is yours. The burden to move to success is your burden. You are the one carrying this luggage and you are the one to load it off yourself.

This brings to memory the other day we had an accident on the way to Mbeya. As the bus skidded many passengers pulled down their luggages and these very luggages blocked the exit door.

Are you blocked?

Paul says in the book of Galatians 5:19-21 "Now the works of the flesh are manifest, which are these; adultery, fornication, uncleanness, lasciviousness. idolatry, witchcraft, hatred, variance, emulations, wrath, strife, seditions, heresies, envying, murders, drunkenness, reveling, and such like: of the which I tell you before, as I have also told you in time past, that they which do such things shall not inherit the kingdom of God.(KJV)......." that these cannot enter the kingdom of heaven. He may not have been talking of prosperity. That might be your own opinion. Whatever the relevance to your search there is a list of blockers here identified with poverty. If the purpose of reading this book is to find the road to prosperity then follow me.

Analyze your blocker.

Extravagance: The dictionary defines this as lust, usually thought of as involving obsessive or excessive thoughts or desires of a sexual nature. Unfulfilled lusts may lead to sexual or sociological compulsions or outbreaks including but not limited to sexual addiction, adultery, bestiality, and rape. At the face of it extravagance appears as excessive or reckless spending, wastefulness, excessiveness or lavishness. If you put a record of your life activities on a weighing scale where on one side you have the virtues and on the other side your life, would you sink or rise? If you were to be tried in a court of law would your activities send you to jail or set you free?

We are all sinners and we sometimes say we are all human. We do not have a license however to suffer poverty for the rest of our lives simply because we were created as human beings (not angels). Is your life enslaved by the desire for sex release?

Bob Marley sang it: Emancipate yourselves from mental slavery......

Analyze your blocker. Is it fornication, rape, perversion, pornography, child molestation, male or female prostitution?

In the same way Greed is defined as Over-consumption. It is derived from the Latin Gluttire, meaning to gulp down or swallow. Greed or gluttony is the over-indulgence and over-consumption of anything to the point of waste or withholding from the needy. At Kipepeo Beach over drinking or over eating or over womanizing can be seen as either a vice or a sign of status. Where food is relatively scarce, being able to eat well might be something to take pride in (although this can also result in a moral backlash when confronted with the reality of those standing outside the fence). Where food is routinely plentiful, it may be considered a sign of self control to resist the temptation to over-indulge.

Study your blocker. In other cultures this list can include eating too much sugar, ice cream or defiling nutritional rules. Define your gluttony.

We can go on defining corruption, laziness, anger, jealousy and pride. Unfortunately that is the work of dictionaries and not of this type of book. Our task is how to get out of the pit; how to put food on our plates; how to sleep with filled stomachs, how to build a roof on our heads and how to grow beyond all this to nothing broken, nothing missing, nothing lacking. Our aim is to have a heart overflowing with joy. We are not stopping there. We want to ensure that we never fall back again into curse. Prosperity must be passable to children and children's children and it is not prosperity yet until it passes to children's children and to children's children and to children's children. I can go on and on and on but there must be a rule of never falling back.

We did not come to these seven cardinal sins by mistake. We trampled upon it on our way searching for prosperity. Here is the story. Abed and I had returned from Mbeya and had sent our invitation to the Chinese investor. The story is at a point when a new company to handle the investment had been registered and an office located. We had spent a month of hard work or head work but not a single dollar had come in. The Task Force was getting stretched and even wondering whether we had not embarked on a time wasting scheme. Members were tired of meetings and meetings and getting nothing in return. One member even declared his intention to quit the group of dreamers and return to his old status. What was better: to die living poor or die dreaming rich?

It was under those pressing problems we sat in JM Mall, Sokoine Street and we faced the problems. We discussed the issues. The spirit of Jesus was there saying why do we put our hands on the plough and then look backwards. Then to my mind came the Seven Deadly Sins. I could not find the right reference in the Bible to pin point our possible weaknesses. Proverbs 6:16 – 19 says (King James Version (KJV) " These six things doth the Lord hate: yea, seven are an abomination unto him:. These are:

    A proud look,
      A lying tongue,
        Hands that shed innocent blood,
          A heart that deviseth wicked imaginations,
            Feet that be swift in running to mischief,
              A false witness that speaketh lies, and

He that soweth discord among brethren.

The list looked like what I was looking for but it did not cover everything. I called my wife Letty who was in Hongkong at the time to fill in the missing gaps. What she could remember were: the feet that are quick to anger, the maid that marries his boss and giving false witness. I called Miro who was in Kuwait then for any reference. As a matter of acknowledgement I quote his sms here: http://en.wikipedia.org/wiki/Seven_deadly_sins"

I bring this point up to say that a taskforce has unlimited supply of resources. We called Kuwait, Hongkong and Heaven to solve the problems that were bedeviling us locally in Tanzania. As I mention this you can sense a smile on my face saying the results of that meeting are the fruits you see today. You can too prosper!

You cannot however prosper by looking at the wrong side of the coin. One side of coin talks politics and another one talks economics. A coin has two faces. Call one virtue and call another vise. It was resolved in that meeting in JM Mall that we should not spend all our time looking at the problematic part of life. There is so much to enjoy and we have a short time to live. We resolved to match every vise with an equivalent virtue and to focus our attention on the virtue side and let the curse die away silently. This is the list we got.

VICE	VIRTUE
Extravagance	Accountable
Greed	Justice
Corruption	Charity
Laziness	Hard work
Complaining	Encouraging
Jealousy	Caring
Pride	Humble

You are encouraged to design your own chart. As you do so you will realize that all your curses cannot fit into seven categories. One sin bears another. Lying is borne by Jealousy.

False Accusation could be borne by Greed or Corruption. Fear could be borne by Laziness or Pride.

Where is your Success Blocker?

If you know where it is you could do this book justice by turning your blocker around and think and practice its equivalent virtue. That is the way we can turn a curse into a blessing. We can turn from poverty to prosperity because the same principles that tie us down are the same principles that can push us up.

This chapter's final declaration is that there is no one who asks a father for a blessing and gets a curse. John 14: 13-14 "And I will do whatever you ask in my name. So do your Father's glory shown through the son. If you ask for anything in my name, I will do it." Now if you belong to the silent majority who would like to turn their life around but lack the courage to do so, simply ask your father in heaven for assistance who says, "If my people forsake their sins and pray to me, I will listen to their prayers and heal the nation".

There is no better way of overcoming the curse than this. If others can certainly too you can! Jane overcame her case. I will tell you the details in another chapter. Just read on.

CHAPTER NINETEEN

DISBELIEF

To overcome a curse you realize you needed a certain form of discipline. Discipline is the power to decide what you want and work towards getting it. There is an alternative to discipline. It is called Disbelief.

Disbelief is defined as Mistrust, Doubt or Skepticism. From what we have said so far in this book, surely this is a good tool for people who want to keep their destiny in poverty or in chaos. It is all a work of the brain. It starts as a thought. Before you can say it in words you think about it. "Let me see what I want to say." Thoughts precede words. In practice we turn words into action. Let us see what we have: Thoughts>Words>Action. In this process Action is an achievement (Accomplishment). Sometimes we do not get what we want. Sometimes we do not get as much as we wanted. Sometimes we get more than we expected. Action depends on our effort. We shall call this Effort our Feelings. I will squeeze the word Feelings between Words and Action. Our formula becomes: Thoughts>Words>Feelings > Action.

I want to turn again to where our thoughts come from. Some say they come from the devil. Some say they come from God. Some say they come from our selves. When we look at this carefully we notice that our thoughts are determined by what we believe. If I cannot see God; if I cannot see the devil; the alternative is, "My thoughts come from me". You believe in the Bible? You believe in the Koran? You believe in the Stars? There you are. Whatever you think follows what you believe.

We earlier on talked about the lifecycle of a butterfly. We saw how it turned from egg, larva, pupa and adult. Turning from poverty to prosperity follows a similar metamorphosis.

The stages of this change are Belief>Thoughts>Words>Feelings>Action.

Again looking at the lifecycle of a butterfly we saw that pulling the insect out of the pupa kills or deforms the butterfly. In fact premature birth has everlasting effect on the life of the kid. The journey to prosperity is the same. Getting out at Buguruni instead of at Malapa though the two stages are near each other blocks your destiny. Put Poverty as your initial stage and Prosperity as your destination then line up the Belief>Thoughts>Words>Feelings>Action system properly. Surely you will get what you want. Surely you will go where you want to go. You will make the changes that you want to make. You will move from poverty to prosperity and you will stay up there with no fear of falling back. Can you imagine anything better than achieving your dream?

Think of it. You will not live the rest of your life to pay your debts. You will not live to build a house or to buy a car. You will not live just to see your children go through college. All that thinking is nothing. You will live to have everlasting joy where nothing is missing or broken. You cannot have children and praise God for them when they are disobedient. You cannot praise God for giving you a wife who screams like a drilling machine. You cannot boast of a husband who treats you like a punching bag. That describes not prosperity but poverty. You have to leave all these pains behind and live beyond riches.

Everyone wants a prosperous life. New Year cards say this all the time. We do not live the way cards say because we add some little nonsense at our Belief>Thoughts>Words>Feelings>Action program. "Dis" is the little virus we add in our formula and everything goes the wrong way around.

Dis is a little nonsense but turns Belief into a strong negative force. Negative forces give negative results. As a tree is known by its fruits belief is known by its action. Think of any scheme, add doubt to your feelings and I can assure you that failure is what you will reap. You do not need experience to know this.

Disbelief is the root cause of most failures. The trouble of all ages is disbelief.

The science of disbelief is that no one is born with it. It does not even exist as we make our progress plans. It waits until everything is well thought out and even said then it comes in as a counter attack force. First it is a thought. It attaches itself to our thinking gene and like cancer seeks to destroy our faith. Our faith mutates or metamorphoses into doubt. Our brain cells are eaten out and we start acting like lunatics. A man is crazy if he expects the same result from different actions. If you think that whatever you will do will lead to failure you are crazy in the absolute meaning of the term. You start thinking of failing. You feel discouraged and you take no reverse action or you do the next silly thing. If you expect to ever prosper with this kind of routine or attitude you must be crazy!

> There is a second chance. Now vote again.
> ( ) Make at least one dollar a day.
> ( ) Make at least ten dollars a day.
> ( ) Make at least a hundred dollars a day.
> ( ) Make five hundred dollars a day.
> ( ) Make one thousand dollars a day

> Is disbelief still your guiding star?
> You can hook it up.
> Abed went to prison and this is what he came out with.

There are seven steps of recreating a man's personality. According to Abed at the time of arrest you still feel strong like a man. When you look at those chains on you and the strength of two or three officers accompanying, you inwardly feel you are a bull and a challenger. You sincerely do not lose that courage until those chains are taken off and you are declared a prisoner.

When you have just been arrested you blame the police for arresting you. Then the moment comes when they throw you in a cell to live with other prisoners. If you ever expected sympathy or understanding from fellow prisoners you got the whole story wrong. Fellow prisoners are bound to bully you so bad that you will long for police protection.

Fellow thieves tell you point blank that you are not a good thief. They call you a spy, a traitor and a pretender at the best. "Save yourself or save us if you are a brave man!" These men assault your very identity until you are totally confused and all you want is to get out of there. Abed calls this assault on identity as Step One. There is often constant threat of physical harm and once caught in it only your captors the police can rescue you. The police of course by your understanding are your worst enemies. They set the terms in this prison. They took away your shoes and clothes. They tell you when to eat and when to visit a bathroom. They dress you up only for the purpose of saving you from nakedness.

There is nothing like fashion in the cell. There you bemuse yourself by saying: We are all equal. We are all dressed in one uniform. We eat in one line. We are all common criminals.

The police throw away your name and reduce you to a number. They call you AP 1234. AP is the derogatory term "Arrested Person" short of Prisoner. They deny you food, sleep and even the right of privacy using a toilet. They make sure your power to think critically or think independently is broken. When they are kind to you they let you talk to a lawyer. When they allow you to receive visitors they record your conversation or make you believe they do. All in all they break your identity and make you lose faith in who you are. Your belief system is raked and ready to accept the "Dis" virus.

Then the police call you out of your cell for interview or what they rightly call Statement Taking. You are asked all questions about yourself, your sisters, friends, grand parents but to the detail of where you were at this hour and minute. They never give you a break until they are absolutely convinced that you are cornered, ashamed and feeling hopeless. This step of awakening guilty feelings in you is Step 2 in developing disbelief. It ends at an introduction of another torture stage by letting you sign your own criminal statement asserting that whatever was written was true, made voluntarily and checked by you and affirmed to be the truth. The opportunity to do changes was given and used and all your rights signed off.

As if that is not torture enough, they take you through Step 3. This is Self betrayal. They are quick to pointing out inconsistencies in your earlier statements and seek critical clarifications. They may quote information received from other trusted sources, friends, fellow prisoners or gangsters. The message is that you are being betrayed by some other people and you do not have to spare them. This betrayal of your own beliefs and of people you feel loyal to increases your shame and sense of loss of identity. The investigating officer gives you the feeling that he knows all about you but wants you to confess your sins. You look like a liar to Mr. Know It All.

I do not know who copies the other: Police or Satan? When you want to prosper Satan says you cannot make it because you cannot invest in business when you have no money. Satan says you are bound to fail this time as you failed before. Satan says who are you to succeed where so and so failed. Satan says forget God's mercy you have let him down a number of times. Satan says you do not belong to your good self anymore. You are guilty. Mr. Know It All uses the same tactics.

The prisoner absorbs and with a broken spirit of mind usually agrees to betray his group of friends and digs himself deeper in self doubt. This session does not end until the prisoner shows psychological or nervous breakdown symptoms like uncontrollable sobbing, deep depression or general disorientation.

When the police are satisfied that the target has lost his grip on reality and has the feeling of being completely lost and alone or is near breaking point —has no clear understanding of who he is or what is happening to him—then and only then they offer a glass of water or a gift to visit a latrine and show some kind of mercy. After a short break the police usually ask whether you would like to return to your cell or finish up the statement taking. Usually you are told that you have a few minutes to go. At this point, as the prisoner you want this torture to end. You decide to continue with this session and end the misery. Usually the session continues at amazingly slow a speed, reading and proof reading the text with endless reminders and signatures at every change. Every prisoner is aware that this session does not end until you express the desire to convert to another belief system where truth and only the truth is told. The police are aware of this feeling. They end the session by promising you going to court.

The journey to court begins with excitement. This is Step 4 of our conversion hypothesis. The prisoner is in a life crisis not knowing who he is, knowing where he is and not sure of what to do, think or say. The police officer identifying himself as an escort is usually friendly, offering you a chance to visit a toilet, a drink of water, a chance to speak on a phone or even asking you what you miss about home. He hopes the judge will be kind and release you. He asks: "What will you do when you are free again? We shall miss you," he quirkily adds.

In a state of psychological breakdown, the small kindness seems huge, and the prisoner may experience a sense of relief and gratitude completely out of understanding to the offering, as if the agent is not a police officer but an agent of salvation. How awkward the feeling of the prisoner is expressed by the speed he wants to return this kindness and seeks legal advice from the escort. At this point, the agent may present the possibility of confession as the quickest way of getting a reduced sentence. Every repeat offender knows that escorts have only one opinion.

Considering all the weeks or months of assault, confusion, breakdown and moments of leniency, the prisoner's reasoning capacity has been completely raked and the bull that entered prison with guards enters court not sure of what he has done wrong. He just knows he is wrong. The judge reads the charge and the bull does not know whether to plead guilty or not. His answer relies on the wishes of his advisor or lawyer. The prisoner is some blank slate and it is the duty of the lawyer to fill in the blanks. The lawyer can fill that emptiness with whatever he wants. Usually the lawyer blames the guilt to the belief system the prisoner is trying to replace. The prisoner too comes to believe it is his belief system that is damaged. The contrast between old and new has been established: The old belief system is associated with shame and pain; and the new belief system is associated with the possibility of escaping that agony.

The defense lawyer works so hard to get the prisoner free. The judge listens so hard as if he is afraid of releasing a guilty man or condemning an innocent to jail. The prosecutor interrupts so much to clean the system of any doubts. The prisoner is a ping pong ball that does not know what to say, think or do.

In the end everything works together for one common good. There is a period called Mitigation. The embattled target is relieved to learn there is an external cause of his wrongness. He is not his greatest enemy. The belief system he was holding to, the company he was keeping in or the circumstances he grew in were the main factors in his wrong doing. He cannot change his history but he can escape the wrong belief system. All he has to do is denounce in his mind all the people and institutions associated with that old belief system, and he won't be in pain anymore. The prisoner has the power to release himself from wrongness by confessing in his mind to acts associated with his old belief system. The prisoner remains absolutely silent but the lawyer swears with all convictions that the prisoner has completed his psychological rejection of his former identity. It is now up to the court to offer the prisoner a new one. This session ends with finding the prisoner guilty or not guilty. Whatever the pronouncement the bull feels: It's not me; it's my beliefs.

Whether the prisoner is set free or returns to jail behaves as a new man once out of court.

Abed calls this Step 5 or Conception or Recreation. Usually those who are returned to jail are treated with leniency. More likely than not are given new cells or promoted to positions of greater responsibility. The police introduces a new belief system in a candy and stick style. As time passes by they treat prisoners according to Abed the way Japans treat their dogs. Good behavior is rewarded but bad behavior is neglected. At this stage, the police stop the abuse; offer the prisoner a taste of physical comfort and mental calm in conjunction with the new belief system. The prisoner is made to feel that it is he who must choose between old and new, good and bad, giving the prisoner the sense that his fate is in his own hands. Conception begins with the prisoner denouncing his old belief system in response to leniency and torment, and making a "conscious effort" or thinking in favor of becoming a new creature. The contrasting belief system helps to further relieve his guilt and the prison officer enhances this growth by putting their hands off him. Eventually the prisoner employs the Belief>Thoughts>Words>Feelings>Action program. If he truly believes that he personally did not maliciously betray anyone or that whatever he did was for someone else's good but not from his selfish motive, being born again is not a difficult choice to make. The new identity is safe, desirable and acceptable because it is nothing like the one that led to his breakdown.

The prisoner may return to court but eventually we see him released. He behaves like one who was not returned to jail.

This Step 6 is what we may describe as Rebirth. It begins with celebrations. There are often rituals or ceremonies to induct the converted believer into his new community. The ex-convict is quick to forgive his past, quick to affirm his commitment to his new life and to pledge the rest of his life to a better life style.

The last stage of conversion is Step 7 described as Recognizance. This is when the actions of a new believer begin to show. He could go to church where he used not to go. He may become a humble spirit. He might give up drinking or womanizing. He might start drawing plans of building a business enterprise. He traps money and designs schemes where money and richness and prosperity will come his way. He becomes religious in all that he does. He believes in discipline and getting what he aimed at. His Belief>Thoughts>Words>Feelings>Action program all come in line. The public recognizes him as success.

You do not need to go through all this beating to get your belief system right. You do not however have to allow whatever thought that enters your head to control your actions. As much as you can say, "let me think about it" gives you the right to suspend using that thought, you can as well expel at will thoughts that could harm your actions. It is your will to say: I will not go deeper in debt. It is your will to say: That extra marital relationship will ruin my finances. It is within your power to say that you will work towards prosperity and you will never fall down again. Neither sickness nor death can take away that dream. It is your right to send away the spirit of disbelief from your thinking and purge your brain from over flowering. Always remember the pruning of Mango tree in Morogoro. (Go to page 160 if you have lost your memory). The Trouble of All Ages: Disbelief.

It was disbelief that kept Jane out of job because she thought she knew no relative in town to employ her. It was disbelief that kept her sewing handkerchiefs in the office instead of learning how to use a phone or a computer because she thought she was not educated enough for such jobs. It was disbelief that almost took away her job .She thought I would not be angry with her for stealing pens and pencils from office since she was my friend's niece. I sent Abed to collect every bit of office property back. It was disbelief that broke her marriage because someone told her it was God's will to block her womb for the way she mistreated her dead grand mother. It was disbelief that kept her stagnant in poverty when she was advised to tithe 10% of her income to Church work and she looked at the instruction as a trick to grow the pastor's belly while leaving her starving. It is disbelief that tells you that you are hearing the voice of man not of God when you are told to get out of your bed very early in the morning and go to unknown offices to fetch your prosperity.

Suppose God told you, "Go into the world and prosper", what would you do? Would you remain skeptical and say, "Show me the money!" Would you rise up and walk? Would you continue in your slumber? Or would you say, "I will not believe it was the voice of God until my bills are paid. I will not believe until I have a new house or a new dress. I will not believe until my children are out of college. I will not believe until I have got a job. I will not believe until I am healed. I will not believe until my problem is solved! I will not believe until...."

The Trouble of All Ages: Disbelief. When we are told to change our status from poverty to prosperity we answer: I am only human. I do not believe in miracles. I tell you today and read it again and again. The same man who turned water into wine can do it again today. Believing in the word power of the same man can move your mountain of debts, problems, poverty into fulfillment, debt free, joy and prosperity. However remember belief is not a gift. It is something we must work ourselves into. The same principles on which disbelief rests are the same principles on which belief works.

The trouble of all ages is disbelief. You can however hook it out of your life. Remember you can catch a woman with a strawberry but you cannot catch a fish with strawberry. You can hook a fish with a worm. You cannot hook a woman with a worm. People like fish are caught by what they eat. People like fish are caught by what they think. When you tell a woman or when you tell a fish, "Wouldn't that be nice for dinner?" You know in your mind that she is hungry or it is hungry. You hook their mind before you hook their bodies.

Disbelief is here to destroy your holy thoughts. Destroy disbelief before it destroys you.

I'm leaving this form for you to fill in. Write in this very book with ink.

"Today, (Date) ———/———/————–
I(Name………………………………………………………of address ……………………… ……………………………. .
and Contact Numbers-Phone ——————–, Mobile —————— Fax—————— and email——— ——————————————-solemnly declare that I have decided to remove disbelief from my thinking system.
Help me God.

Signature: ………………………………………………………..
Witness:………………………………………………………………
………………………………………………………………………………
………………………………………………………………………………
………………………………………………………………………………
………………………………………………………………………………
………………………………………………

This is legal document. You cannot fill it carelessly. Read the notice below.

Desire to Change.

Any person can change one's life from good to bad or from bad to good but must have a personal desire to make the change.

No excuses.

There are no excuses for changing your way of thinking. You are not changing because you have been forced to or you fear a certain punishment. You are above the law. The desire to change puts all other thoughts irrelevant and puts you above the law. It makes you the master of your destiny and a commander of your regiment. You are the boss of your temple. You are your own pastor. You have overcome the past. You are the boss of today and the master of tomorrow. You are not changing because you want to prosper. You are not changing your thinking because you want to have a free mind. Changing is not a fault and has no excuses. Do not entertain any thought that wants to reason with your decision to change. Anything that comes with the power of "Because" must be stopped before it infects your thinking. As you download a new computer program you must always be weary of some hidden virus. Computer experts' advice: Do not download anything from the internet to avoid viruses. To keep your thinking clean, do not accept any excuses whether it comes to support or oppose your belief.

Take immediate Action.

Today's decision must be implemented today. Do not decide to get belly fats off today and put off the love for candies until tomorrow. If you want to get out of debt today do not put off stopping borrowing until all credit cards are paid off. Go back to Deuteronomy 30 and see how everything had to be done 'today'.

Moses confronted his men with this tough talking in Deuteronomy 30 in the quoted verses.

Verse 11 "Now what I am commanding you today.........
Verse 15 "See, I set before you today life ………………..
Verse 16 "For I command you today……………………..
Verse 18 "I declare to you this day……………………..
Verse 19 ".This day I call heaven and earth as witnesses against you …………………………………………………...

Once you have a desire to change, you have no more excuse to do so or not to do so. The time for action is right now. Take immediate action and sign the form above.

Change your self-perception.

You have signed yourself into the regiment for change. You have put your ink against procrastination, excuses and stubbornness. You have to change your way of thinking. You have to control your thoughts. If your secretary is becoming more attractive and more responsible than your wife, fire the secretary but do not contemplate divorce. Yes I repeat," Fire, fire, fire the secretary. If that secretary is you, get fired. And you woman, if your male boss is making passes at you, resign. Do not think of his honor. Such a man has no honor to lose.

Take the first steps against disbelief. Control your words. Then control your thoughts. Think only of those things that will drive you forward towards your goal. Forget or dismiss all those thoughts that want to drive you backwards. Forget your history. Forget where you came from. Forget what you have gone through. Forget all the pains you have suffered. Forget all those who have failed and meditate upon those who are inspiring. Focus on your goal and move forward.

When you change your words and you change your thinking, you will change your feelings. Your feelings will determine how you determine your decisions. Your decision will determine your action. Your action will determine your habit. Your habit will determine your character. Your character will determine your destination. This is how the road to prosperity looks like:

Words>Feelings>Decisions>Action>Habits>Character>Prosperity.

One day Mr. Kato told Abed something about words. It was in a lesson to teach him salesmanship. Mr. Kato had a big hardware store. In one week he wanted to introduce a new tool to his customers. He couched half of his salesgirls to greet their customers by, "You don't need this new tool, do you?" The other half said, "You need this tool, don't you?" Guess what? With all the same Japanese kindness and mannerism the first group with their negative approach sold only 30% of their weekly stock. The second group using as many words as the first group sold 55% of their stock. Surely the difference laid nowhere else but in the power of their words.

In the following week Mr. Kato reversed the roles of the salesgirls and the sales equally reversed. There is power in words. Negative thinking takes the air out of your balloon but positive thinking propels you to prosperity.

Mr. Kato did another experiment. One group asked: Would you like one of these? Another group asked: Would you like some of these? Again the second group beat the first one in sales.

There is power in words. "I cannot do it." Say this and you are bound to fail. "I will try." "Yes I can." These are the words of the successful men and women you admire every day. This was the character of the five people you listed in the first chapter of this book.

> Jesus Christ went to a fig tree. He talked to it.
> Jesus: Hi man, I'm hungry.
> Fig Tree: I have just a shade here. Sorry, no figs.
> Jesus: You good-for-nothing-tree. I'm looking for something to eat not for shades. You will not waste my time again.

This is a true story. It was not thoughts. Those who were with him heard and 24 hours later saw that his curses had come true and the tree had withered. Words have power. The same man who turned water into wine; the same man who talked to a tree and the tree obeyed; looked at a mountain and said not metaphorically but realistically that whoever says to that particular mountain , with no doubt in his heart and; believe or trust in what he was saying , would have the mountain move physically. You need tractors, bull dozers and bombs to move a mountain. Yes?

No. You need power of the mouth. Moses said in Deuteronomy 30: "11 Now what I am commanding you today is not too difficult for you or beyond your reach. 12 It is not up in heaven, so that you have to ask, "Who will ascend into heaven to get it and proclaim it to us so we may obey it?" 13 Nor is it beyond the sea, so that you have to ask, "Who will cross the sea to get it and proclaim it to us so we may obey it?" 14 No, the word is very near you; it is in your mouth and in your heart so you may obey it.

Disbelief if allowed can come in. You can say Moses was not talking to us. Jesus meant a mountain of issues but not the physical movement of the big hill. Issues understandably can move at the power of words but not heaps of stones. Mr. Kato's experiment was not scientifically controlled. His conclusions were not valid. We can develop any kind of disbelief if we allow the way we process our thinking to go doubtful. We can stop and look back. We start admiring those old-good-days and the desire to climb mountains vaporizes.

Never go back.

This is a rule. Never go back. This is the most important decision you can take against disbelief. Never go back. Talk to yourself and say three times: I will never go back. I will never go back. I will never go back. Hardship, abuse, persecutions, failures or whatever will never force us back to our vomit. This decision quarantines your thoughts. When the Dis Virus attacks it finds that your antivirus program is ready and running. The decision catches the virus and stops it from entering your system. Say three times: I will never go back. I will never go back. I will never go back. I will never go back to poverty. I will never go back to poverty. I will never go back to poverty. This means you will have to go forward to prosperity and you have to claim every territory you capture and decide never to go back.

Never go back to those circumstances that led you down. If you gave up drinking never go back to the pub again. If you gave up smoking never go back to the same shop that used to sell you cigarettes. Never ring back to that secretary you just fired. Never call back that boss you just denounced. Never go back. Never go back to that jail again. Never go back to visit fellow prisoners. Never go back to greet that kind escort. Never go back. However stupid a dog you might be never return to your vomit.

The deceptive part of disbelief is that one which wants you to go where you do not want to go. Call in discipline. Say it in words that you have already been delivered out of the pit. You are a new creature and you cannot go back to your mother's womb again. "One more time?" This is lasciviousness. Apply breaks to your habits. Go forward if you want to see change. Do not go back to: It is right because it feels good. Stay away from unwise emotional entanglements. They will carry you back the way Abed was carried to prison. Do not go back to your old self. Check your life stages.

Belief>Thoughts>Words>Feelings>Decisions>Action>Habits>Character>Prosperity.

To help you stand we suggested getting you a witness as you filled in the form above. This was done to ensure that you never think of breaking the oath. Remember the fifth commandment against disbelief is: Never go back.

Stop waiting for outside assistance.

This rule comes from the same Deuteronomy 30. Do not wait for others to advise you. Do not say: Who can help me? God is a member of your task force and he is willing to help you without creating any preconditions. Take the law in your own words. Prosper.

Do not disbelieve.

The seventh commandment is the very root of all successes. Believe. Believe in yourself. Believe in your thoughts. Believe in your words. Believe in your feelings. Believe in your decisions. Believe in your actions. Believe in your habits. Believe in your character. Believe in your destiny. All you need to grow from poverty to prosperity with no possibility of returning is a wise belief system. The Trouble of All Ages: Disbelief

CHAPTER TWENTY

PROSTITUTION

In the past few days we have been discussing the issue of disbelief. We saw disbelief as the very tool essential to keeping you in poverty or in chaos. It is the cornerstone on which failure is based. I asked you in the last pages to overrule disbelief in your thinking. I hope you did because my next statement requires more belief than understanding.

"In Tanzania there is a fish that lives on chicken and chips." Do you believe me?

Given my background in fishing and given that my knowledge is based not in laying the nets in the sea but in lying and watching on the beach, would you believe me more? If I told you that my years of stay at the Butterfly Beach taught me that shrimps have their hearts in their bodies, would you trust my expertise?

If I could tell you that there are creatures like bats that have never seen the sun in their lives would you agree? In fact there are bats that spend their entire lives in caves, and if forced to fly out during day time they keep their eyes closed! These have never seen the sun. Some are born blind because without light there is no point seeing.

Did you know that in Tanzania there are frogs that give birth to young ones instead of laying eggs? Yes they are there in Uluguru, Udzungwa Mountains and in the Southern Highlands of eastern and southern Tanzania. When you walk in this region you are not scared of stepping on a frog but on a frog jumping on your neck. They are called Treefrogs.

Did you know that there is life on the moon? I remember some woman asked me this. I went into a long explanation opposing her but she explained, "There is life on the moon depending on which woman you have gone with!" She told me that in 1969 Americans went to the moon. For 40 years they have never gone back. Why? On their return they destroyed the rocket they had used and all the first astronauts later died off. But more important the first astronauts came back with a negative report that there was nothing to see on the moon. There was nothing to inspire another trip. It appears as if the short hours they spent on the moon were a wasted time. If they had gone with their wives or girlfriends they could have come back with: There is life on the moon.

The speaker was none other than Jane. From what we have said so far about her you do not expect much from her head, do you? She told me about that woman whose husband went manual. She told me that human beings are prostitutes by nature. Every normal woman is a prostitute. Every normal man is a prostitute. We are all prostitutes. What varies is the degree we accept our behavior and blame others for what we all do. Define prostitution as 'the renting of one's body for sex in exchange for money.' No wonder why it is called the "World's Oldest Trade Practice."

What's wrong with that? Nothing much until you choose to think about it seriously. Are prostitutes really men-sucking vampires flying out of their alleys in the cover of darkness or roaming blindly during day time looking for food, accommodation or running away from the police? Are prostitutes innocent fellow human beings victimized by the gluttony of the male race for sex? Are they really innocent when they are responsible for spreading AIDS and other Sexually Transmitted Diseases? Are they victims or targets of lust?

What is your view of prostitution? Should it be wiped out or tolerated? If it is bad why should it be tolerated and if it is not evil why should it be persecuted?

Some people have embraced the hunters' view that the best way of shooting prostitution down is by bringing it up in the open. Get it out of the alleys and make it like an ordinary business practice. In brief legalize it. License it. Baptize it something like 'Sex Trade'. Make it honorable and dissociate prostitution from the stigma that goes with it. In short stop blaming prostitutes for spreading STD and AIDS. Encourage condom use. Teach in your churches that the foundations of Israel lie at the kind action of the prostitute who hid God's spies as they were scheming out an attack. The spies stayed with this woman (doing what we all do) and gave her protection in the end. She spied on the land and the enemies of Israel were defeated. Jesus defended prostitution by telling the woman caught red-handed, "None condemns you so don't I."

Legalize it. Call it a sport. First contain it in special bars and districts. Then move it around until it can participate in the Olympics. It does not in fact hurt people like boxing or wrestling does. It could be a nice pass-time! Legalize it. We could even tax it and raise revenue for the government. One wonders why we do not legalize corruption and theft and raise revenue for the government.

This trade is as old as mankind itself. If we cannot get rid of it let us get something out of it. Why don't we legalize poverty and stop trying to change to prosperity? Poverty has been with us for so long and it will always be. There will always be poor people among us but we must fight not to be those poor people.

Other people argue otherwise that prostitution disgraces society and should never be allowed to survive. Ban it in all its forms. Persecute it. Arrest those who employ it. Those who hire it and those who rent it should be arrested. Blame it for child trafficking, divorce, sexually transmitted diseases and the economic disaster it has caused by creating so many orphans. The number of orphans in Tanzania for instance mostly from AIDS, is estimated to almost 2 million out of a population of 38 million. Show this figure in the campaign against prostitution. The answer lies in blaming and abusing the trade until all reasonable people will flee from it. Prostitutes eventually will either lose the desire to rent themselves out or their customers will turn to marriage as an alternative way of living. It is true. Whatever changes your way of thinking will change your way of living.

Common sense tells you that prostitution may be bad but it is here to stay. It is the profession of all ages. It has been with us from time immemorial. In Tanzania HIV/AIDS is the greatest single threat to the country's socio-economic development. It is placing an increasing burden on limited resources through rising medical expenditures, absenteeism from work, labor shortages, and training of replacement labor. AIDs has no cure. Whereas there is no figure linking AIDS directly to prostitution it would be but an interesting coincidence that in towns of Iringa, Mwanza, Dodoma Kigoma, Dar es Salaam, and Arusha where prostitution is well spread AIDS is equally well spread.

It is also said that some traditions still favor marrying virgins. Children of as young an age as 12 are given in marriage. For some unknown reason, just as fish may choose a worm and a woman chooses strawberry, some girls here reach puberty while below the age of 13. Not only that. Society is changing. Many young girls here prefer marrying men of their father's age claiming young men are irresponsible and beat and easily disband their wives. Plainly put Jane said, "Women have aunties to teach them marriage life but men have no such a person. Like wildlife they hunt around until they are mature. They never learn to love until they have broken many hearts. That is why young women say, 'No man is too old as long as he stands.'" Prostitution is not for the young and strong. It is for all ages. Wherever there is a poverty gap between men and women the bridge is prostitution.

You often hear girls say to the men, "Thank you very much for your kindness. I have no money or any other means to pay back. Leave me your phone number I will call you when I am free."

The trend of leaving prostitution to uneducated women is slowly changing. There are a number of educated women and men that have gone into practice to substantiate their income gaps. Pimps in tie and suits are widely seen on the streets of the above mentioned towns in growing numbers. Lady prostitutes (Is there such a term?) are turning to prostitution to get that extra income needed to run their households. The idea of single mothers is catching on in Tanzania.

There are unconfirmed reports that Tanzanian girls are lured to resort towns by promises of hotel jobs or riches and trips abroad, but instead are given work in bars or are turned into prostitutes. Some girls are lured into the job by men promising them school fees and the goodies education brings. Others are taken by "Uncle Sum" picking them from school and driving them home. Everyone hates lining up and fighting to get into a crowded bus. If old and married women accept such lifts what but a 16 year old student would say? If you can bear generalizations, men talk of Tanzania women as pick-and play girls and women consider all men married or not married as unfaithful lovers. Prostitution is just a game!

Is prostitution really bad? Did God really say: You must not use your bodies for sex? Is sex really bad? When domestic workers (maids) flee abusive employers and turn to prostitution for survival is it prostitution to blame or employers? It is reported that girls are trafficked from Tanzania to South Africa, the Middle East, America and Europe for prostitution the way vegetables, minerals are trafficked. If it turns out that there are many girls in those countries in this illicit trade is it the girls to blame? Should we blame the countries where they come from? Should we impose economic sanctions on those governments that fail to stamp out exporting of human beings and leave the importers free? What should we do? Perhaps we should put more money in research and find out exactly why prostitution has eluded us for centuries and centuries. Perhaps the answer is not very far. It is in your heart and mouth.

> Desire to change
> Stop excuses.
> Take immediate action,
> Change your perception
> Never go back to old habits or thinking. Look forward
> Take personal responsibility.
> Stop waiting for someone else.
> Believe in your success.

These were the steps that we saw in the previous chapter that lead to change. They are true all the time. They can change you from poverty to prosperity. They can change you from whatever sort of personality you have to the one you desire to have. We have to practice them. I believe the only way one can get out of trouble is by going through it. You cannot dodge trouble or jump out of it. Go through it. If in any way you are affected by prostitution or its associates like pornography, child trafficking, STD, marital strains or divorce, go through your rough days.

Prostitution

Has your husband walked out and gone to a prostitute? Has your spouse turned to prostitution? Do not despair. There is a way out.

I told you in the beginning of the book that there are no hidden secrets to prosperity. I chose to be open to you and we will be open up to the end.

It was discovered that the accident we had when we were going to Mbeya was not caused by mechanic failure but the stubbornness of our driver. Close to where we crashed there was a road sign reading: YIELD. Its message to all drivers was that we had to change lanes and give the one behind us the right-of-passage. The right of way in this special circumstance belonged to the car behind us. In proper driving practice we had to let this vehicle overtake us.

We were all sleeping and we never saw this. A car came behind us and as it was trying to overtake us our bus driver denied it the right to pass. We were squeezed out of the road. Our driver used excessive force on the breaks to save us from dropping down the valley. Our tires overheated and we suffered a puncture.

In fighting prostitution we do not have to follow a good idea but a God idea. The God idea is to see this woman caught in adultery, offer her protection–not condemnation– and then release her, "Woman sin no more." We do not have to read the statement halfway ("None condemns you, nor do I.").

Now that Jesus has been killed, buried and gone we have to yield to the counsel of his successor. Yielding to the Holy Spirit might not make us popular but will certainly make us successful and powerful. Imagine what would have happened had our driver yielded to the passing vehicle! How many hours and worries would we have saved? Yield to the Holy Spirit. The question comes" "How can we do that?" (Go back to page 39).

We align our thinking with the thinking of God. We no longer look at the man we want to marry as good "because he is handsome" or "because he has money" but "because he is faithful." We do not need to get used to misery. We need to adapt our living to the likeness of the tree frogs who have learnt that there is more freedom up there than down under. We may look strange but we will find our names in the book of life the way

Treefrogs have found their name in the Desire of All ages. Yield to the Holy Spirit. Ask yourself always, "Lord what do you want me to do?"

Jane says prostitution requires training and practice. It is not a simple profession. It demands restrain and discipline. It has women and men of different backgrounds all competing for one customer. It requires salesmanship of a high degree. You need humility, hard work, persistence and firmness if you are to succeed. Is it the same as all other professions? No. In prostitution you need to get used to your misery but in other jobs you do not have to.

What however is true of prostitution is that whoever can sell her body successfully can sell anything else successfully. You must give yourself a good value. Look the customer in the eye and state your price. You must be willing to negotiate but you must be firm. You must be able to look in the eye of the customer and tell him how much you are worth. You must be straight that you are doing a job and this is your living. Do not sell at any cost. You must not go cheap. You must smile even when you are trembling and sweating. You do not have to feel confident to be confident. You must overcome your fear always if you are to make that man dip his hands in his pockets and give out the money.

You need tactic and style to undress an honorable gentleman and tell him to do as you say without saying "why." You need to make your customer overcome his fear. Give him a sense of urgency but not of panic. You may be afraid of being arrested but your fear must not show. You may be afraid of catching some dreadful disease from your client but you must overcome your fear. Prostitution is not a game for cowards but for men and women who can control their fear.

Do you remember what I said about the psychology of prostitution on page 1?

Prostitution has rules of its own. For instance, you need not identify men into categories but to take each one as some piece of tool which you can take in and throw out as you please soon after it has lost its usefulness. To be a good prostitute you must never fall in love with your customer. You must be like that dog (Jasper) who loves without expecting marriage in return.

The institution of marriage remains the greatest danger to prostitution. Those who oppose my view must stand up and tell us why Satan wants divorce.

There are at least seven commodities essential to life: shelter, water, sanitation, schooling, information, healthcare and food. This is what you expect to get in marriage. Look at how divorce can wreck them all. Jane says when her marriage broke down all the seven commodities went away with it. She lost everything including her dream to make a living. She turned to prostitution. At first it was a part-time job but later on she realized that two part-time jobs do not make one full-time employment. She quit as my secretary to do something else.

Now Jane says to avoid prostitution or for those in it to come out of it they must not stop dreaming of the good days ahead. Do not stop dreaming of prosperity. The Desire of all ages is prosperity. Keep the dream alive. Turn from poverty to prosperity and stay up there. I remind you that Jane typed this manuscript and assumedly approved the references said of her.

I have been repeating myself several times in this book. I can do it again here. Jane has given us two important ways of changing our lives. She says (1) Yield to the Holy Spirit and (2) Do not stop dreaming of prosperity. Dreams are tiny images of seeing yourself debt free. Dreams are tiny images of seeing yourself in a house not under mortgage but your own. Dreams are tiny images of seeing yourself relaxing and napping in your husband's arms and calling him your own. Never lose those dreams you made up in your mind as you read Chapter 5. Persecution, old age, pain, sickness or opposition should never steal your dream. There are many dream-thieves around you but ask," God show me your way." and fight on.

The dreams I'm talking about are not the dreams that come to you after a strong drink or after a sleepless night. I'm talking about the dreams you had when you were healthy and sober. I am talking about those dreams you sang to your mother, "

> When I was just a little girl
> I asked my mother what should I do
> Will I be pretty ?
> Will I be rich ?

This is what my mother said
Que Sela Sela whatever will be will be,
The future is not ours to see,
Que Sera Sera.

Never let these dreams of your childhood go away. Let nobody not even your mother steal away your destiny and there is no other destiny but prosperity. Those dreams signify your real life. This is the life full of righteousness, peace and joy. This is the life program you and God agree on. Learn to love this life. Protect it. Live it. It is the best you can have.

When you get this feeling that you cannot leave the miserable lane you are in; when you get this feeling that you cannot change for the better; when you get this feeling that the new life will be tougher than the old life then the time to change has come.

When you are attacked by doubt, realize the war has become tough. When the going becomes rough, you have to become tougher. It means the war has intensified because you are about to overcome your weakness and take your first enemy's stronghold. The enemy in his despair throws one of his strongest missiles to you. He only uses this firearm against soldiers who have faith. This ballistic missile is called Doubt. He does not use it unless he has noticed you have faith. This is the time to drive the devil crazy. Deny him your attitude. Deny him your joy. Hit him further by saying, "God is on my side. I know God is good. I do not know how he is going to get me out of this. I cannot figure him out but I am changing right away". Then yield to the Holy Spirit and take the privilege of being God's follower. Lean on God's wisdom and power.

This sounds like reinventing yourself. Every good prostitute knows his product and how to pack it. If you are a street vendor, no matter the weather you need a short skirt, heavy foundation on your face, perhaps a bag or night gaggles. Holding a mobile phone in your hands could be an advantage. A strong perfume and a drunken look is a good gesture. Do not look like an angel from a church. You need some streetwise intelligence!

So Jane says as much as a prostitute can reinvent oneself so are the ones who want to quit. Remember your dream and go back to it. Think seriously of what your purpose in life is. Are you just to live as someone's pillow forever? Are you some tool to give someone else pleasure when you are getting none yourself?

Jane clarifies that prostitutes are not meant to enjoy what they do. A prostitute must "come" as quickly as possible to maximize the number of men she can lie with in a day. A prostitute must not welcome returning customers because those are the guys who want to pay 'next time'. These are the men who keep bargaining your price downwards. If you enjoy your customer he may get stuck on you and treat you with jealousy like you are his house wife.

To reinvent yourself properly for any reason is to go back and search your original purpose. Do not align yourself with the world opinion but with God's opinion. What did God think of you before he put you in your mother's womb? What did God want you to be when he put you in your mother's womb? What did God want you to be when he put you out of your mother's womb?

In all the situations above you seemingly played no part. Then you were born. As a little girl or boy you started designing yourself. You talked to your parents of what you would be as an adult. Surprisingly your parents could sit and listen. You had a purpose in life.

So there was God's purpose in creating you and there was your purpose in growing up. It is these two purposes that determined what you grew into. If these two pointed in the same direction you would never make a prostitute. If these two disagreed you would grow into chaos. You cannot change God's purpose. Like revenge, leave that work to him. It is only your purpose you can manipulate. Refocus your image. Reinvent yourself. Remember the first commandment of change: Desire to change. It is not far from you (Page 157).

For Jane marriage broke down. Her income could not sustain her any more. She lost her purpose of living. To put it better she changed her purpose. Drew new plans. She asked God to bless her plans and he answered, "Did you consult me in the beginning?" She was irritated and she chose to walk in her own direction.

God's purpose, Jane's first purpose and Jane's second purpose were no longer in line. Whereas in Jane's first purpose she saw herself as God's chosen instrument in the second plan she counted herself as God's Forsaken. From that time her life was not a process of growing up but of growing into (something).

She lied to me of her whereabouts. She lied to me when she lost concentration at work or when she dozed in the middle of taking instructions. She lied to me many times. Jane grew into a lady prostitute. She had one leg in the church and one leg in the brothel. That way she could fish men of all types.

She boasts of her experience. If there were ten prostitutes and there was only one sex tourist she would be the one to catch that man. She knew how white men come to Africa with a notion that black women will do anything for their "In God We Trust" dollars. At first sight she would be that African woman. Success in prostitution means being all that your client expects you to be.

If she saw some man with a tattoo, holding a cigarette and drunk she would tell herself, "Jane take the first move. You are in the right place at the right time". In this job to move to the top you must be the first one to know of a new guest in Jerusalem. You had to keep in touch with hotel owners, taxi drivers and security guards. Under the Tanzania Penal Code, not only prostitution is illegal but even benefiting from the proceeds of the business or to procure or assist someone to engage in prostitution are also against the law. Surprisingly to drive one into prostitution as in the case of Jane is not illegal. To survive in this profession you need a wide network of information.

Jane was strong in this field. She knew when the American Marines would be in town for instance. She knew when the Parliament would seat in Dodoma and of course that meant she knew when to travel to Dodoma. She knew which team was playing football in the national stadium. She knew when to move her stand to Ohio Street near Movenpick Hotel or to Virginia Pub in Kinondoni. This information coupled with a good weather forecast greatly determined her daily bread.

Her success however lay in her principle of not worrying about her circumstances. "As long as there is a parliament there will be laws" she often said. As long as there is a law there is a chance of breaking it. Keep your eyes and ears open. You will know the existence of a police raid when it is still at a planning stage.

Prostitution

Police raids against prostitutes are common in Dar Es Salaam. Statistics show that such raids hardly catch anybody. When they do, they catch some young fish which is not worth carrying in the net. They often release these under-age girls with a warning. Keeping them in rehabilitation homes has to wait for overseas donations! On one hand one would not like to create the impression that prostitution is the passage to free education. On the other hand one would not like to drive prostitution underground where it would be harder to monitor.

Jane says all the health threats and the police ambushes cannot convince one to give up this trading practice. Blaming the practice on men or on women or on both does not help either. She had blamed her misery on her husband. She had blamed her life on her education. She had blamed her life on the rich exploiting the poor. She had blamed her life on her priest. Nevertheless the pain did not go away. She came to the conclusion: Blame does not take away pain.

As you read this you realize Jane turned away from prostitution and from all the evil it has. Jane says she overcame the habit when she decided to take her happiness in her own hands. Jane came to a very important discovery that no one else but herself was responsible to make her happy. She discovered that happiness lay in her feelings and if she was going to make a change she was going to tackle her feelings.

We saw it in the last chapter: Thoughts>Words>Feelings>Action. Jane says when you change your thinking you change your living. To change your living however you must change your feelings.

If you are tired of being broke; if you are tired of your job; if you are tired of how the world perceives you; if you are tired of yourself sign the form below.
I (Name) …………………………………..

(1) I want to change my life.   Sign…………………………..
(2) I do not want to remain mediocre. I do not want my life to remain as it is now.
                              Sign…………………………..
(3) I'm ready to reinvent my life   Sign…………………………..
(4) I will not lose my image again.   Sign…………………………..

This is the beginning of our guided tour.

Now we have to focus our energy towards our feelings. Get a blank piece of paper. An A4 white photocopier paper without any lines can do. Have a box of matches, a cigarette lighter or anything that can light a fire nearby.

Look at this paper as though you had never seen it before. It would be helpful if you could sit comfortably down on a pillow or on a soft pad. The key word is comfort. Roll your mind back to a point when you were as innocent as this paper. Look at nothing else but this paper. Your task is to rub your memory out until it is as clean as this paper before you. Remember what upset you one hour ago. Remember one thing you did, thought, heard or saw which you ought not to have done. Remember what you ate or drunk when you should not have done so. Think of every moment that you regret to have lived.

Extend the time span to two or three hours. As you drive your life in reverse you will meet some bumps and painful memories. Do not quit at this time. You may feel like vomiting or crying. You may feel angry or irritated again. You have to press past all these feelings to the new beginning. These are labor pains. Either way you have to suffer. You will have either to suffer the pain of changing or the pain of not changing. Better suffer changing.

Extend the spiritual cleansing to a day's time, a week's time, a month's time. You may go back years and years into your life. Plough out those painful memories. Keep the paper in your focus.

Sometimes you may feel there is a pain too big to overcome. It might be as big as Mt. Morogoro or Kilimanjalo. Remember Hosef and climb further. You may have to throw away your mobile phone. You may have to throw away your photo album. You may have to break that favorite CD. These are but labor pains.

There is a story of four beggars who used to sit at a border fence of a certain country. War broke up between their country and their neighbors. There was no more food at the border crossing. The men told themselves. There is nobody to beg from and if we sit here we will starve to death. If we go deeper in the countryside we will surely die. If we crossed to the enemy side they may either shoot us or let us live. Either way we could die.

One way had a glimpse of hope but betraying your country is a bad choice. They had but to move quickly. They crossed into the enemy side. Fortunately on the night they crossed a wrong story had entered the enemy camp that the beggar's country had joined an alliance with a reckless country and the two were attacking that night. The soldiers fled. The beggars found an empty camp. They ate to their full and there was no attack.

Thinking of living you might be feeling like those beggars. You might feel you have nothing but a plateful of bad choices. Do not be afraid of losing what you have. Let go of your corruption and false hopes. If what you have is from God do not be afraid of losing it. God can give it back. If it is not from God why don't you get rid of it anyway?

Are you afraid of losing a customer? God will give you a husband. You lose weight to get health. Health is wealth. The way to prosperity is to lose all that which does not pay and replace it with that which brings gains.

Press past the anger. If you were awfully offended and you felt like murdering somebody in revenge press harder on passed this point. Do not jump to a new step before you overcome this anger. There are four things God told us not to touch: Revenge, Anointing, Glory and Tithe. These he calls his and touching them is robbing him of his responsibility. The rest of our actions is ours. Changing your feelings is not one of the free gifts from heaven. You have to do it yourself.

Press past pain and get to victory. Blaming does not remove pain. Two wrongs do not make one right. Overcome evil with good. Forgive the one who hurt you. Give the greatest forgiveness to the one who hurt you most. Let go of the bad things that you know of your husband or spouse. Let go of the bad things that you know of your parentage. Let go of what you know of your race. Let go of what you know of your history.

Press past your feelings. Own your feelings, attitudes and choices. You can find faults with many other people but you cannot change any one of them. You can only control your body and what is built in it. You cannot change your husband however much you love him. All you can do is to change yourself and the husband may follow. It is the husband to drive himself to you not you to pull or seduce him. Drive your own wagon until you have reached that blank page of your life. This small image of a blank page is the innocence God wanted you to be. I will cut the story short that God wants you to be like him, act like him, think like him. You cannot however come to this point of holiness with all your history unless forgiveness makes you faultless. Jesus did not forgive you in secret. He stood on top of a mountain. He stood on top of a tree. He could have remained on the ground and be trumped upon like anybody else. He could have remained unnoticed like all other frogs we do not mention here. He chose however to be noticed like those Treefrogs. He spoke loud and clear. He spoke in presence of journalists, scribes, policemen, government officers. "Father, Forgive them for they do not know what they are doing." It is by this pronouncement that you were declared innocent. Forgive one another and you will be clean. Make right choices while still hurting.

Finally take that paper that has caused you so much pain and burn it. Yes. I know the feeling. Why should I burn a clean white paper? Burn it. It highlighted your sins. Burn it. It brought you a lot of pains. Burn it and do not feel guilty about it. If Jesus without sin was hung on a cross why can't an innocent paper burn?

The Koran teaches that the person of innocent Jesus was not hung on a cross but Satan. It was the person of sin that was hung up instead. The image of God was not hung on the cross but the sin of man. Let your feelings burn and as the flames burn, burn in your heart all those past pains. Bad feelings need to be burnt away with real fire. Burn those feelings away.

Jane recalls vividly the day we went through this with her. We got a snapper fish and burnt it.

It all started with a trip to the Mafia Islands.

Mafia Island lies off the mouth of the Rufiji River in Southern Tanzania. It has two trading centres Kilindoni (the District Capital not to be confused with Kinondoni the "Prostitute capital" of Dar Es Salaam) and Utende.

From Dar Es Salaam we went by lorry to Kisiju. The journey was like a trip from poverty to prosperity. It was lengthy, wobbly and uncomfortable. I'm told we could have used a small aircraft from Dar Es Salaam but the cost was so high that my guides did not think of suggesting it.

Prostitution

We arrived at Utende. This is thought to be a place of tourist attraction. The few roads on the island were in poor conditions and to go from place to place we had either to rent bicycle taxis or foot the distance. Surely Mafia needs someone to carry it to the bottom of the ladder. Mafia is one of the least developed parts of an undeveloped country. Going to Mafia was like going to the moon. There was nothing to see. There were no newspapers, bookshops or libraries. I was told there were two internet cafes but both were not working at the time because electricity which comes once in a while on the island was off that day. Do not expect running water in such circumstances of course. Have some streetwise intelligence!

The people in Mafia looked poorer than the island itself. All of them men, women and children came out wrapped in a rectangular piece of cloth called Kanga. It is a piece of cloth worn and designed without any sense of fashion. It is just like a plain table cloth. It has no line of stitches around it. Its body is an open background with a sentence of words at its bottom. I was warned that this wrapper had not to be despised because it was the only property the people were proud of. They called it Tanzania's National Dress.

Kanga is the gift lovers give. Husbands give it to their wives. Mothers give it to their children and friends share it. You can sleep in it. You can wear and walk in it. You cannot do without a Kanga.

Advertisers and politicians use it. It is not a simple 6x4ft rectangle cloth but it is the message board of town.

The most thrilling part of a Kanga is not its color or seamless pattern but the motto it carries.

Popular mottos were:

Our man (It had a picture of Jakaya Kikwete).
Don't just love me in good times; don't abandon me in bad times.
Don't blame the ant, it won't finish all the sugar.
It's strange for a dry coconut to try breaking a stone.
I knew they would cause you jealousy a lot.
Better ask me than spying on me.
I'm settled because to plan is to make a choice.

I won't revenge but I won't forget.
A poor man's capital is his body strength.
The one who denied you is the one who gave me.

We went with Jane and Abed and we wanted to buy a Kanga that would remind us of our visit. I bought <u>To Plan is to Make a Choice</u> for Jane and for Abed. Kangas take their names from their slogans.

We then walked until we reached Kilindoni Motel where we had to stay for a night. I say it that way because we had one choice. We sat down and ordered what has become to be the standard meal in all bars and restaurants in Tanzania. It is chicken and chips. When you sit with a woman in Tanzania in such a place you do not need to ask what she might eat. You may ask what she might drink. For eating 99% of the times it will be chicken and chips.

It was there we bought a snapper.

I bought this fish. We hired a stove and sat around it. I did not order for spoons or folks. I was told some foods taste better with hands and fish is one of them. We bought a bottle of oil and a matchbox.

We talked about our business trip and all that we were planning to do that night. Then a moment of strange sacrifice came.

The Swahili word for snapper is Changudoa. In Tanzania prostitutes are called Changudoa (or CD in short). It is not clear why they take the name of that innocent looking snapper fish. The term refers to women who sell their bodies for gain (money, food, drink, clothes, shelter, schooling, health), otherwise known as commercial sex workers. The term is commonly used and is a bit derogatory. It is however softer than Malaya or prostitute. There is no equivalent term for men prostitutes except the term Numb or Skin Dead.

At first Jane felt particularly offended by using the term so openly as if we clearly meant to insult her. She saw this as the usual despising language men use against women. In fact she demanded an apology. She kept using a term like Numb or Skin Dead to refer to us men. We were sitting so close to the fire yet we could not feel the heat. We were skin dead.

We sat around the fire gazing at that fish pressing hard to go beyond all the pains, the hatred, the experience we had suffered. The trip to Mafia was judged as misconceived but not an accident. We told Jane that a problem is not a license to be rude. You can never know your real self until you see yourself under pressure. She too hit back. We were nursing her wounds without touching her. Our love was like that of a prostitute. It was empty. It had no life. It was like a CD put in a drive but inactivated. We claimed to be Christians yet we were mistreating people. As employers we were bossing ourselves around as if we had no God in heaven. We trusted our riches. We loved to give advice though we would take none.

It hurt though we could not admit it. She accused us of behaving like Christians who did not believe in resurrection. She called as Sadducees. She said we were white tombs hiding the rot inside. We were to her everything bad she could imagine. We were worse than men who bought her and walked away without paying. We were rapists, hooligans, Sons of Snakes. The Moslems who rejected Jesus as a God and honoured him as a prophet were more sensible than us Christians who called him a God and yet could not obey him.

In the end nobody was interested in eating anything. We poured oil onto the fish and let it burn. It burnt until it was charcoal black. We said goodnight to each other but none meant it. Jane says at that very moment she felt, "I have no excuse for this prostitution, let it go right now" but she wasn't going to talk to us.

Jane woke up in the morning having given her Kanga a new meaning. She said she was again born again.

We asked Jane why it did take her so long to see the light. Her answer quoted five elements.

(1) Pride. She wanted to do things her own way. She did not want to accept that there was a problem in her life.
(2) Fear. She was simply afraid of taking a new step in her life. She could not imagine what else she could do. What if she did not succeed in her new venture?
(3) Rebellion. She wanted to annoy God just like a child refuses to switch off a TV or a computer to annoy parents.

(4) Laziness. It was just going to be hard to change. She had said it a number of times that it was hard to change her life. It had therefore become hard.
(5) Ignorance. She had never thought about it seriously. She hated being called Changudoa but she took prostitution as a job to take her out of poverty.
(6) Belief: She was not a prostitute but a Commercial sex worker.

Prostitutes love chicken and chips. What I told you in the beginning is true. "In Tanzania there is a fish that lives on chicken and chips."

This however is not the end of the story.

We gave Jane a surprise gift. We flew back from Mafia to Dar Es Salaam by plane. You can imagine the excitement of being in the skies. You too can fly from the stage of poverty you are on to prosperity. I want you to do that and to swear as Jane did: I will never go back.

Jane confessed that the woman with a husband who had gone manual was her. (She agreed I could write this). That was her first marriage. She got her first baby when she was only 16 and she left when she realized there was no reason to suffer "simply because she had married a wrong boy when she was at school."

She saw the second marriage as the continuation of her first marriage. She kept her first life from her husband as a closely guarded secret. She sealed off any contacts with her children and she did not communicate with any relative who knew about them. She was eventually convinced that as she was nursing nobody, she was a mother to none. Secrets have power and they have power to destroy. The second marriage broke down too.

Allow me to go back to what I have just said. Secrets have power. Whoever you share a secret with has power over you. You can see how Jane has controlled me in the story of the man who went manual. The power of secrets is destructive. The way Jane kept her secret meant she could not fully understand her second husband. She kept thinking that as she was hiding some information from him, he too was hiding something from her. Suspicion arose. What started as a feeling became a habit. When a habit is repeated persistently it becomes a character. The character determines the action. For Jane that action was the breaking up of her second marriage and turning to prostitution.

Jane and I agreed to break this story. It is against decent journalism to disclose the source of one's story. Whether I have to obey men or God is up to you to judge. He says: Confess your weaknesses to one another. By this the world will know that you're my followers. There is pride in being God's followers. The road to prosperity from poverty has no hidden secrets.

Some prostitutes excuse themselves for being what they are by blaming having a history of sexual abuse, having grown up without love from their parents or from significant adults in their lives, being enticed by a friend or by peer pressure from a group of friends and need for money, food or accommodation. Those who used drugs prior to their involvement in prostitution mention their addiction as a major reason for renting their bodies out for money or drugs. I have not heard of those who do it for the fun of the game.

The theory that prostitution has been with us for so long and if we cannot beat it we should live with it is based on wrong grounds. The idea that prostitution is an individual's sexual orientation and like other forms of human rights regulating it is unconstitutional is corrupt itself. You can get into it and like poverty can get out of it.

I now confess. Offering Jane a job was not for the sake of pleasing her nephew Abed. In fact I learnt later on that Abed was not her nephew at all but some old classmate. He found her when he had just broken up with his girlfriend. Suffering brought them together. In the end he told his own story, led his own life, borrowing Jane's experience. We can see that example on page 130. God does not put us in trouble but knows how to take us out. In bringing us all together he had a plan in mind. It worked out well for me, Jane, Abed and you. What do you think was the plan?

CHAPTER TWENTY ONE

Corruption

There is one thing I didn't tell you in the chapter on prostitution. As my pen started writing about legalizing and taxing prostitution I started laughing out loud. I could not believe where my head was getting such an idea from. I re-read the text before printing this book and I decided that though the idea might be crazy I was not to feel guilty publishing it after all it was not originally my idea anyway.

Well, that is no defense. Ok, ok, ok. I must be held accountable for each and every idea in my head. We do not have to listen to every single thought that comes into our heads. We have the authority to chase some back, to suffocate others and reject or accept those we choose using our freewill power. Corruption too enters our mind this way. It starts as somebody else's idea or offer and then it becomes our guilt. It is no defense to say, "Not guilty. I did not initiate it."

At the time I wrote the last chapter I was of the view that governments can fight poverty by widening first their tax base. With increased resources they would have more funds at hand to spend on poverty-relief measures like free primary schooling, affordable medication and distribution of medicated bed nets for pregnant mothers and children- under-the-age-of-five, give every citizen sanitized drinking water and perhaps a right to vote. These are the benchmarks the world counts as measurements in changing a nation from poverty to prosperity.

With such nice goals in mind if taxing prostitutes could be feasible, why not? One expert however told me that if it takes more money to collect a tax than the amount that can be collected, forget levying the tax. If for centuries it has been impossible to hunt down prostitutes for some good reasons would it be any easier to hunt them down to pay taxes?

Police on the face of it may not be corrupt but fearing to drive prostitution underground may render them incompetent. It is this incompetence or inefficiency to deliver public service which is defined as corruption. I repeat. Corruption is incompetence or inefficiency in delivery of public service.

By this definition there is nothing racial or nothing cultural in corruption. Where there is a gap between poverty and prosperity there is inefficiency in delivery of services. True to say: The bigger the gap, the greater the corruption. By retrospection poverty and corruption are as associated as poverty and prostitution are. By conclusion bridging the gap between poverty and prosperity is eliminating corruption. By the way, what came first a chicken or an egg?

Let me continue with this theme. Go back to Page 14, the fourth paragraph. "However, there should be no poor among you, for in the land the LORD your God is giving you to possess as your inheritance, he will richly bless you, if only you fully obey the LORD your God and are careful to follow all these commands I am giving you today." (Full stop). "For the LORD your God will bless you as he has promised, and you will lend to many nations but will borrow from none." (Full stop). You will rule over many nations but none will rule over you. (There is another Full Stop here). Continue, "If there is a poor man among your brothers in any of the towns of the land that the LORD your God is giving you, do not be hardhearted or tightfisted toward your poor brother".

I guess what I am saying here is that a fight against poverty is a fight against corruption. The same weapons usable against poverty are the same weapons usable against corruption. Whoever can take a stand against poverty can take a stand against corruption. You can read again the text above but find and replace 'poor' with 'corrupt' and you will get what I mean. I confess it was not my intention to quote the text out of context. I believe the same Lord who hates poverty hates corruption as well.

Way back in the year 2000 the Tanzania's Commission of Science and Technology was given the task of researching, assessing and eliminating corruption. I know you may wonder how such an assignment came to such a commission.

I call it despair. The government first suffered from a number of complaints and ridicules from the public that it had failed to deliver on its campaign against corruption. Churches came out openly to read Micah 7 and 'found and replaced 'Israel' with 'Tanzania' and the story remained accurate.

Look at it: The Misery of Tanzania.

1 "How miserable I am!
 I feel like the fruit picker after the harvest
 Who can find nothing to eat.
 Not a cluster of grapes or a single early fig
 Can be found to satisfy my hunger.
2 The godly people have all disappeared;
 Not one honest person is left on the earth.
 They are all murderers,
 Setting traps even for their own brothers.
3 Both their hands are equally skilled at doing evil!
 Officials and judges alike demand bribes.
 The people with influence get what they want,
 And together they scheme to twist justice.
4 Even the best of them is like a brier;
 The most honest is as dangerous as a hedge of thorns.
 But your judgment day is coming swiftly now.
 Your time of punishment is here, a time of confusion.
5 Don't trust anyone—
 Not your best friend or even your wife!
6 For the son despises his father.
 The daughter defies her mother.
 The daughter-in-law defies her mother-in-law.
 Your enemies are right in your own household!"

The Government got alarmed. Worse still the election date was drawing near and nearer every day. Government officials behaved more-or-less like the article than they could deny it. Newsmen depicted officials' family-life misfortunes as prophesy that had come true.

Blame is not a tool for fighting corruption. It can neither wipe it nor cover it. Denial had been tried and failed. A new tactic had to be tried otherwise the end of Nyerere's 'Teachers Union' had come to an end. The solution was to combat corruption from its stronghold and to do the job thoroughly well was to start by spying out corruption in its strongholds. The government loaded the task onto the commission. The Justice Ministry was judged too weak to investigate itself. The Police Crime Investigation Department could not be trusted either. A commission to be credible had to be independent. Corruption had grown from an art to a science. Of all commissions the Science and Technology was the only one suitable for the job.

Corruption and bribery go together. In fact the Oxford dictionary defines corruption as the perversion or destruction of integrity or fidelity in the discharge of public duties by bribery or favour.

In my situation when I left Mbeya with a letter inviting the Chinese investors my local advisors blamed me for not getting the MOU signed, on not using my brain. "Tanzania is like Heaven. You do not get what you pray for but you get what you deserve". My challenge remained, "You may get what you want but you may not want what you get."

Logic said that if I had given a little bribe (may be as small as a chicken or a glass of beer or a mustard seed) I would have got that letter without even riding down to Mbeya. Warning: When you are in a situation that makes such suggestions, stop and think where that voice comes from. If it brings life, it is from God. If it brings worry, fear, condemnation, imprisonment, fines and restlessness, it is from Satan. If it is from some companion of yours you will hear it with your own ears. You can take him aside and say," "Get behind me; for you are not setting your mind on God's interests, but man's." If he or she persists in disturbing you it is better you cut off his lips or cut off your own ears instead of letting your thoughts be polluted.

If the voice is from you, it will come in as first opinion and will not need being seconded, argued or supported. If it does persist, tell it loud and clearly that you are not going to think about it. That annoys most thoughts and forces them to walk out on you. Do not call them back. Let them go. Without your head they will roam the universe and without a head to enter, they will fall down and die in the wilderness. Bad thoughts can be eliminated that way.

A bribe has the power of a propeller that drives ships across the seas or directs airplanes across the sky. When you hook an officer with a bribe you can drive him left and right the way a rope in a horse's mouth drives the animal and even controls its speed. Jane told me that just a little wink of an eye can make a police man quiet or blind. A little word of "I will see you later, Officer," could make her earn her daily bread. Such few words could mean that when arrested she could stand in the dock but the judge would certainly release her simply with a warning. Jane would be back from court to the street with pride. This could be good for Jane's reputation but bad for justice as a whole. When corruption enters society it attacks the justice system first and turns it 'skin dead.'

The trick bribery plays is wonderfully simple. The law requires the police to take every detainee to court within 48 hours. When you promise the officer "a little something" he would delay your file past the hour. In court the judge would ask, "Where are your accusers?" The officer would lament that due to heavy workload the files were still laying in the office of the Director of Prosecutions. As a matter of routine the judge would set the condemned free. Legally one cannot be remanded when there is no accuser.

I'm writing this chapter with a lot of sensitivity because my words might hurt so many people and this could seriously affect my book sales. Guilt hurts. My critics will not understand how I come to praise Tanzania for fighting corruption and yet my own characters' lifestyle shows that corruption is still strong and growing.

Corruption. Corruption. Corruption. What can I compare it to? It is similar to homosexuality. It begins as a joke, then a group, a movement and finally a right. It is conceived in one mind. Then it enters into another mind. Then one body and another body get together. Then the two bodies become one. Then one-by-one one becomes a group. The group becomes a club. The club becomes a movement. The movement gains strength. The movement goes to court. The court obeys the rules and judges not in the movement favour. Then the movement demands the court changes the rules. The court does not change the rules but changes the interpretation. The movement returns to court and presses its demands again. The court follows the constitution and the new light. The movement wins the case. ~~Homosexuality~~ Corruption becomes a right.

Corruption can be spread by association or by inheritance. Like all other viruses it can mutate its genealogy and interchange its weapons from protective to defensive. For instance it uses temptation as its offensive weapon and none of us can claim to be immune from temptation. By temptation I mean 'pressure attempting your flesh'. I saw that when I was watching those 'gazelles' at Butterfly Beach. Men who can be called 'real men' know what it means looking at a beautiful, naked, living, flesh of a weak gender. Temptations will always be with you. It is the way you control your feelings that determines your habit, character and action. If you say you are beyond temptation you are but a liar. If you are not, tell us in which world you live that the devil has never reached. Corruption can also use "Emotional Sickness" – 'pressure-attempting-your spirit' and you start seeing your ideas as "I was only obeying orders" or "God told me."

Tanzania's Prevention of Corruption Act No. 16 of 1971, classifies corruption offences as follows:

1. Corrupt Transactions S.3 (Bribery)

A person is said to have committed an offence under S.3 (1), when such a person by himself or in conjunction with any other person, corruptly solicits, accepts or obtains or agrees to accept or attempts to obtain from any other person any advantage as an inducement to or reward for or otherwise in account of any agent, doing or forbearing to do or having done or for bore to do, anything in relation to his principal's affair or business.

The second category of a corrupt transaction offence is when any person by himself or in conjunction with any other person, corruptly gives, promise or offers any advantage to any person, whether for the benefit of that person or another person, as an inducement to, or reward for doing or forbearing to do or having done or forbearing to do anything in relation to his/her principal's affair or business.

The advantage can be a gift of any property, (movable or immovable), reward or favour discount, bonus, commission, employment etc.

A principal can be an employer, a beneficiary under a trust estate as if it were a person, any person interested in the estate of a deceased person, the estate of the deceased person and the authority or body of the persons in which a public office is held.

Agent for the purpose of this section means and includes any person in employment of or acting for another, a trustee, an administrator or an executor and public officer.

Where any person is convicted of an offence against this section he/she shall be liable to imprisonment for a term not exceeding ten years or to a fine not exceeding fifty thousand shillings or to both such imprisonment and fine. However if one of them decides to associate himself in acts of corrupt transactions for the sole purpose of helping to unearth corrupt practices the law protects such a person.

Are you a liar or not? Are you a well disciplined soldier? Are you a carrot, an egg or a coffee bean?

I am told the Commission of Science looked at how man can be one thing to one and another to another and decided that corruption in man cannot be pinned down if truth remained relative. It had to search for the source of corruption not for just how wide it had spread. A gift had to be defined as a gift and a bribe a bribe. A fine had to be forbidding not just affordable. The deterrent effect imposed by the US$ 50 fine (a fine not exceeding fifty thousand shillings) which any sex tourist could offer without thinking twice was no longer to be taken as impressive but abusive.

The feasibility study identified data flow patterns and their reporting mechanisms within and across various government sectors as defective. Districts had many political, economical, social and administrative responsibilities. Under the local district administration were education and health services delivery, tax collection, business licensing, council election supervision, roads-water-electricity supply infrastructure, housing construction and maintenance, waste management and keeping law and order. Most of these tasks were manually processed and were largely ineffective and inefficient. Corruption was born by a slow flow of information which invited bribery in the delivery of these public services.

Like all other temptations or emotional sicknesses, corruption comes in when you are hungry, tired or overloaded. Having one situation is bad enough but the poor have all. Avoid these three situations and you will certainly turn from poverty to prosperity. Above all else keep sober. This is as much a medical prescription as "Lose weight, gain health"

Computerizing the local government in Tanzania was proposed as the solution to mending this trust deficiency. This was a medical prescription and Kinondoni District took the trial test.

The goal of the research team was finding a way that would boost good governance, revenue collection and service delivery without putting excessive costs and extra burden to tax payers.

Kinondoni District starting with only two computers in 1998 developed computerized databases for various services and records, such as health, education, birth, marriage and death. This facilitated good governance and accelerated public services and the compilation of various social service reports. The process of registering and issuing birth, marriage and death certificates became a pay-and-get affair and corruption or bribery (in the narrow sense of the word), was almost wiped out of this sector. The job became so easily done and no worker was demanding money for moving and lifting piles of dusty files in search of some number.

Imagine life before computerization. See yourself getting a marriage certificate after you are already divorced or imagine your partner leaving you and marrying somebody else and you cannot lay any claim because there was no marriage certificate issued to you or it came when he/she had already been taken by somebody else. And that guy knowing the rules of the game better than you knew bought out his certificate before wedding. He kept his wedding a secret. The fact she kept living with you when she was married to someone else meant that you are the one who was cheating and liable to punishment. Computerizing ended this malpractice. I was told and I do not know whether this was true or where it used to happen that before computerization men accused of polygamy could stand up in court and deny having ever been married before to so-and so by simply saying, " I do not remember having ever married you."

The project was then extended to the management and processing of matters pertaining to foreign trade and investment. Corruption fled from this area too. Government Revenue was increased and the district increased the computers to the hundreds of them it has today. The Kinondoni experience shows that corruption should not be legalized nor taxed.

As public outcry about victimization, favoritism and corruption in taxation procedures went down the government directed all districts in the country to adopt the Kinondoni experience. The Teachers' Party (renamed The Liberation Party) won the elections. Tanzania now is looked at as one of the countries in Africa that are ready and willing to fight corruption.

On May 17, 2006 the United States signed an accord with the Tanzanian government giving the country up to $11.15 million in assistance to develop a multi-sectoral attack on corruption. An independent bureau against corruption was created with a goal that read, "Develop an investment climate with local capacity to fight corruption, strengthen the rule of law for good governance and increase oversight of public procurement."

When we think of those gallant soldiers who first went out to fight corruption with only two computers we see men who succeeded because they did not fear to tackle the job. The job must have looked big and tough. They did not say: "We cannot do it or we cannot try it because we cannot do it so well". All they did was to align their confidence, determination, decision and action in the pattern of one straight thinking:

Belief>Thoughts>Words>Feelings>Decisions>Habits> Character> Action.

Success is for men and women of character. These are people who insist on doing what is right even if they do not want to do it. They do what is good even if they do not feel good. These are men and women who know that it is their inalienable right to do what is right and legal. They do good persistently, out of habit and that eventually defines their character. Blessed are you if your name is added to one of these.

Nothing is impossible for those who believe in success. If you set your mind to turning from poverty to prosperity and you earnestly convinced yourself that you could, surely you would. It is your brain that keeps you in poverty. The common thing is to load the problem over the devil. I am not a devil's advocate and this is not written in Satan's defense but if finance is your weakness, the devil is not interested in that bit of you. Military intelligence teaches to strike the enemy before he strikes you. Military intelligence recommends striking the enemy in his stronghold. What is the devil to get out of your weakness? If there is no money in your pockets how can an intelligent thief steal your pocket? When you burnt your list of obstacles you burnt your weaknesses. Spend no energy in reclaiming your lost territory. Determine your stronghold and that is what to protect. The devil is only interested in your strongholds. If faith is your stronghold doubt is going to be cast at you. If your marriage is based on love, protect your affair. Hatred, bitterness, envy, doubt, suspicion are all poised to attack your stronghold. If knowledge is your stronghold await new data that will attempt to change your belief theory. When the constitution is your strength corruption will demand that you change the interpretation and call a bribe a gift or a she a he

When "Our Man" President Jakaya Kikwete took office he made a public commitment to continue the "war on corruption" as waged by his predecessor. Words have power. When you make them with your mouth especially to the public then you have your life at a balance. The public knows clearly that 'a glass of water' is not the same as 'a water glass'. Kikwete had to follow his words with action otherwise the punishment foretold would befall him.

The death of Corruption in Tanzania now is near. How do we know that? Our benchmarks show an increased number of pregnant mothers receiving mosquito nets, more children are enrolled in the Primary one school entrances and ……..the world says so.

"However, there should be no corrupt among you, for in the land the LORD your God is giving you to possess as your inheritance, he will richly bless you, if only you fully obey the LORD your God and are careful to follow all these commands I am giving you today. For the LORD your God will bless you as he has promised, and you will lend to many nations but will borrow from none. You will rule over many nations but none will rule over you. If there is a corrupt man among your brothers in any of the towns of the land that the LORD your God is giving you, do not be hardhearted or tightfisted toward your corrupt brother".

By interpretation this is not to mean being light on your brother. It simply means warn him, if he doesn't listen warn him again but in presence of a trusted witness. If he further does not listen expose the matter to the family and if he does not break down leave him to the world. Police and prison will take care of him.

When a fish is getting rotten it starts from the head. To save the fish you have to cut off the head. When we see the head of family tolerating mistakes or silly excuses we must know that not only his death is near but that the death of the entire clan is near. It is better that one man dies instead of the whole nation.

Have you ever heard of Temple Prostitutes? They were not living in hostelries and guest houses. I told you before that corruption could live in those very assemblies scheming against it. It mutates like a virus. The war against corruption must twist in time from a physical battle to a spiritual battle and sometimes back. We must be ready for these changes and avoid uprising corruption otherwise we glorify and worship it. Corruption turns from a physical give-and-take of a bribe to a way of thinking, a way of doing things, a way of living. Fighting corruption is not a war limited to chasing thieves and thugs. That was just in the beginning. Now it has become like political football with strongholds in high places.

Kikwete went on record. He fired the Director of the Central Bank, fired a Commissioner of Police, and reshuffled his cabinet, all within three years, in an effort to clean the country of the disease of corruption. Corruption like prostitution can hide in high offices too!

America heard about this and decided to raise government assistance to Tanzania. President Bush– The Most Powerful President of the World then– chose to visit Tanzania to sing with Kikwete a victory song against corruption. With him was a package of US$ 698 million to bless the government's socio-economic activities. Kikwete was given the power and authority to spend US$ 373 million on road and airports infrastructure development, energy –US$ 206 million and US$ 66 million on water supply. This amount of money could be spent within five years but more could be given if Tanzania showed results. In fact from Tanzania President Bush called his Congress back home and asked them to approve more money to alleviate poverty in Africa.

This gesture may have come too late for President Bush critics said. He made this offer on his farewell visit to Africa as he was to leave office by the end of the year. President Bush said his visit was late but good enough to show that it was not all grim that comes from Africa. "You are a strong leader," Bush told Kikwete. "I'll just put it bluntly: America doesn't want to spend money on people who steal the money."

For Kikwete the funding meant he could win another four years of presidency. By our benchmarks this could mean a development towards democracy. Kikwete said Bush had come to leave some kind of legacy in Africa with a positive note. This was a good observation considering that Bush's approval ratings as a head of state had fallen so low. His reputation had changed from the most powerful man in the world to the worst president America had ever had.

President Bush could have been blamed for having been blind throughout his presidency but he could be praised for having opened his eyes once and seeing in an instant the victory Tanzania had over corruption.

A little investment in 2 computers Tanzania made yielded almost US$ 700 million in a period of ten years. An investment in a smile brings love. A little 'Thank you' or "I will see you Officer" brings heavy rewards. Think of how a small word 'Sorry" cures so many ills. I will return you to the theme. You can turn from poverty to prosperity. Do not say you have no money to invest. If you have the idea, someone else surely will have the money and will be willing and proud to put it into your plan. Just be honest and prepared to use money from someone else's pocket wisely. Do not say the task is too big. Plant the seed today. It will grow. If you have a desire to live in a clean house, you start by buying a broom. If you want to live debt free, start by stopping borrowing. If you want to gain health, curb your appetite. If I had told you to do some great thing, would you not have done it? How much more, then, when I tell you, 'Decide to believe in yourself and prosper'!

Corruption stinks.

When President Bush arrived at Mwalimu Julius Nyerere International Airport the man who had arranged the trip; the man who had led the government as the Prime Minister he had come to thank, was nowhere to be seen.

President Bush arrived in Tanzania on February 16th 2008. Just a week before Prime Minister Lowassa had tendered his resignation to President Kikwete. His integrity had been questioned in a report by a Parliamentary Committee investigating the awarding of a contract to Richmond Development Company LLC of Texas, USA for the supply of electricity to Tanzania Electric Supply Company Limited (TANESCO).

The visiting President Bush though was the former Governor of Texas and his home was in Texas was not implicated. According to the report, the Prime Minister used his position to circumvent the rules and influence the bidding process in favor of Richmond Development Company of Texas. The Prime Minister in doing his duties chose not to know that Richmond Development was essentially a bogus 'briefcase company', which fabricated and forged documents used during the bidding process and could not deliver on any of its promises. Against advice the Prime Minister committed the government and people of Tanzania to a life of no electricity but with a bill of thousands of US dollars daily to Richmond. Indeed it was a rare occasion when parliamentarians of all parties united and put aside their political ideological differences to criticize the way and the manner government leaders were thinking, doing and living.

Corruption cost Lowassa his post as Prime Minister.

Lowassa had an extensive background in both parliamentary issues and government affairs. He served as Minister of State in the Prime Minister's Office (1986-1990). He grew up to the rank of bidding for nomination as the ruling party's presidential candidate in 1995. He was unsuccessful but appointed Minister for State, Vice President's Office - Environment & Poverty in 1997. Following the Tanzanian general election in 2000 he was appointed Minister of Water and Livestock Development. He gained a high profile as a Minister. Kikwete won the 2005 election and he announced his nomination of Lowassa for the position of Prime Minister. Parliament overwhelmingly confirmed the nomination, with 312 votes in favor and two opposed, and Lowassa was sworn in, December 30th, 2005.

As overwhelmingly he was elected he was overwhelmingly dismissed.

The law in Tanzania reads: When a public officer solicits or accepts or attempts to obtain any advantage without lawful consideration or for a lawful consideration which he knows or has reason to believe to be inadequate, from any person whom he knows or has reasons to believe to have been, or to be, or to be likely, or about to be, concerned in any matter or transaction with himself as a public officer or having connection with the official functions of himself or of any officer to whom he is subordinate; is said to have committed an offence under section 6 of the Prevention of Corruption Act No. 16 of 1971.

The same law says: When any person knowingly gives to any agent or any agent knowingly uses with intent to deceive his principal, any receipt, account or other document relating to his principal's affairs or business and which contains any statement which is false or erroneous or defective in any material particular and which to his knowledge is intended to mislead the principal, he/she shall be guilty of an offence and shall be liable on conviction to imprisonment for a term not exceeding five years or to a fine not exceeding twenty thousand shillings, or to both such imprisonment and fine.

Whereas the law did not come out to name Lowassa as the person being referred to above by-and-large he was the one. Due to public outcry President Kikwete relieved Lowassa of his duties and dissolved his cabinet.

Bush arrived to the airport to be received by a Prime minister he had never heard of before. For his part Kikwete was described as a tough leader. It was not easy to move against a prime minister of Lowassa's popularity and experience. Within the same month Kikwete was elected the President–in–Chief of the African Union. This sounds like fulfilling the prophesy: "You will rule over many nations but none will rule over you."

Lowassa went down without a fight.

He had bravely sat through a parliamentary session where he saw a colleague every after colleague stand up and speak against him. Finally when he was given a microphone (perhaps to defend himself) he could not say anything but to announce that he had submitted his resignation to the President.

Corruption is the worst smear a person's character can ever suffer. Remember that in our journey to prosperity Character comes close to the final stage. It is after you have gone through so much that your character comes to prominence. The devil or whoever your enemy is aims at assassinating your character to prevent you from your life rewards. Be on guard always. Defend your character persistently. Keep your habits unchanged. Persevere and endure in good works. Nurse your character.

There was no point for the former Prime Minister to stand up and fight for his name or office. Corruption is like a skin disease called Leprosy. It comes up and attacks places like the face which you can hardly hide. The only medicine for corruption is power to look beyond the case. If you are caught in the smear any attempt to wriggle out of it raises the stench and dirties you further.

Lowassa handled his downfall with impressive dignity. Within days of his resignation some parliamentarians were grateful for the way he did not plunge the country into a constitutional crisis or legal battles that could have endangered the nation. In neighbouring Kenya at the time the Prime Minister and the President over there were fighting each other and thousands of people were dying. Several newspaper articles appeared praising Lowassa's 'courage' in resigning over the Richmond corruption scandal and accepting the responsibility and his mistakes in a gentle man's manner. The committee that called for the Prime Minister's resignation instead was attacked as unprofessional and incompetent. It had handled a very serious case but without any seriousness that the case demanded. Instead of proving Lowassa corrupt beyond any reasonable doubt they had only managed to prove that some form of corruption had occurred. Lowassa was let off as a mere scapegoat, treated unfairly particularly that he was not given a chance to defend himself and yet the allegations against him were unfounded.

This world's wisdom is simultaneously foolish. Mwakiteme, the man who legally performed his duties as the Chairman of the Parliamentary Investigating Committee and who single handedly brought down the government of his schoolmate (Mwakiteme and Lowassa reportedly attended the same law school) was instead blamed for his work. Mwakiteme's committee set out to unravel corruption and punish whoever was caught without fear or favor. He got the Prime Minister as the prime suspect. He netted and wrestled him down. For his reward he received a barrage of criticisms. Surely it is true as it was written, "Criticize not and ye shall not be criticized; condemn not and ye shall not be condemned" or "do not be hardhearted or tightfisted toward your corrupt brother."

Mwakiteme almost went into hiding. Brethren, if any person is overtaken in misconduct or corruption of any sort, you who are not corrupt should set him right and restore and reinstate him, without any sense of superiority and with gentleness, keeping an attentive eye on oneself, lest you should be tempted also.

The events that followed indicated that Lowassa was not finished yet. Speaking on the Television of the Nation (TvT) one Saturday night, Lowassa said his resignation from the premiership on the basis of "collective responsibility" was not without precedence. Ali Hassan Mwinyi, once resigned as Home Affairs minister and later on went to become the country's president. The story is that some vigilantes thought of fighting witchcraft in Tanzania by attacking and killing everyone suspected of being a witch doctor. The police failed to stop the killings and the minister under whose administration the police department fell resigned.

Mwinyi resigned as Home Affairs Minister in the first phase government of Mwalimu Julius Nyerere in 1978, accepting accountability for the police inefficiency in protecting innocent civilians of Shinyanga Region. However he bounced back first as the President of the small island of Zanzibar and then in 1985 took over as the elected president of the United Republic of Tanzania replacing the very president who had fired him.

This is what Lowassa said: "I opted to resign on the basis of collective responsibility (over the Richmond power generation scandal). But this is not the first time. Mzee Mwinyi did it as Home Affairs Minister; Peter Siyovelwa also resigned as Internal Security Minister; and Peter Kisumo resigned as Regional

Commissioner. However, none of them was even in Shinyanga when those killings took place."

Lowassa appeared not to be looking at his wounds but at life after healing.

You might be suffering from a stinking level of poverty as found in Africa conveniently termed "Extreme Poverty" or what medical cycles describe as "Coma" or in numerical terms "Earning less than a dollar a day". You might be an occasional sufferer who only pays bills on demand or when you receive the final notice. You may be this guy who earns from hand to mouth; eats to live or you may be the rich fool. Whatever predicaments you are in count it as joy. Do not allow pressure to overcome you. Confuse trouble by smiling at your circumstances. Remember what I asked you before: Suppose God told you, "Go into the world and prosper", what would you do? Would you remain skeptical and say, "Show me the money!" Would you rise up and walk? Would you continue in your slumber? Or would you say, "I will not believe it was the voice of God until my bills are paid. I will not believe until I have a new house or a new dress. I will not believe until my children are out of college. I will not believe until I have got a job. I will not believe until I am healed. I will not believe until my problem is solved! I will not believe until....."

You might be accused of corruption. Look beyond the trial. If your own strength and messages from dear friends are breaking your courage employ patience. Patience is the only emotion that can stand heavy pressure. Faith may wear out but Patience survives because the latter is consistently and constantly the same. Lowassa acted with prudence when he addressed a rally in his Monduli Constituency and insisted that he would not quit politics and that he was ready to serve the country in any capacity. He proved it to us by his gesture that it is not circumstances that may steal our joy and future; it is our attitude. You do not have to be full of joy to be joyful. Start with the little you have and let it grow.

Corruption and joy are related. Whereas Corruption makes you sick, condemned and crashed, joy energizes you, gives you recovery and drives you forward. When you are hard pressed joy is better that happiness. Happiness depends on what you have. Joy depends on what you know. If you know you will eventually merge out victorious joy will drive you to victory. It is when you are on your victory party that happiness comes in. Joy comes in before happiness. Do not let your circumstances tie you down, rejoice.

Corruption is an old disease. It has been with us from time immemorial. The fact that it has lived with us for so long does not make us legalize it however. Some of those guys we know today accused of corruption may have inherited it from their parents or cultivated it as they learnt to grow. On the charge of corrupting under age children many parents are guilty. What do you expect to become of a child who is always rewarded for doing the wrong things? You often hear a mother pleading to a two year old, "Come my darling. Do this and this I will give you a candy."

A mother pleads to her teenage daughter, "If you wash dishes I will give you ten dollars." Rewarding children for the good things they do is not the problem but paying them that they may do what they are supposed to do is the root of corruption.

I now confess having enjoyed myself watching children playing beach football at the Butterfly. I sometimes laughed myself silly and even gave some candies to some kids. The funny bit of it was that when some kids saw that they were losing the match, they moved the goal posts or changed the rules. It is such kids I gave candies. Forgive me.

"Train up a child in the way he should go: and when he is old, he will not depart from it". Proverbs 22:6/KJV

Read the story that follows and answer the questions. You are advised to read it three or four times before attempting to answer the questions.

2 Kings 5: Naaman Healed of Leprosy

[1] Now Naaman was commander of the army of the king of Aram. He was a great man in the sight of his master and highly regarded, because through him the LORD had given victory to Aram. He was a valiant soldier, but he had leprosy.

[2] Now bands from Aram had gone out and had taken captive a young girl from Israel, and she served Naaman's wife. [3] She said to her mistress, "If only my master would see the prophet who is in Samaria! He would cure him of his leprosy."

[4] Naaman went to his master and told him what the girl from Israel had said. [5] "By all means, go," the King of Aram replied. "I

will send a letter to the King of Israel." So Naaman left, taking with him ten talents (about 350 kg) of silver, six thousand shekels (about 70kg) of gold and ten sets of clothing. ⁶ The letter that he took to the King of Israel read: "With this letter I am sending my servant Naaman to you so that you may cure him of his leprosy."

⁷ As soon as the King of Israel read the letter, he tore his robes and said, "Am I God? Can I kill and bring back to life? Why does this fellow send someone to me to be cured of his leprosy? See how he is trying to pick a quarrel with me!"

⁸ When Elisha the man of God heard that the King of Israel had torn his robes, he sent him this message: "Why have you torn your robes? Have the man come to me and he will know that there is a prophet in Israel." ⁹ So Naaman went with his horses and chariots and stopped at the door of Elisha's house. ¹⁰ Elisha sent a messenger to say to him, "Go, wash yourself seven times in the Jordan, and your flesh will be restored and you will be cleansed."

¹¹ But Naaman went away angry and said, "I thought that he would surely come out to me and stand and call on the name of the LORD his God, wave his hand over the spot and cure me of my leprosy. ¹² Are not Abana and Pharpar, the rivers of Damascus, better than any of the waters of Israel? Couldn't I wash in them and be cleansed?" So he turned and went off in a rage.

¹³ Naaman's servants went to him and said, "My father, if the prophet had told you to do some great thing, would you not have done it? How much more, then, when he tells you, 'Wash and be cleansed'!" ¹⁴ So he went down and dipped himself in the Jordan seven times, as the man of God had told him, and his flesh was restored and became clean like that of a young boy.

¹⁵ Then Naaman and all his attendants went back to the man of God. He stood before him and said, "Now I know that there is no God in all the world except in Israel. Please accept now a gift from your servant."

¹⁶ The prophet answered, "As surely as the LORD lives, whom I serve, I will not accept a thing." And even though Naaman urged him, he refused.

¹⁷ "If you will not," said Naaman, "please let me, your servant, be given as much earth as a pair of mules can carry, for your servant will never again make burnt offerings and sacrifices to any other god but the LORD. ¹⁸ But may the LORD forgive your servant for this one thing: When my master enters the temple of

Corruption

Rimmon to bow down and he is leaning on my arm and I bow there also—when I bow down in the temple of Rimmon, may the LORD forgive your servant for this."

[19] "Go in peace," Elisha said.

After Naaman had traveled some distance, [20] Gehazi, the servant of Elisha the man of God, said to himself, "My master was too easy on Naaman, this Aramean, by not accepting from him what he brought. As surely as the LORD lives, I will run after him and get something from him."

[21] So Gehazi hurried after Naaman. When Naaman saw him running toward him, he got down from the chariot to meet him. "Is everything all right?" he asked.

[22] "Everything is all right," Gehazi answered. "My master sent me to say, 'Two young men from the company of the prophets have just come to me from the hill country of Ephraim. Please give them a talent (about 34kg) of silver and two sets of clothing.'"

[23] "By all means, take two talents," said Naaman. He urged Gehazi to accept them, and then tied up the two talents of silver in two bags, with two sets of clothing. He gave them to two of his servants, and they carried them ahead of Gehazi.

[24] When Gehazi came to the hill, he took the things from the servants and put them away in the house. He sent the men away and they left.

[25] Then he went in and stood before his master Elisha. "Where have you been, Gehazi?" Elisha asked. "Your servant didn't go anywhere," Gehazi answered.

[26] But Elisha said to him, "Was not my spirit with you when the man got down from his chariot to meet you? Is this the time to take money, or to accept clothes, olive groves, vineyards, flocks, herds, or menservants and maidservants? [27] Naaman's leprosy will cling to you and to your descendants forever." Then Gehazi went from Elisha's presence and he was leprous, as white as snow.

Question Time!
(1) To a five year old how would you describe who Elisha and Naaman were?
(2) Complete the statement: Gehazi was to Elisha as Naaman was to the King of Aram as Elisha was to……… ………………

(3) Why did the letter of the King of Aram annoy the King of Israel?
(4) "Are not Abana and Pharpar, the rivers of Damascus, better than any of the waters of Israel?" Who said this, to whom and why?
(5) According to the Servant girl what was stopping her master from being healed was (a) lack of faith (b) lack of knowledge (c) disbelief (d) doubt on the part of the master. Choose one.
(6) Naaman was a good soldier, a good husband and a good leader. Find examples to support this statement.
(7) Why didn't Elisha accept a gift from Naaman? If you were Lowassa would you accept a gift from Richmond?
(8) Compare Naaman and Mwinyi.
(9) Find three crimes you could accuse Gehazi of.
(10) What role did the devil play in this scandal?

The visit of President Bush reminded Tanzanians of a man who went to war without an exit strategy. They saw a warrior of Naaman's strength but with leprosy in the face. Some pockets in the country like the University of Dar Es Salaam held protests that Kikwete should keep himself clean and not associate with people with bad names. A Tanzanian proverb says: "Bad company corrupts good morals."

Association is one of the offensive weapons used by people who want to accuse others of corruption. In every case of corruption you hear the receiver being associated with the characteristic behavior of the giver. Lowassa was aware of this. Asked to respond to allegations that Richmond was linked to people close to him, he said: "I don't know who owns Richmond. It is a crooked company."

To shake off corruption, dissociate yourself from all acts of the devil. When someone tries to give you a gift so that you may do some favour for him, say, "I do not know you."

When you feel angry at yourself for being too easy on someone you could easily have taken a bribe from, say, "Not for the cost of generations of leprosy."

When they return to you calling a bribe a gift, say, "As surely as the LORD lives, whom I serve, I will not accept a thing."

When they try to persuade you to do something against your character, say, "Go in peace."

And then run to your stronghold. Get this book and run through chapter 5 quickly. Redefine yourself.

I am a son of God.

By his strides and I'm healed

If God is for us who can be against us?

This war is not against flesh and blood but the spirit.

Dress yourself in the armor of God.

This behavior will certainly give you defense against corruption but to enjoy your character you must add more data to what you know. Joy comes from knowledge. Go online. Go to any Bible site and search for references of corruption or bribery.

I went to http//: www.Bible.com and found the following. Read these references. It is fine just to read the verses but it is better to read the whole chapter. It is a matter of choice.

( ) Make at least one dollar a day. ( ) Make five hundred dollars a day. ( ) Make at least ten dollars a day. ( ) Make one thousand dollars a day. ( ) Make at least a hundred dollars a day.

Your task is to make your face be like Naaman's boy face! The Bible says, "My people die for lack of knowledge". The people who miss out the opportunity to change say, "I did not know that" or "I was never told so". You should make time to read just a little more than you usually do. Take a quick look at your schedule. Find a few moments to just escape from it all. Try just to read a little harder. It's worth it. Joy comes from knowledge.

http://bibleresources.bible.com/keywordsearchresults.php?keyword=corrupt%2C+bribe&multiplemethod=any&version1=49&numpageresults=25&sortorder=bookorder&page=3

Genesis 6:1 (Whole Chapter)

[*The **Corrupt**ion of Mankind*] Now it came about, when men began to multiply on the face of the land, and daughters were born to them,

Genesis 6:11 (Whole Chapter)

Now the earth was [Deut 31:29; Judg 2:19] **corrupt** in the sight of God, and the earth was [Ezek 8:17] filled with violence.

Genesis 6:12 (Whole Chapter)
God looked on the earth, and behold, it was **corrupt**; for [Ps 14:1-3] all flesh had **corrupt**ed their way upon the earth.

Exodus 23:8 (Whole Chapter)
" [Deut 10:17; 16:19; Prov 15:27; 17:8, 23; Is 5:22, 23] You shall not take a **bribe**, for a **bribe** blinds the clear-sighted and subverts the cause of the just.

Exodus 32:7 (Whole Chapter)
Then the LORD spoke to Moses, "Go down at once, for your people, whom [Ex 32:4, 11; Deut 9:12] you brought up from the land of Egypt, have [Gen 6:11] **corrupt**ed themselves.

Leviticus 22:25 (Whole Chapter)
Nor shall you accept any such from the hand of a foreigner for offering [Lev 21:22] as the food of your God; for their **corrupt**ion is in them, they have a defect, they shall not be accepted for you.'"

Deuteronomy 4:16 (Whole Chapter)
So that you do not [Deut 4:25; 9:12; 31:29] act **corrupt**ly and [Ex 20:4; Lev 26:1; Deut 5:8, 9; 27:15; Rom 1:23] make a graven image for yourselves in the form of any figure, the likeness of male or female,

The list looks so long and exhaustive. There is a temptation to flip over the next few pages and omit all these references. For the reason that our mind is corrupt we tend to feel:
> "I don't have time for this... And, this is really inappropriate during work.
> "I will read this later perhaps on Sunday night or maybe tomorrow."
> "I don't want my boss or my colleagues to find me reading this kind of stuff. I will read it in the privacy of my home".

The criterion of judging a picture pornographic or not is simple. If you are ashamed of it, it is pornographic. The criterion of judging an act corrupt or not is simple. If you are ashamed of it, it is corrupt. If you are tempted to hide some action, do not do it. It is corrupt.

Every reference carries (Whole Chapter) to remind you that repetition teaches. I want you to read the whole chapter as often as you see the word, 'Whole chapter.' This is not for my own good but yours. My appeal that you read the whole chapter comes from the same heart saying why should you be satisfied with headlines when you could read the whole story? Don't you see any advantage in being better informed?

Deuteronomy 4:25 (Whole Chapter)
"When you become the father of children and children's children and have remained long in the land, and [Deut 4:16] act **corrupt**ly, and [Deut 4:23] make an idol in the form of anything, and [2 Kin 17:17] do that which is evil in the sight of the LORD your God so as to provoke Him to anger,

Deuteronomy 9:12 (Whole Chapter)
" [Ex 32:7, 8] Then the LORD said to me, 'Arise, go down from here quickly, for your people whom you brought out of Egypt have acted **corrupt**ly They have [Judg 2:17] quickly turned aside from the way which I commanded them; they have made a molten image for themselves.'

Deuteronomy 10:17 (Whole Chapter)
" [Josh 22:22; Ps 136:2; Dan 2:47; 1 Tim 6:15; Rev 19:16] For the LORD your God is the God of gods and the [Rev 17:14] Lord of lords, the great, the mighty, and the awesome God [Deut 1:17; Acts 10:34; Rom 2:11; Gal 2:6; Eph 6:9] who does not show partiality nor [Deut 16:19] take a **bribe**.

Deuteronomy 16:19 (Whole Chapter)
" [Ex 23:2; Lev 19:15; Deut 1:17; 10:17] You shall not distort justice; [Prov 24:23] you shall not be partial, and [Ex 23:8; Prov 17:23; Eccl 7:7] you shall not take a **bribe**, for a **bribe** blinds the eyes of the wise and perverts the words of the righteous.

Deuteronomy 27:25 (Whole Chapter)
' [Ex 23:7; Deut 10:17; Ps 15:5; Ezek 22:12] Cursed is he who accepts a **bribe** to strike down an innocent person.' And all the people shall say, 'Amen.'

Deuteronomy 31:29 (Whole Chapter)
"For I know that after my death you will [Judg 2:19] act **corrupt**ly and turn from the way which I have commanded you; and evil will befall you in the latter days, for you will do that which is evil in the sight of the LORD, provoking Him to anger with the work of your hands."

Deuteronomy 32:5 (Whole Chapter)

"[Deut 4:25; 31:29] They have acted **corrupt**ly toward Him, They are not His children, because of their defect; [Matt 17:17] But are a perverse and crooked generation.

Judges 2:19 (Whole Chapter)
But it came about when the judge died, that they would turn back and act more **corrupt**ly than their fathers, in following other gods to serve them and bow down to them; they did not abandon their practices or their stubborn ways.

Perhaps what I have set is the simplest of all exercises. What if I told you to show this page to ten of your friends? What if I told you to send emails to whoever is in your address book and specifically state that the Desire of all ages Page 150 says, "Leave your evil ways and follow me," would you send them?

> "I do not know people on my list who could like this kind of stuff."
> "This is a well thought out scheme to advertise the book."
> 'Leave your evil ways and follow me.' "There is no such reference on Page 150".

Imagine there was a registration book for all that wanted to prosper. The form required you to fill your first name, middle name, surname, street address, telephone numbers, email address, your credit card number, your pin number, date of validity, social security number, nationality and everything that defines you, would you do it? Would you be scared of having your identity stolen? Would you fear of someone finding out your hidden corrupt self?

What if I said if you did all this all your credit history would be wiped away, would you then fill in the form? Would you risk your life today for a better tomorrow?

1 Samuel 8:3 (Whole Chapter)
His sons, however, did not walk in his ways, but turned aside after dishonest gain and [Ex 23:6, 8; Deut 16:19] took **bribe**s and perverted justice.

1 Samuel 12:3 (Whole Chapter)
"Here I am; bear witness against me before the LORD and [1 Sam 10:1; 24:6; 2 Sam 1:14] His anointed [Ex 20:17; Num 16:15;

Acts 20:33] Whose ox have I taken, or whose donkey have I taken, or whom have I defrauded? Whom have I oppressed, or [Ex 23:8; Deut 16:19] from whose hand have I taken a **bribe** to blind my eyes with it? I will restore it to you."

2 Chronicles 19:7 (Whole Chapter)

"Now then let the fear of the LORD be upon you; be very careful what you do, for the LORD our God will [Gen 18:25; Deut 32:4] have no part in unrighteousness [Deut 10:17, 18] or partiality or the taking of a **bribe**."

2 Chronicles 26:16 (Whole Chapter)

[*Pride Is Uzziah's Undoing*] But [Deut 32:15; 2 Chr 25:19] when he became strong, his heart was so proud that he acted **corrupt**ly, and he was unfaithful to the LORD his God, for [1 Kin 13:1-4] he entered the temple of the LORD to burn incense on the altar of incense.

2 Chronicles 27:2 (Whole Chapter)

He did right in the sight of the LORD, according to all that his father Uzziah had done; [2 Chr 26:16] however he did not enter the temple of the LORD. But the people continued acting **corrupt**ly.

Nehemiah 1:7 (Whole Chapter)

" [Dan 9:5] We have acted very **corrupt**ly against You and have not kept the commandments, nor the statutes, nor the ordinances [Deut 28:14] which You commanded Your servant Moses.

Job 6:22 (Whole Chapter)

"Have I said, 'Give me something,' Or, 'Offer a **bribe** for me from your wealth,'

Job 15:16 (Whole Chapter)

How much less one who is [Ps 14:1] detestable and **corrupt**, Man, who [Job 34:7; Prov 19:28] drinks iniquity like water!

Job 15:34 (Whole Chapter)

"For the company of [Job 8:13] the godless is barren, And fire consumes [Job 8:22] the tents of the **corrupt**.

Psalm 14:1 (Whole Chapter)

[*Folly and Wickedness of Men.*] [*For the choir director. A Psalm of David.*] The fool has [Ps 10:4; 53:1] said in his heart, "There is no God" They are **corrupt**, they have committed abominable deeds; There is [Ps 14:1-3; 130:3; Rom 3:10-12] no one who does good.

Psalm 14:3 (Whole Chapter)

They have all [Ps 58:3] turned aside, together they have become **corrupt**; There is [Ps 143:2] no one who does good, not even one.

Psalm 15:5 (Whole Chapter)

He [Ex 22:25; Lev 25:36; Deut 23:20; Ezek 18:8] does not put out his money [I e to a fellow Israelite] at interest, Nor [Ex 23:8; Deut 16:19] does he take a **bribe** against the innocent [2 Pet 1:10] He who does these things will never be shaken.

Psalm 26:10 (Whole Chapter)

In whose hands is a [Ps 37:7] wicked scheme, And whose right hand is full of [Ps 15:5] **bribe**s.

Psalm 53:1 (Whole Chapter)

[*Folly and Wickedness of Men.*] [*For the choir director; according to Mahalath [I.e. sickness, a sad tone]. A Maskil of David.*] [Ps 10:4; 14:1-7; 53:1-6] The fool has said in his heart, "There is no God," They are **corrupt**, and have committed abominable injustice; [Rom 3:10] There is no one who does good.

As you continue reading through these references you get some kind of conviction. You start seeing references which specifically talk to your mind. Do not jump over them easily. Yes aligning Belief>Thoughts>Words>

Feelings> Decisions>Habits> Character> Action creates some cricking sound. It is the irritating sound of a screw driver in a wall. In the middle of the pain, rejoice because you are being aligned for prosperity.

Psalm 53:3 (Whole Chapter)

[Rom 3:12] Every one of them has turned aside; together they have become **corrupt**; There is no one who does good, not even one.

Proverbs 15:27 (Whole Chapter)

He who [Prov 1:19; 28:25; 1 Tim 6:10] profits illicitly troubles his own house, But he who [Ex 23:8; Deut 16:19; 1 Sam 12:3; Is 33:15] hates **bribe**s will live.

Proverbs 17:8 (Whole Chapter)

A [Prov 21:14; Is 1:23; Amos 5:12] **bribe** is a charm in the sight of its owner; Wherever he turns, he prospers.

Proverbs 17:23 (Whole Chapter)
A wicked man receives a [Prov 17:8] **bribe** from the bosom To [Ex 23:8; Mic 3:11; 7:3] pervert the ways of justice.

Proverbs 21:14 (Whole Chapter)
A [Prov 18:16; 19:6] gift in secret subdues anger, And a **bribe** in the bosom, strong wrath.

Proverbs 29:4 (Whole Chapter)
The [2 Chr 9:8; Prov 8:15; 29:14] king gives stability to the land by justice, But a man who takes **bribe**s overthrows it.

Why is it that the truth hurts and yet a lie soothes?

Why are we so sleepy in church but right when the sermon is over we suddenly wake up?

Why do we want to keep books of this nature closed and yet we would like to read soap magazines from cover to cover?

Why is it so hard to talk about God and how good he could be but yet so easy to talk about some corrupt stuff and how funny it could be?

Why is it so easy to delete a Godly e- mail, but yet we forward all the corrupt ones without fear or favour?

Ecclesiastes 7:7 (Whole Chapter)
For [Eccl 4:1; 5:8] oppression makes a wise man mad, And a [Ex 23:8; Deut 16:19; Prov 17:8, 23] **bribe corrupt**s the heart.

Isaiah 1:4 (Whole Chapter)
Alas, sinful nation, People weighed down with iniquity, [Is 14:20] Offspring of evildoers,Sons who [Neh 1:7] act **corrupt**ly! They have [Is 1:28] abandoned the LORD, They have [Is 5:24] despised the Holy One of Israel, They have turned away from Him.

Isaiah 1:21 (Whole Chapter)
[*Zion* **Corrupt***ed, to Be Redeemed*] How the faithful city has become a [Is 57:3-9; Jer 2:20] harlot, She who was full of justice! Righteousness once lodged in her, But now murderers.

Isaiah 1:23 (Whole Chapter)
Your [Hos 5:10; Mic 7:3] rulers are rebels And companions of thieves; Everyone [Ex 23:8; Mic 7:3] loves a **bribe** And chases after rewards. They [Is 10:2; Jer 5:28; Ezek 22:7; Zech 7:10] do not defend the orphan, Nor does the widow's plea come before them.

Isaiah 5:23 (Whole Chapter)
[Ex 23:8; Is 1:23; 10:1, 2; Mic 3:11; 7:3] Who justify the wicked for a **bribe**, And [Ps 94:21; James 5:6] take away the rights of the ones who are in the right!

Isaiah 33:15 (Whole Chapter)
He who [Ps 15:2; 24:4; Is 58:6-11] walks righteously and speaks with sincerity, He who rejects unjust gain And shakes his hands so that they hold no **bribe**; He who stops his ears from hearing about bloodshed And [Ps 119:37] shuts his eyes from looking upon evil;

Jeremiah 6:28 (Whole Chapter)
All of them are stubbornly rebellious, [Jer 9:4] Going about as a talebearer They are [Ezek 22:18] bronze and iron; They, all of them, are **corrupt**.

Ezekiel 16:33 (Whole Chapter)
"Men give gifts to all harlots, but you [Is 57:9; Ezek 16:41; Hos 8:9, 10] give your gifts to all your lovers to **bribe** them to come to you from every direction for your harlotries.

You may have heard of a story of a Pastor named Thomas. Any story about Thomas might be as doubtful as the meaning in the name. I put this story here but I have failed to verify the origin of it. If it happens to be a lie consider it a parable. If it is true thank George Thomas. If there is a man like George Thomas I think he owes me advertising fee!

There are reasons to doubt the truth of the story. The event is in England but the currency quoted is neither British Pounds nor Euros but American dollars! The story of Naaman uses the Talent as the exchange currency and that makes the story real given the time it talks about. If Naaman had to pay Ghehazi in Tanzanian shillings we would have a right not to print his story in this book.

On further analysis we recognize the language style not to be that common in England. Perhaps this town New England is not in England at all. It could be just as far apart as Dar Es Salaam is from Jerusalem.

Well, all these are excuses to corrupt your mind against the story. This is another example of how corruption enters our thinking system.

This is what the story says:

There once was a man named George Thomas, pastor in a small New England town. One Easter Sunday morning he came to the Church carrying a rusty, bent, old bird cage, and set it by the pulpit.

Eyebrows were raised and, as if in response, Pastor Thomas began to speak, 'I was walking through town yesterday when I saw a young boy coming towards me swinging this bird cage.

'In the bottom of the cage were three little wild birds, shivering with cold and fright. I stopped the lad and asked, 'What you got there, son?'

'Just some old birds,' came the reply

'What are you gonna do with them?' I asked.

'Take 'em home and have fun with 'em,' he answered 'I'm gonna tease 'em and pull out their feathers to make 'em fight. I'm gonna have a real good time'

'But you'll get tired of those birds sooner or later. What will you do?'

'Oh, I got some cats,' said the little boy. 'They like birds. I'll take 'em to them.'

The pastor was silent for a moment. 'How much do you want for those birds, son?'

'Huh?? !!! Why, you don't want them birds, mister. They're just plain old field birds. They don't sing. They ain't even pretty!'

'How much?' the pastor asked again.

The boy sized up the pastor as if he were crazy and said, '$10?'

The pastor reached in his pocket and took out a ten dollar bill. He placed it in the boy's hand. In a flash, the boy was gone.

The pastor picked up the cage and gently carried it to the end of the alley where there was a tree and a grassy spot. Setting the cage down, he opened the door, and by softly tapping the bars persuaded the birds out, setting them free.

Well, that explained the empty bird cage on the pulpit, and then the pastor began to tell this story.

One day Satan and Jesus were having a conversation. Satan had just come from the Garden of Eden, and he was gloating and boasting. 'Yes, sir, I just caught the world full of people down there. Set my trap, used bait I knew they couldn't resist. Got 'em all!'

'What are you going to do with them?' Jesus asked.

Satan replied, 'Oh, I'm gonna have fun! I'm gonna teach them how to marry and divorce each other, how to hate and abuse each other, how to drink and smoke and curse. I'm gonna teach them how to invent guns and bombs and kill each other. I'm really gonna have fun!'

'And what will you do when you get done with them?' Jesus asked.

'Oh, I'll kill 'em,' Satan glared proudly.

'How much do you want for them?' Jesus asked

'Oh, you don't want those people. They ain't no good. Why, you'll take them and they'll just hate you. They'll spit on you, curse you and kill you. You don't want those people!'

'How much?' He asked again.

Satan looked at Jesus and sneered, 'All your blood, tears and your life.'

Jesus said, 'DONE!'

Then He paid the price.

The pastor picked up the cage he opened the door and he walked from the pulpit.

Ezekiel 16:47 (Whole Chapter)

"Yet you have not merely walked in their ways or done according to their abominations; but, as if that were [1 Kin 16:31] too little, you acted [2 Kin 21:9; Ezek 5:6; 16:48, 51] more **corrupt**ly in all your conduct than they.

Ezekiel 20:44 (Whole Chapter)

"Then [Ezek 24:24] you will know that I am the LORD when I have dealt with you [Ezek 36:22] for My name's sake, not according to your evil ways or according to your **corrupt** deeds, O house of Israel," declares the Lord GOD."'

Ezekiel 22:12 (Whole Chapter)

"In you they have [Ex 23:8; Deut 16:19; 27:25; Mic 7:2, 3] taken **bribe**s to shed blood; you have taken [Lev 25:36; Deut 23:19] interest and profits, and you have injured your neighbors for gain by [Lev 19:13] oppression, and you have [Ps 106:21; Ezek 23:35] forgotten Me," declares the Lord GOD.

Ezekiel 23:11 (Whole Chapter)

"Now her sister Oholibah saw this, yet she was [Jer 3:8-11; Ezek 16:51] more **corrupt** in her lust than she, and her harlotries were more than the harlotries of her sister.

Ezekiel 28:17 (Whole Chapter)
"Your heart was lifted up because of your [Ezek 27:3, 4; 28:7] beauty; You [Is 19:11] **corrupt**ed your wisdom by reason of your splendor I cast you to the ground; I put you before [Ezek 26:16] kings, That they may see you.

Are you thinking of someone you have just read about in this book?
Are you thinking of yourself?
I did not mean to cause you sorrow but are you somehow guilty?

Daniel 2:9 (Whole Chapter)
That if you do not make the dream known to me, there is only [Esth 4:11; Dan 3:15] one decree for you For you have agreed together to speak lying and **corrupt** words before me until the situation is changed; therefore tell me the dream, that I may [Is 41:23] know that you can declare to me its interpretation."
Daniel 6:4 (Whole Chapter)
Then the commissioners and satraps began [Gen 43:18; Judg 14:4; Jer 20:10; Dan 3:8; Luke 20:20] trying to find a ground of accusation against Daniel in regard to government affairs; but they could find [Dan 6:22; Luke 20:26; 23:14, 15; Phil 2:15; 1 Pet 2:12; 3:16] no ground of accusation or evidence of **corrupt**ion, inasmuch as he was faithful, and no negligence or **corrupt**ion was to be found in him.
Amos 5:12 (Whole Chapter)
For I know your transgressions are many and your sins are great, You who [Is 1:23; 5:23; Amos 2:6] distress the righteous and accept **bribe**s And turn aside the poor in the gate.
Micah 3:11 (Whole Chapter)
Her leaders pronounce [Is 1:23; Mic 7:3] judgment for a **bribe**, Her [Jer 6:13] priests instruct for a price And her prophets divine for money Yet they lean on the LORD saying," [Is 48:2] Is not the LORD in our midst? Calamity will not come upon us."
Micah 7:3 (Whole Chapter)
Concerning evil, both hands do it [Prov 4:16, 17] well The prince asks, also the judge, for a [Amos 5:12; Mic 3:11] **bribe**, And a great man speaks the desire of his soul; So they weave it together.

Zephaniah 3:7 (Whole Chapter)
"I said, 'Surely you will revere Me, [Job 36:10; Ps 32:8; 1 Tim 1:5] Accept instruction 'So her dwelling will [Jer 7:7] not be cut off According to all that I have appointed concerning her But they were eager to [Hos 9:9] **corrupt** all their deeds.

Malachi 2:8 (Whole Chapter)
"But as for you, you have turned aside from the way; you have caused many to [Jer 18:15] stumble by the instruction; you have [Num 25:12, 13; Neh 13:29; Ezek 44:10] **corrupt**ed the covenant of Levi," says the LORD of hosts.

Romans 1:23 (Whole Chapter)
And [Deut 4:16-18; Ps 106:20; Jer 2:11; Acts 17:29] exchanged the glory of the incorruptible God for an image in the form of **corrupt**ible man and of birds and four-footed animals and [Or reptiles] crawling creatures.

Romans 8:21 (Whole Chapter)
That [Acts 3:21; 2 Pet 3:13; Rev 21:1] the creation itself also will be set free from its slavery to **corrupt**ion into the freedom of the glory of the children of God.

1 Corinthians 15:33 (Whole Chapter)
[1 Cor 6:9] Do not be deceived: "Bad company **corrupt**s good morals."

2 Corinthians 7:2 (Whole Chapter)
[2 Cor 6:12; 12:15] Make room for us in your hearts; we wronged no one, we **corrupt**ed no one, we took advantage of no one.

Galatians 6:8 (Whole Chapter)
[Job 4:8; Hos 8:7; Rom 6:21] For the one who sows to his own flesh will from the flesh reap [1 Cor 15:42] **corrupt**ion, but [Rom 8:11; James 3:18] the one who sows to the Spirit will from the Spirit reap eternal life.

Ephesians 4:22 (Whole Chapter)
That, in reference to your former manner of life, you [Eph 4:25, 31; Col 3:8; Heb 12:1; James 1:21; 1 Pet 2:1] lay aside the [Rom 6:6] old self, which is being **corrupt**ed in accordance with the [2 Cor 11:3; Heb 3:13] lusts of deceit,

2 Peter 1:4 (Whole Chapter)
For by these He has granted to us His precious and magnificent [2 Pet 3:9, 13] promises, so that by them you may

become [Eph 4:13, 24; Heb 12:10; 1 John 3:2] partakers of the divine nature, having [2 Pet 2:18, 20] escaped the [2 Pet 2:19] **corrupt**ion that is in [James 1:27] the world by lust.

2 Peter 2:10 (Whole Chapter)

And especially those who [2 Pet 3:3; Jude 16, 18] indulge the flesh in its **corrupt** desires and [Ex 22:28; Jude 8] despise authority. Daring, [Titus 1:7] self-willed, they do not tremble when they [Ex 22:28; Jude 8] revile angelic majesties,

2 Peter 2:19 (Whole Chapter)

Promising them freedom while they themselves are slaves of **corrupt**ion; for [John 8:34; Rom 6:16] by what a man is overcome, by this he is enslaved.

Revelation 19:2 (Whole Chapter)

[Ps 19:9] BECAUSE HIS [Rev 6:10] JUDGMENTS ARE [Rev 16:7] TRUE AND RIGHTEOUS; for He has judged the [Rev 17:1] great harlot who was **corrupt**ing the earth with her immorality, and HE HAS [Deut 32:43; 2 Kin 9:7; Rev 16:6; 18:20] AVENGED THE BLOOD OF HIS BOND-SERVANTS ON HER."

If the entire world could hear the words of George Thomas what would happen? Or if the words of George Thomas could make sense to you, would you have anything in your life that you would ever attempt to change?

It may be hard for you to accept but sooner or later, you will need to acknowledge the fact that our bodies are bombarded by a huge number of thoughts, perhaps in thousands every minute and a vast amount of that finds its way into our brain. Some thoughts come through the foods that we eat daily, some through drinks, some through the air that we breathe in and some through our eyes, skin and ears. Health experts believe that these thoughts create a long list of diseases spreading from heart diseases to cancer and lunacy. Wise people are now putting aside some time and energy to remove these body corruptions and start a new and healthier way to prosperity

If you were ever given a chance to live your life again, a brain detox and a change in your daily activity plan may be just the thing that you need for a better, prosperous future.

There are plenty of means to change your belief system and some may necessitate some changes in the way you sleep and the way you wake up. If you were living in some relationship which you know pretty well is against God's law and then in the other ear you hear God loud and clear offering you the chance to make money; offering you the opportunity to live beyond riches on the bargain that you break that relationship, you would opt for methods that you are comfortable with. For the most part, failure to complete a journey to prosperity is mainly because you have chosen regulations that change your daily life too much and later find it hard to stick with the rules. Do not be too hard on either yourself or on your corrupt brother. If you are really interested in anti-corruption measures and want to move quickly to prosperity you can begin the detoxification process by reducing the amount of authority you give to yourself and surrender more and more to someone who is ready and willing to carry it. There is always someone willing to help. Depression is caused by carrying more than you can lift. Casting your burden on someone else gives you rest. You will discover that you would love your new life at the start but fatigue and boredom will come in to reverse your thinking. This occurs because you want to have some help but you do not want to get your mind off the task.

What actually happens is that when you chase ugly thoughts out of your head, your brain becomes less congested, clean and clear. You feel good and strong. The expelled thoughts meanwhile are out roaming the universe looking for whom to devour. They find none and reinforce themselves, regroup and return to recapture their lost territory. Should they find you unaware they will destroy your stronghold and re enter their old fortress.

It is therefore very important that when you win the first battle against corruption you do not leave your new stronghold unguarded. Bring in a new tenant stronger than you. He will guard your home and train your ear to sieve through what it hears, train your eyes to choose what to see. He will above all train your mouth to speak only after thinking and also train it not to allow in foods that have high level of alcohol, saturated fats, or sugar. Smoking has also been identified as one of the major contributors to corruption. It cannot be by mare coincidence that most criminals are smokers. He will stop your mouth to smoke.

You are very safe with your trainer resident in your brain. Soon or later you will not be led by your feelings. You will believe in the existence of absolute truth. Your thoughts will follow your belief and lead your feelings. You will think before you speak and speak before you act.

You will become a very efficient person in all that you do. At delivering public service you will be praiseworthy. The world will look at you and call you Corrupt-Free. They will honour you with a promotion. That is what happened when Lowassa fell. His unknown secretary Pinto was appointed the new Prime Minister. We have many reasons for rejecting corruption.

Renewing your mind will bring you many rewards. Lowassa could have gone to jail. On the Thursday following his resignation many Legislative Counselors from the ruling party called for arrest and seizure of his assets. No such punishments ever came out. Lowassa did not exhibit fear but renewal of the mind.

Remember this when you are caught under a campaign of smear. Forget yourself and reach out to please someone else. Do exactly what Lowassa did. Instead of hiding and engaging himself in a monologue he went out to a public rally and left his shameful past behind him and looked towards the future. He did not seek justice but mercy.

It is shameful to be poor. Work on getting rich. Do not despair because justice may not rule in your favour. Where justice fails we still have mercy. Mercy is a fine for all sins. Our bail is paid by mercy. Make up your mind to spend the rest of your life happy. You cannot be selfish and happy at the same time. Change your attitude and seek good out of every situation. Move on and make others happy. In pleasing others you will find your own joy. Turn this habit into your character. Practice good manners persistently. When your head tells you to receive a bribe and your mind says, "Don't", follow your mind. It will not be long before you reach prosperity. The promise of this book is that God will take care of all the revenges you deserve and he will supply your needs. He will overfill you with joy. That is prosperity. To hell with corruption! Forward with prosperity. To hell with poverty. Forward to Prosperity. The desire of all ages is Prosperity. Let us go and get it.

CHAPTER TWENTY TWO

GOLD

This storybook now takes you back to a time after the Chinese Investor had visited Mbeya.

The company had just completed an Environmental Impact Assessment and Feasibility Study on the Chunya Gold Project in the Lupa Goldfields. Chunya is one of the eight districts of Mbeya Administrative Region. A mining license application had been submitted to the relevant authorities and approved. The company's intention was to develop the project into a profitable mining operation but more importantly volunteered to use part of its profits to build schools, hospitals and roads. It would pay taxes as usual. With increased resources the government would have more funds at hand to spend on poverty-relief measures like free primary schooling, affordable medication and distribution of medicated bed nets for pregnant mothers and children- under-the-age-of-five, give every citizen sanitized drinking water and perhaps a right to vote. These are the benchmarks the world counts as measurements in changing a nation from poverty to prosperity.

Abed made a deal. He went to Chunya and convinced small mine diggers not to sell their gold nuggets to collectors in Tanzania. They would get better value for their gold if they sold it to China directly. They had to do this quite quick before mineral-hungry neo colonialists would come down to Chunya to eat up the land. Abed argued that poverty is slavery and a poor man shall always be a slave to the rich; a borrower shall be a slave to the lender; a poor landowner shall mortgage his property and live like a squatter. We cannot pull ourselves out of the pit but we can avoid being buried down the pit. If we pulled ourselves together other than pulling ourselves down we would turn this living from crab race to human race.

Who would carry the gold to China or who would bring a buyer from China down to Tanzania?

The answer was me.

I was introduced by Abed to the local council officials in Lupa and to the Mbeya Region Area Commissioner for Mines.

The arrangement was that permit would be given to Abed's company to export 50kg of gold to China. The buying company however would be required to pay on behalf of the miners all the taxes and expenses prior to the export. The miners would entrust their gold to the Lupa Council. The council would give Abed the gold. Abed and I would travel to China together. I would sell the gold at least US 25,000 per kilogram and all the amount I would make above that would be my payment. I would remit US 1,250,000 from China within five days after sale to the council who would in turn distribute it to the miners each according to ones collection. Each miner would pay Abed a commission of 5% of the money one would receive.

All went well. A shipping agent was found. He advised that cargo would be airlifted from Mbeya to the tax free port of Hongkong. We checked all the documents and all looked fine.

Abed and I flew from Mbeya to Dar Es Salaam. There was some more paper work to be done in Dar including obtaining visas to Hongkong. The buyer from China would collect and pay for his goods on arrival at Hongkong.

We were booked on Qatar Airways flight. At 1.00 pm we were at Julius Nyerere International Airport awaiting a 2.30 pm plane to Hongkong. The agent arrived at 1.30 pm and gave the Export Licence, Certificate of Ownership and the air ticket to Abed. He however said that the goods had been only airlifted to Doha, Qatar. As we would change the planes there, we would pick up the goods and carry them as extra heavy hand luggage to Hongkong. All the expenses and permits for the change of cargo status had already been made. We were convinced this arrangement gave us an extra chance to ensure that our cargo was on board.

We arrived in Doha. We went to claim the cargo. There was no such cargo. We were advised to check with the shipper. I hate to say this but my mind opened up that we had been cheated. We quickly decided against missing our connection to Hongkong. Empty handed we flew to Hongkong.

We arrived at the airport. My wife Letty, children Faith, Grace, Justice and Joy were all there. My friends and officials from the Chinese Investor company were there. Security guards were there. What was not there was happiness. Grief was there.

I could not explain where the cargo was. How had I lost the cargo? This was Abed's second visit to Hongkong. He hated Hongkong the first time. He feared it this time.

Abed phoned his mother in Mozambique. She said she would pray for him. It sounded like usual Christian rhetoric. It wasn't. She asked him what he wanted her to pray for. She explained that whatever one prays for in the name of Jesus, with belief, one gets. She told him to believe first that the cargo would be found before she prayed that it could be found.

"Yes, Mum," he answered.

I told you at the beginning of this book that it is not what you feel that changes your circumstances. It is what you believe. Do you believe that Abed recovered the gold?

If you say, 'I don't know,' I will reserve my answer too but I will ask you another question. Do you believe the baptism of John was fake or genuine? I mean that guy who wore animal skins and went baptizing people, swearing at them as brood of vipers and calling them to leave their ways and follow him. We call him John the Baptist but by whose authority was he baptizing?

Let me paraphrase my question. Do you think that Abed could recover the gold? There is a difference in the two questions above.

You have heard of the story of a man called Jonah?

This was a man who was sent by God to carry some message to people of one city but thought it wiser to carry the message to a different city. He heard God loud and clear but thought it wiser to go to Tarshish instead of Nineveh. He boarded a ship of men who clearly did not believe in God but left the ship when they were converted. He told them his story and they believed him. Like in a funny movie they threw him off board. God sent him a rescue fish that swallowed him and vomited him on land after three days.

People die because of lack of knowledge. Call it ignorance. There is a book of Jonah in the Bible you can read the full story for yourself. The question is: Do you think Jonah stayed in the fish belly alive or dead? Asking the question the other way: Do you believe Jonah died for three days and three nights and came back to life when the fish vomited him out?

I do not accept, "I do not know" for an answer. Do you believe he died in the fish belly or not?

Jonah himself describes his life in the fish belly. The book of Jonah says, "From inside the fish Jonah prayed to the LORD his God." What does this make you think?

He said: "In my distress I called to the LORD, and he answered me. From the depths of the grave I called for help, and you listened to my cry. You hurled me into the deep, into the very heart of the seas, and the currents swirled about me; all your waves and breakers swept over me".

Do you believe that Abed could recover the gold? Abed's mother told him to pray and believe in his heart that he had already got whatever he prayed for even if he had not seen the results of his prayer yet.

Jonah said, 'I have been banished from your sight; yet I will look again toward your holy temple.'

We are what we believe.

"The engulfing waters threatened me", said Jonah. "The deep surrounded me; seaweed was wrapped around my head. To the roots of the mountains I sank down; the earth beneath barred me in forever".

What do you think or believe this 'forever' thing mean? Do you believe he died in the fish belly or not? What was the result of Jonah's belief?

"But you brought my life up from the pit, O LORD my God." Do you believe he was talking about his hard circumstances or he was referring to resurrecting from death?

"When my life was ebbing away", (or when it seemed all over), "I remembered you, LORD, and my prayer rose to you, to your holy temple".

What was Jonah's prayer? What was Abed's prayer?

Jonah remembered the message he was carrying to Ninevah. He recited it to the Lord. He said, "Those who cling to worthless idols forfeit the grace that could be theirs." He added a persuading argument, "But I, with a song of thanksgiving, will sacrifice to you. What I have vowed I will make good. Salvation comes from the LORD."

Salvation comes from the LORD. Where does prosperity come from?

"And the LORD commanded the fish, and it vomited Jonah onto dry land." Do you believe Abed recovered the Gold?

"Chances are that if he did it was a miracle".

We are what we believe. If you believe, "Those who cling to worthless ideas forfeit the grace that could be theirs." you could start composing your Thanksgiving song now. If God could command a fish to rescue Jonah can you still say, "Where shall my help come from?"

Abed's mother insisted that recovery of gold depended on what Abed believed and wanted to pray for. She told him of Prophet Ezekiel and the miracle of dry bones. The prophet found himself in middle of a valley full of human bones. He walked through them a number of times to recognize that they were very dry.

God asked the prophet, "Son of man, can these bones live?" This is what I asked you: Do you believe that Abed could recover the gold?

The prophet answered, "O Sovereign LORD, you alone know." In defense the prophet believed that whatever God said was possible. His answer was not an "I don't know". So God told the believer, "Prophesy to these bones and say to them, 'Dry bones, hear the word of the LORD! This is what the Sovereign LORD says: I will make breath enter you, and you will come to life. I will attach tendons to you and make flesh come upon you and cover you with skin; I will put breath in you, and you will come to life. Then you will know that I am the LORD.'"

So he did as commanded. As he did, there was a noise, a rattling sound, and the bones came together, bone to bone. He looked as tendons and flesh appeared on them and skin covered them, but it was noticed there was no breath in them. They were like dead bodies.

This is what happened to Abed. Yes there were moments when he could feel that he could recover the gold, or the insurance company could compensate him or the local council could give him a reasonable period of time to pay up the miners. A miracle could happen to turn dry bones to dead bodies and that would be it!

Then God said, "Prophesy to the breath; prophesy, son of man, and say to it, 'This is what the Sovereign LORD says: Come from the four winds, O breath, and breathe into these slain, that they may live.' "So he prophesied as he was commanded and breath entered them; they came to life and stood up on their feet—a vast army.

Now do you believe prayers can perform miracles? Do you believe Abed mother's prayer could return the gold?

Then God said these bones were those people who say, "Our bones are dried up and our hope is gone; we are cut off.' Therefore prophesy and say to them: "This is what the Sovereign LORD says: O my people, I am going to open your graves and bring you up from them; I will bring you back to the land of Israel. Then you, my people, will know that I am the LORD, when I open your graves and bring you up from them. I will put my Spirit in you and you will live, and I will settle you in your own land. Then you will know that I the LORD have spoken, and I have done it, declares the LORD.'"

Having read this lesson this far do you believe the gold was recovered? If you were Abed what would you tell your mother to pray for? Would you pray that the judge may be lenient? Would you pray that the swindler may burn in hell? Would you pray for forgiveness or mercy?

What Abed needed was a miracle. He locked himself in his hotel room and prayed. He prayed and did not doubt. He went through the scriptures his mother referred to and studied them the way he studied his father's Letter from the Grave. He swore not to doubt. There are moments when scary thoughts wanted to enter his head. He slapped his face and said to them: I will not think of you.

Abed cried, "Teach me, O Lord, to follow your decrees; then I will keep them to the end. Give me understanding, and I will keep your law and obey it with all my heart. Direct me in the path of your commands, for there I find delight. Turn my heart towards your statues and not towards selfish gain. Turn my eyes away from worthless things; preserve my life according to your word. Fulfil your promise to your servant so that you may be feared. Take away the disgrace I dread, for your laws are good. How I long for your precepts! Preserve my life in your righteousness."

Do you believe Abed recovered the Gold? Do you believe Jonah died for three days and three nights and came back to life when the fish vomited him out?

This is what Jesus said of the incident, ""A wicked and adulterous generation asks for a miraculous sign! But none will be given it except the sign of the prophet Jonah. For as Jonah was three days and three nights in the belly of a huge fish, so the Son of Man will be three days and three nights in the heart of the earth."

Was Jesus for three days and three nights dead or alive in the tomb? What do you believe? It is what you believe that guides your thinking. If he was there alive then he did not rise again from death or there is no resurrection what so ever. If you believe he died then you can think that death is not the end of life. You can believe that dead bones could live again and Abed could pray and recover the gold. We are what we believe. The purpose of this book is to make you believe that even if our bones are dried up, our income is below US$ 1 a day but our hope is not gone; we can raise from poverty to prosperity.

Abed returned to Tanzania. Saying farewell he told us that he was going back to Tanzania to pick up the cargo. There was no sign of it at that moment. He did not know how he was going to do it but his faith saved him. He made a lot of money and like Jonah he said, "What I have vowed I will make good." He did.

How did he do it?

Man is snared by his own words. Your words can give you comfort or can scare you. The process you go through formulating those words can be literary a burden to you. If it is too heavy it creates stress and depression and if it is light and easy it creates joy and happiness. The way you make out your words follows your feeling, thinking and believing.

Jesus used his words positively. He said, "I'm the Truth, the Way and Life". These are very nice qualities to have and each one of them brings peace to the beholder. You cannot sit on a chair unless you trust it is firm. You cannot seek treatment from a doctor whose qualifications you do not trust. The first principle of the belief theory is to know whom or what you believe in.

When you believe in a great God, a Miracle worker, Deliverer, Rewarder, Redeemer then you are expecting miracles, deliverance, rewards and redemption. It is whom you believe in that determines what you believe and it is what you believe that determines what you think. It is what you think that determines what you feel. And it is what you feel that you get. If you have no spirit of expectancy there is no need to pray. Go to hell! Otherwise if you have faith and do not doubt, not only can you solve a problem but you can tell a mountain to come and it comes or to go away and it obeys.

If Abed could make it you too can. There are moments when plans look like dry bones, lost ventures, dead bodies; do not lose hope. Here are old, proven strategies to reclaim your time and feel less rushed and less stressed. Yes, there is a chance to move from poverty to prosperity with no possibility of falling back.

Dr.Luke in a book called <u>Luke</u> talked of a farmer who went out to sow his seed. As he sprayed out the seeds some fell along the path. Some were trampled on and some were eaten up by birds. Some fell among stones and just dried up soon after germination. Some fell among weeds which choked it up with time. The rest fell in the farm and grew up well in yields.

Jesus explained that actually the seed is the word of Truth. Those along the path are the ones who hear the word and doubt comes and takes away the belief from their heart and they are filled with suspicion, fear and acrimony. Those who fell among stones are double minded people who cannot live long with their faith. Roots cannot penetrate stones. With moisture plants may germinate but they are doomed to die in a short space of time. Those who fell in the weeds are people whose faith cannot carry them through their situation. They are choked by worries, riches, pleasures and failures. They never mature. They die young. They die poor. They retire in poverty. To them prosperity is a figment of imagination. There are those however who grow up in the farm they were meant to grow in. Those who live to the character they were created in. These live to prosperity.

In the beginning of this book I said that the writing has not been easy. I started with great excitement but after writing a few chapters I realized that I was not writing what I wanted to write and instead I was writing what I did not want to write. For months I gave up the project then I had a dream and I saw words clearly inscribed on a wall: God, Gold, You and Godless. I stayed hours in bed half awake and half asleep trying to interpret my dream. This book is the result of that vision. If I were to title it anything else, I would have called it: God, Gold, You and Godless

We were seated in a hall listening to an American Revival Church Evangelist who had just been released from the dungeons of the dictatorial communist regime of China. He had been arrested for carrying books across the border. They charged him as a smuggler and yet all he did was to give some 500 Bibles to his friend in China.

The audience of course was divided. Some were saying indeed the speaker was a smuggler others were calling him a liberator. Like Abed's father he was both a hero and a felony.

On the notice board were those famous words: God, Gold, You and Godless. May be this was the theme of the discussion. On the pulpit however were a globe and a fruit to the best of my description that looked like a pumpkin with peelings of a banana.

I wanted to eat this pumpkin but the peelings were a menace. As I peeled off one layer a new layer quickly grew up replacing the old one. I tried to peel as fast as I could but the faster I peeled the faster too grew the replacements. I lost the speaker busy peeling this fruit. Eventually I got a knife and just sliced the peelings off. I cut deep and deep into the fruit removing several layers. I noticed one thing. The out layer was yellow. I peeled that off. Then inside was another layer of water melon. I peeled that too. There was another layer of a carrot. There was another layer of another unknown fruit. I peeled off one layer and I found another layer. Peeled that layer off and found another one. None of these layers were edible .They were just peelings.

I asked God, "What does this mean?"

He answered, "You cannot mix your things with my things."

I warned the light-hearted. Looking for prosperity can be scary. This might be getting tougher. I know what I am saying is true because I wrote the book and I went back editing and editing it a number of times but the more I read it the more I got scared of my own writing. Yes, you can be scared of your own writing as parents can be scared of their own children!

It was scary. What was wrong with me? How were my plans different from God's plans?

We are told that when we pray we may not get what we pray for because God studies our motives and sees that what we say with our hearts is different from what we say with our lips. We need to line up our prayer life such that what we pray is indeed what is in our hearts and indeed is what we believe.

I kept on peeling. Two peelings off and one peeling on. Three peelings off and two peelings back. Five peelings off and three peelings anew. Eventually all peelings were removed and I had a small golden seed. I tried to cut it. It could not be cut. I tried to scratch it and it could not be scratched. I put it in boiling water. It was not a carrot. It was not an egg. It was not a coffee bean. I put it in a bottle of Sulphuric acid and it could not change. Wow, I knew what I had. It was gold!

This chapter is about gold.

Abed returned to Tanzania. Saying farewell he told us that he was going back to Tanzania to pick up the cargo. There was no sign of it at that moment. He did not know how he was going to do it but his faith led him.

The rest of the story is found in Abed's telephone message box. These are private exchanges between Abed and his mother. They are reproduced with special permission. They have not been presented in any special order. I wanted to arrange them in a kind of question and answer form but I could not have been accurate. I have left this for you to do. As an academic exercise, pull out all Outbox messages and all Inbox messages and arrange them in the order that to you they may have happened. Sincerely this can turn out to be a memory-improving task.

Outbox: I have called the Shipper's Number and the Airport Police answered. They said they would brief me later. Maybe he was trying to steal out the cargo. I believe God is answering. Our mission is not in doubt.

Outbox: This time I do not fear. We shall overcome. May our vision be met.

Outbox: This is real ministry. I can understand Luke 4:41. God rebuked Satan attack.

Outbox: Luke 14:1-14 pray because just woke up with fear that I have the collateral but the shipment documents not yet with me till now. Pray I get them early morning. They were due today. Opened Bible to Luke

Outbox: I was in church. It is ok to avoid gossiping and divisions to mention the need without mentioning names.

Outbox : On the way to pick up 3kg of collateral, test at govt office and pay. Pray this is critical time. Jane is not here. I wanted to wait for her but my shipper is in hurry. Pray.

Outbox: Praise our victory is at hand. The meeting that broke down the last obstacle took only 5 min but we had worried for 3 days. Casting trouble to Christ is a way of solving problems.

Outbox: Phil1: 9-11

Outbox: My concern the people might be pretending there is a problem and they ask for more money or not send the cargo.

Outbox: Positive thinking is my direction. Doubt is the opposite of faith. The burden is not mine. Anyway if they had wanted to play tricks why do they keep calling me? My trust not in them but in Savior.

Outbox: Airway Bill 157-14127643 on Qatar Airways leaving Jun 22 Arriving 23 at 4.30 pm can be seen at www.qrcargo.com

Outbox: This morning we see commissioner about rescuing cargo. My mind says they were tricking us but GOD protected us. Chinese wants to pay but I said wait till I check up first.

Outbox: We should look to God not to circumstances. We pray to HIM not to them.

Outbox: When we pray he is in our midst. Let us claim our success.

Outbox: Cannot looking now for cargo agency feeling not easy carrying it. The men at airport may create excuse to disturb us, so we cargo it.

Outbox: After prayer I asked for wisdom. See 1 John 3:21-4.6

Outbox: Last time I had no money so I did not go to see but there is so much around. Want see easy. Trials start after saying ok. Pray for sign and guidance.

Outbox: woke up to pray. Today pay or not pay.

Outbox: Money arrived. Tomorrow shipping.

Inbox: so tired I want to sleep . SMS you later.

Inbox. Can chat now.

Inbox: Still at work.

Inbox : Read Matthew 21: 21-22

Inbox: It is true we have already experienced in other cases. Power is in His word. Speak with your lips that those people will not be able to cheat but to do the business properly.

Inbox; Prophesy that there would be no problem and that they send the goods. Nothing is impossible with God. His word is our shield and protector.

Inbox: I am not worried if GOD is giving those wealth to us. No one can stop because all things are possible to God.

Inbox: May be that is a message from GOD for us.

Inbox: Before you told me God told you, 'Don't mix up my work with other things' may be this is the other thing God is talking about. Just calm down ask God what to do next.

Inbox: Pray to God to give you wisdom. Open the Bible and read and what God is telling.

Inbox: Okey know that in everything God is in control. Just have hope, faith and belief and it will be done.

Inbox: Isaiah 12: 1-6 only when day come people sing, praise GOD now comfort me his anger has ended, he is our savior, trust him, not be afraid, give us power and strength, people rejoice, give thanks to God, tell nation he is great, sing to the Lord Holy God is great, he lives among his people.

Inbox: Praise the Lord the Holy Spirit is leading me. I always pray for God's protection over my children, you and and I need to do that also for 2 other or more people. Pray together God is in midst of them all. Tell this to others too.

Inbox: Amen just claim it. Fear is from Satan, hope faith and belief is from God. He will give us victory as he used to do in the past.

Inbox: Yes God is in control and he knows our motives, the money we get can build hospitals, schools, roads, etc in Africa.

Inbox: Yes, Sirach 48:20 but they prayed to the merciful Lord, the Holy one in heaven who quickly answered their prayers and sent Isaiah to save Hezekiah and his people from the attack of Sennacherib.

Inbox: When there is a big problem praise and worship God. Apply it when you face challenges in your life and GOD will show his miraculous supernatural power.

Inbox: Satan wants to frighten you. Rebuke him to leave you in the name of Jesus. Amen.

Inbox: Just need for you and me to pray for God's protection on those goods that no loss on the way, nobody will be in trouble, clear them in custom easily and get our share ASAP.

Inbox: Yes Jesus said believe what you pray you have already received. Surely your father in heaven will do it.

Inbox: In the message we need to prophesy that the gold people won't cheat us and that our God will give us victory.

Inbox: You need to pray. I did and opened the Bible at Ezekiel 37. The Valley of Dry Bones. God told Ezekiel to prophesy to the bones. He did and God brought them back to life. Then they knew God does whatever he promises.

Inbox: Good. GOD gives you wisdom. Use it. We need to enjoy GOD every day, have jubilee and to have a deep intimate relationship with HIM.

Inbox: Ok. He wants us to trust and believe in him alone as we pray.

Inbox: That is what my spirit is also telling me.

Inbox: Ok .pray peoples' cooperation to handle business properly, not cheat that we have successful business deal. Isaiah 30:18 The lord is awaiting your prayer.

Inbox: Did u see the gold? Ask God to give you sign to pay or not. Only God knows what to do. Pray money not lost.

There are moments when you are about to achieve something good and an interruption occurs and you lose your focus. It is said Pope Simon Peter 1 walked on water while his eyes were focused on Jesus. He walked on and on like Abed's father. What made him sink where Abed's father did not was one moment when he looked at the storm and lost his site. He took his eyes off faith, off self-confidence, and sank. We should not trust in circumstances but in God. The circumstances might be as good as our Dar-Hongkong arrangements but the devil knows belief removes doubt and belief can lead to success and success can lead into trusting God and therefore not good for him.

He manipulates the circumstances so that your faith may not grow. You are partakers of a divine nature. Claim your victory over your circumstances for whoever believes can move mountains Dr.Luke said. He was a trustworthy doctor. Truly, truly, I say to you, "We give glory to God not to circumstances. We pray to God not to circumstances".

The city of Tanga in Tanzania has a story of its mayor who went to war. A grenade was thrown at him He commanded the grenade in the name of Jesus not to explode and it obeyed. Who is this man that even grenades could obey?

This gift is for whoever believes. This is why I said to you and I have I said it before but I can repeat it here. When you stay with poor people you realize one other factor why they never move out of poverty. They move in circles. When a rich man consults you and you give him an advice he values, he immediately leaves whatever he is doing and implements the advice right away. The poor are not like that. They go away as if determined and then they start thinking negatively of your advice. "What if this problem arises?" they say. The next day they will be having complaints and excuses. We must not grow weary of helping others or better put we should not be worn out by others.

We should peel off excuses. Peel off condemnation. Peel off self pity. Peel off saying we are not good enough. When we were at Mafia Island Jane told us that she could not peel off prostitution because she was not good enough for Christianity. When she peeled it off however she became the lady of fortune she is today. She is the Mary Magdalene of our time.

Abed arrived in Tanzania. He swore to tell the truth and only the truth. It was difficult for him of course. Satan kept on reminding him that it was because of telling the truth that his father was executed. Like father like son his life was going to end. Abed struck at the devil: He would rather die for a cause other than live a life of a common criminal.

God is pleased when we move back to him other than doubt him. We are not redeemed by gold or by dollars or by the blood of our fathers. We were ordained to prosper by the blood of Jesus Christ. Satan hates confession especially this kind of confession. I surely tell you this sentence can affect this book sale.

If however Abed recovered the gold so can you recover whatever you have ever lost. You cannot lose your prosperity. I tell you the truth. Abed recovered the gold. Knowing your destiny makes you walk with purpose. Integrity is always rewarded. Peel off all malice and all guile and insincerity and envy and all slander. You cannot mix belief with doubt. You cannot mix faith with fear. You cannot mix God's spirit with human spirit. You must lose one and gain the other. You have only one choice here. Abed picked the right choice. He opposed himself against lying. He opposed himself against putting up a front. He opposed himself against pretending that he was better off than everybody else. He opposed himself against making others believe what was not true. He forgot himself and he recovered the gold.

CHAPTER TWENTY THREE

MEMORY

Let me start this chapter by asking you whether you are happy with what you have read so far. Are you happy? How happy are you? Are you going to keep this happiness forever? Do you want to be happy once in a while or consistently happy? If you were given a choice to keep yourself happy or to keep others happy what choice would you take? Who is responsible for your happiness?

Now think deeper. In a world full of extreme pain, dysfunction, distress, social problems, and death or similar problems for those in contact with the afflicted person, who can be but unhappy? How can we be so insensitive to a world bedeviled with injuries, disabilities, disorders, syndromes, infections, isolated symptoms, deviant behaviors, and atypical variations of structure and function? Who can be happy in a world which God himself once wanted to disown? Who can be happy in a world drenched in poverty, chaos, prostitution and corruption?

A disease is an abnormal condition of an organism that impairs bodily functions that the victim may not act whole or at ease. We say the victim is diseased. We say the country is poor.

Some diseases such as flu are spread by contact or by inhalation. Malaria is transmitted by mosquito bites. Sexually transmitted diseases are spread by prostitution. Some diseases can be beaten by changes in lifestyle, changes in hygiene or changes in eating habits. Many diseases (including some cancers, heart disease and mental disorders) have a propeller or a gene in our bodies that they use to direct our lives. There are other diseases like pregnancy, poverty, hunger, thirst and aging which are transmitted from one generation to another, go detected but hardly treated.

A condition may be considered to be a disease in some cultures or areas but not in others. Similarly poverty is generally considered to be undesirable due to the pain and suffering it may cause but in certain spiritual contexts we ask God to curse our enemies with it. Poverty can be used as a weapon against corruption. Prisons are built to reverse ones fortune to poverty. When a man is sent to jail some people will celebrate others will wail. It is all a question of our attitude. If you consider Tanzania a poor country you may not invest in it but if you look at its mineral resources you may call investing in Tanzania a golden opportunity. You could make much money, easily and with joy. You could meet your life needs and you could define your life as prosperous.

Many poor people are treated like mosquitoes. When mosquitoes bite someone, they do not inject own blood or the blood of an animal or person bitten into the next person. The mosquito injects saliva, which acts as a lubricant so that it can feed more effectively. Yellow fever and malaria can be transmitted through the saliva. For biting human beings all mosquitoes are given a cover punishment. All must be beaten to death. They may be suspected of spreading AIDS despite what we already know that HIV does not reproduce in insects, and therefore cannot survive in the mosquito long enough to be transmitted in the saliva. Poor people are lazy. They may write on your car insults or steal rear mirrors. Mosquitoes do not actually travel from one person to another after ingesting blood, sucking from one and vomiting into another. These insects need time to digest the blood meal before moving on. Poor people do not steal cars. They would need fuel. They write words like 'Wash me' on dirty cars only. Think of it the other way. They are only writing an application for a car washing job!

Sicknesses confer on the victim the right to being looked after by others and in return an obligation on the sick person to seek treatment and work to become well once more.

Poverty is deprivation of those things that determine the prosperity of life, including food, clothing, shelter, safe-drinking water, opportunity to learn and to enjoy the respect of others. Poverty confers on the victim the right to being looked after by others and in turn an obligation on the poor person to seek assistance and work to become well once more.

The psychology of positive thinking always picks something good out of a mess and focuses its success on that. We do not need to curl and condemn our entire existence into unhappiness simply because we have been found with a 'poverty' virus. It is our obligation to seek assistance and work to become well once more. Every individual is responsible for one's own happiness.

I have often said how I admired the young men and women reading this book. I in the same strength condemn the young men and women who read this book and do nothing about what it says. They read it the way we often read a Bible or a Koran. We agree with the authors that it is a good book full of wisdom but choose to follow our own foolishness, anyway. On my part book sales push me towards prosperity and I therefore seek your assistance to push me forward. I believe, think, feel, say and act like a millionaire. By behaving like a millionaire I become one. If you cannot see the difference between me and a millionaire it means I have reached the end of the journey. .

I have said it before that we have to change our poverty-driven stinking thinking to prosperous-driven glory and glamour thinking. I said before that it is not a question of how to change one's thinking but actually what to do to change the thinking. I called the Desire of All Ages a guided tour to prosperity. I have therefore decided to walk you through steps that might improve your memory.

What is the name of the man who took me to Morogoro? If you could not remember find the name on page 159. If you knew just read on.

The idea of telling you to open the book and read again is giving you one technique of improving your memory. Good thinking depends on good memory. As much as you are responsible for your own happiness you are responsible for your own thinking and you are responsible for keeping your memory sharp. Using your right finger as a pen, write the name in your left palm. Reverse if you are left handed. This air-writing can help you remember telephone numbers or help you check your bill in a store. It is environment friendly. The savings on ink you might make by the end of the year could be significant enough in your drive towards prosperity.

When you try to cram names or phone numbers in your head you may feel the stress as physical pain in the brain. You were advised in the above chapter to sweep out bad thoughts from your head and rent your brain to a new tenant. The new tenant will teach you to write on your palm with your finger, train you to talk with your hands. Scientists now agree that delegating some talking to the hands, eyes and mouth saves the latter from talking all the time. People who gesture with their bodies talk less yet communicate more. The reduced task on the mouth allows the mouth to spare some time and talk after thinking. Psychologists now agree that lowering your stress level by delegating your work to some other people, or creating Task Forces lowers your stress and limits chances of suffering from depression. Without depression you will be left with untreated anger as the only known cause of your poverty. Purging negative relationships and thoughts out of your life will speed you up to prosperity. Instead of choosing one-dollar-a-day income you may be able to pick 10-dollars-a-day.

Now I hope you know that it was Hosef who took me to Morogoro.

Why did he take me to Morogoro? To eat mangoes or to show Morogoro mines.

These could be right answers but the untold reason is that Hosef was born in Morogoro. I learnt in doing work on this book that there is some strange nature in man that pulls every man back to his home. Investments begin at home. For that same reason Abed started business life by investing in Mozambique. Kato invited Abed to Japan and majority of people invite you to invest in their own home areas. The main reason why we go back home is to sleep. Sleeping is so much related to death that in it we find rest. "Sleep on it" when you are faced with a problem or difficult decision. It is fine to have a free weekend or free time and do nothing to occupy it. If someone comes and asks what you are doing tell him that you are not riding a dead donkey you are busy resting. Deciding to go to bed and going to bed without doing anything else in between (no TV, no music or no phone call) improves your sleeping, memory, decision making and speeds up your transit to prosperity. You will then have more time in life to enjoy your goodness. You will retire young and retire rich.

Another exercise is here for you. What does Belief>Thoughts >Words>Feelings>Action mean to you? In terms of what you eat how can you change your diet to improve your wealth?

Discussing what you have read with other people can greatly improve your memory. In your own words can you recall the story of Namaan? If you can tell it as if you were an eye witness then you could consider joining a book club? By mastering the story and how to put it to others in a manner they can understand will improve your chances of convincing your Task Force of your new plans. Talking is sifting ideas, sorting them out, rearranging them and packaging them into proper words. The way you speak reflects the amount of wisdom in your head. Giving the public to choose between calling you wise or dumb is giving them too many choices. The foundation of prosperity is wisdom. Work on your memory. Work on your thinking. Work on your wisdom. This is your investment.

You need to exercise your brain as much as you would need to exercise your legs. It is said that when Mr.Mwinyi lost the post as the Minister of Internal affairs overlooking the police during the riots, he undertook to running across Zanzibar Island as his morning exercise. The end result of it is that many young men joined his team, pushed him to electing him the President of Zanzibar and then of Tanzania as a whole. A mare physical exercise can move you from poverty to prosperity. Exercise improves blood flow in the brain, improves your memory and thinking. With improved thinking, you can speak articulately, feel good, behave well and act prosperous. You are not prosperous when you are eating fast foods and chips or when you cannot meet your needs. When you act prosperous you are prosperous. The purpose of this guide is to see that you can turn from poverty to prosperity with no chance of falling back. What makes people fall back is loss of memory.

In this chapter we have already mentioned five ways of improving your memory. Count them off your fingers. Start by clamping your fingers in a fist and release one finger one by one as you recall the different ways of improving your memory.

You can see how this finger-talking is a great tool in improving your memory. If you cannot get the five tips you may re-read the chapter and this will do great to your memory. The number of times you read the word 'memory' in this paragraph enforces what this chapter is all about. Reputation assists learning. You may even discover that more than five tips to improving your memory have been mentioned. Now you can improve this hand exercise by doing more of those jobs than can be done with your fingers in a fist. Run up a flight of stairs, jog to work, sing aloud, dance around, grab your child or wife's hand and jump on the bed together.

You are responsible for your own happiness and no one can enjoy it for you. I say someone can spoil your happiness but no one can enjoy it for you. If you want to tell others that you are really happy carry a rose flower or scent your desk with rosemary perfume. True prosperity is like a smile on the face; it cannot be hidden. Spread it around. As I said before prosperity is a journey not a destiny. Keep on moving and enjoying it not up to the end of your life but beyond your life span. It is nice to be rich! You can join Yoga classes and improve on meditative exercises. This can improve your reasoning capacity and add up to skills indispensable to critical thinking. We get wisdom from different places and learn how to use it properly. Surely we have means of growing from poverty to prosperity. It is what we do with this wisdom that counts in the end.

What have you decided? ( ) Make at least one dollar a day; ( ) Make at least ten dollars a day; ( ) Make at least a hundred dollars a day; ( ) Make five hundred dollars a day; ( ) Make one thousand dollars a day.

Remember Hosef again. He was not poor because he was lazy but he could not pay much attention while talking fixing the phone. When people fail to remember it is often because they did not take in the information in first place. When the brain checks for it in its library it returns, "File is empty." Jane could not recall peoples' names or numbers she did not record. She was a beautiful secretary, punctual and most of the time in office but in the end she had to quit because two half-time jobs do not make one full–time job. Abed taught us that one trick to getting attention is paying closer attention. Stop multitasking and be fully present. It is rude to go lunching with your friend and keep talking on the phone. Turn off the TV when you are reading the Desire of All ages. You will be more likely to remember the place's name when the conductor calls Buguruni, Buguruni Buguruni. You will not get off the bus at Buguruni instead of at Malapa. Your memory will create enough space to map the red roof top of La Promise Hotel on the conductor's words. You will be able to say: "Susha" without hesitation. (A little hesitation however short will make you get off the bus at a wrong stage). Stopping multitasking will train your eyes only to see what they want to see. You will see prosperity not wealth. You will see success in life not graduating at college. You will build houses and live in them. You will have a good time and enjoy it. You will not continue in your slumber. You will jump to the first opportunity to make money and grow rich. You will not wait for God to reveal himself to you. You will claim your promise. All these are guaranteed! (Author's Note: I had written these in bold letters and swore on earth and in heaven that they were true. I had offered my head if they failed. I was advised by the editorial staff not to put them in bold because human beings are corrupt by nature. I settled but still claim the truth in the statements).

Research says challenging our brain keeps it active. Overworking our brain keeps it dull. If you wanted to improve your thinking and had a choice between challenging the brain and overworking it, what would you choose? Challenge your brain to sleep an extra hour. Challenge your brain to learn the lyrics of Olivia John Newton's "Hopelessly Devoted to You." Think of how many years Olivia has given you to learn her song and you have failed. Learning a new song improves your auditory and verbal power. This improves your talking. It can assist your Belief> Thoughts>Words>Feelings>Action programme. Do whatever it takes to grow prosperous. Improve your memory. Health is wealth. If you can learn the lyrics then you can recite Isaiah 58.

When you cannot focus on information, you cannot acquire it effectively, and you can never remember something you did not learn in the first place! What does Isaiah 58 say?

Now draw the ladder showing the journey from poverty to prosperity. Show all the stages you have to go through and indicate with "Here I am" where you are at the moment.

CONGRATULATIONS

CHAPTER TWENTY FOUR

SUCCESS

Suppose God told you……..
Yes.. yes.. yes…… . . This is a cheering end. Celebrate your victory. Celebrations cement success.

Just 'picture' God told you, "Go into the world and multiply" will you take a second wife? Will you look for another partner? Will you throw your current boyfriend or girl friend out of the window? What will you do?

Now that you are given a chance to live your life again, will you ever consider marrying the same woman or man again? Will you cast your vote for the same politician again? Will you ever go back to the same school you went through again?

Assuming you were living in some relationship which you know pretty well is against God's law and then on the other hand you hear God loud and clear offering you the chance to make money; offering you the opportunity to live beyond riches on the bargain that you break that relationship, will you say, "That must not have been God speaking?" Will you pray, "Dear God, give me one more day or one more weekend?"Or will you plead, "God save my face!"

Let us go deeper. I warned the light-hearted. Looking for prosperity could be scary. This was getting tougher. I knew what I was saying was true because I wrote the book and I went back editing and editing it a number of times but the more I read it the more I got scared of my own writing. Yes, you can be scared of your own writing as parents can be scared of their own children!

What will you do if you had said, "It is futile to serve God. What did we gain by carrying out his requirements and going about like mourners before the Lord Almighty? But now we call the arrogant blessed. Certainly the evil doers prosper, and even those who challenge God escape"?

This is the second part of the above question. What will you do if you had consulted your pastor and he told you, "Malachi 3:16: Then those who feared Lord talked with each other and the Lord listened and heard"?

Will you consult that pastor again or will you look for a doctor or a lawyer? Tell me. Will you say that you are running crazy? What will you think? Will you say you might have been dreaming or those were works of great imagination?

I know this God-thing is scaring and may not do well to the marketing of this book. I challenge those who feel this way that wouldn't they go to a cinema because the film showing is scary? I go deeper! God is saying to you, "Go into the world and prosper", what will you do? Will you remain skeptical and say, "Show me the money!" Will you rise up and walk? Will you continue in your slumber? Or will you say, "I will not believe it was the voice of God until my bills are paid? I will not believe until I have a new house or a new dress. I will not believe until my children are out of college. I will not believe until I have got a job. I will not believe until I am healed. I will not believe until my problem is solved! I will not believe until....I die"

If you ever feel that you would like to put off that silent voice for another day; or if you feel that acting upon such a voice immediately might ruin your reputation or hurt other people's feelings, or if you ever feel that the message might be alright but the timing might be wrong, trust me you are reading the right book. If you are not convinced yet check it up in Malachi 3:16: A scroll of remembrance was written in God's presence concerning those who feared and honoured his name. Verse 17 says the Almighty saw the list and remarked, "They will be mine in the day when I make up my treasured possession. I will spare them, just as in compassion a man spares his son who serves him".

I do not know about you. You may be the guy who thinks prosperity is determined by fate at birth. You may think some people are created to be happy and others are there to suffer. You may think one cannot change one's fate. What I am saying here is different. I know that suffering teaches perseverance and perseverance teaches patience and patience teaches faith and faith leads to action. Having said all that I do not mean there is no Gain without Pain. You can surely turn from poverty to prosperity by reading this book.

In my earlier book, <u>Face to Face With Grief</u> (A Psychological Approach to coping with suffering)(ISBN-13: 978-988-98555-1-2) I made a great statement. I said , "You are what you think". I have been humbled by the great number of people who have called me up to say how much they have been helped by reading that book. I want to suggest to those who have not read the book yet to get a copy right now. If you can do it today, why wait for tomorrow? This I am making might be the biggest advertisement for <u>Face to Face with Grief</u> but I owe no one any apology. It is on record. You can turn your life around from surviving to thriving by simply changing your thinking. I am standing on that ground to add an afterthought. It is not what you feel that matters. It is what you believe.

You may argue otherwise but you do not have to feel good to be good. To be good just do good. If you think it is hard just try it. Practice makes perfect. The process has nothing to do with your feelings! Feeling angry shouldn't make you angry. It is just like hearing insults. You choose when to call an insult an insult. Sincerely you can feel hungry yet have no desire to eat. You do not have to feel forgiving before forgiving or feel forgetting before forgetting. You want to do it, simply do it.

A few minutes ago I felt like licking my elbow. I tried it and failed. I tried so many times and failed as many. So I came to the conclusion: One cannot lick one's own elbow. You may feel like doing it yet you cannot. Our actions cannot be directed by our feelings.

If you want to change your belief do not allow your feelings to control your thinking system. You can write this down: "My feelings, you are mine. That does not make me yours."

If you want to gain understanding seek knowledge. You will again see the distinction between the righteous and the wicked; between those who serve God and those who do not. What I promised by reading this book through is that you would see ways of walking to prosperity through your circumstances. You will not listen to those who discourage you. You will not listen to those who criticize you. You will listen to those who know that as you prosper they too prosper. They will encourage and support you.

Just as I was writing this book my nephew sent me this text message: "Uncle please send me U$ 5000 being school fees. Send to this account Fred … (surname withheld) Ac No 295120987001, Trust Bank."

I called my sister and asked what Fred was doing lately. She told me he had just got married and was working as a primary school teacher. His wife was a perfect price for those who love carelessly.

I therefore knew why he needed the money. I sent Fred this message. "Sorry I cannot help you at this time." I left out the reason that led me to this decision. You know what? I did not believe him.

Face to Face with Grief presented a psychological approach to coping with suffering. As it was at the time of writing so it is today 'a wonderful title for people recovering from tsunami, terrorist attacks, floods or earthquakes. It restores self confidence into people who have lost loved ones, friendships, jobs or sources of income. It shows the way forward after some devastating news. Without belittling your feelings for the loss of your loved ones, demeaning the pain of joblessness and poverty and blaming you for your circumstances, it uses the counseling and experience of others to dig you out of your own grave. It helps the reader to modify and control ones anger, doubts , hatred and helps one to think through one's goals, guide one's life course decisions and let one think and design one's lasting relief from one's problems'. The quotation was from the book cover.

Many people have been helped by that book. Rising sales could be a measure of this success story. I did not write that to pat myself on the back but to say that if you missed a boat that could take your life from surviving to thriving, do not worry yourself out another boat to take you to the land of richness, money, overflowing joy, wealth and prosperity was ready to sail.

I am talking to people who have ever lost an opportunity. Do not give up. Close to where I am there is an advertisement. It reads, "If you lost a rainy day," says God, "Do not worry I will create another one for you another day". In the same city I saw another signboard reading, "Pray before you are prayed for." Suppose you were divorced once or twice or let us say you have ever been divorced or you are contemplating divorce, and …..a beautiful woman or this awesome guy comes along and says, "This is me to dry your tears" what would you do? Wouldn't you marry him or her?

I am a counselor by profession. I asked a friend of mine Hosef (you have read about him) this question and he answered, "I would marry her."

I said, "Hosef, one woman almost made you crazy and another one almost made you take your own life. You have just been divorced not once and not twice. Would you consider marrying again?"

This book, "The Desire of All Ages: How to Make Money and move from Poverty to Prosperity with no falling back", is a practical guide to changing one's life from poverty to prosperity. I called it the guided tour from poverty to prosperity. In this book you have found a practical plan on how to market yourself and your services. You have found the common causes of failure in life and how to conquer those circumstances. Those who have lost their fortunes and those who are just beginning to make money must appreciate the value of having a guided tour from poverty to prosperity.

Writing this book has not been easy. I started with great excitement but after writing a few chapters I realized that I was not writing what I wanted to write and instead I was writing what I did not want to write. For months I gave up the project then I had a dream and I saw words clearly inscribed on a wall: God, Gold, You and Godless. I stayed hours in bed half awake and half asleep trying to interpret my dream. This book is the result of that vision. If I were to title it anything else, I would have called it: God, Gold, You and Godless

Once this was said some felt, "Oh God I have just landed myself on those other "Make it Rich schemes." *If you felt that way, my advice was: Throw this book right away and ask for a refund.* I wrote that in italics for their easy reference. Anyone who read this book that far and stopped there was entitled to full refund with no questions asked. Check Page 11 for your reference.

I knew there was a great wall between poverty and prosperity. In fact this is what I saw in the dream. I saw a picture of a world. In this world there was an economic ladder on which was tied the fruits of prosperity. Everyone was trying to climb that ladder. Some people ran in teams called countries and some people ran on their individual merit. The entire human race was competing. Developed countries were right at the top of the ladder and developing countries were right down on the base. The division was so big that one could see the ladder as covered in different colors. What however made the greatest difference between the rich and poor was the point at which some people would quit. The poor quit at the beginning and the rich never quit.

There was also another difference. The poor, I mean those who stayed permanently poor, were down the ladder complaining and abusing their situation on the exploitation by the rich. The rich however, I mean the rich who got to the top and remained there, were always grateful to the poor who pushed them up and were always helpful to the poor. It is kind of silly but they were not worried that if the poor grew rich (they the rich) would lose their prosperity. The only people I saw rise and fall were the mean who grew rich and remained mean. I saw an ex-millionaire who had been so hard on himself. He had been too mean even to put food in his own mouth. He fed on chips and fast foods. He knew it was better to give than to receive, yet he could not follow through.

Poverty is multifaceted. Not every person was on the ladder. The people in extreme poverty were stuck away in the mad far from the ladder. To these even to live was an act of courage. The hardest part of their struggle was getting to the first step. In fact some of them were not even looking in the direction of the ladder at all. They were not resting either. They seemed to be running in circles. There are moments they appeared to be going towards the ladder but either they stopped short of it, bypassed it or just changed direction and swam away. In front of this lot were those who were at the bottom rungs. These survived because they had some ray of hope. Though their development was sometimes uneven and slow, they were generally making some progress. They reminded you of that guy who said, "Jesus, if only I could touch your garments, I would be healed."

I quoted this "guy" because she was as desperate as most of us could be; yet she survived the circumstances. She did not wait for her circumstances to change but worked through her circumstances. Read the story for yourself in Mathew 9:21.You will see what I mean. In fact her story ranks among those in which Jesus was quoted saying, "Your faith has healed you." She believed that the end justifies the means and that kept her hope alive.

The greatest challenge of our time is that you cannot go up unless you start climbing and to start climbing you need to reach the ladder. Poor people are people who have failed to become rich. Poor people are not failures. If you do not start building a house you cannot fail to finish it. A failure is a person who starts on a task but gives it up before accomplishing it. If you do not start, (you are safe), you will never fail! Failing once or twice does not make you a failure. Succeeding once or twice does not make you a success. You have to fail repeatedly, persistently and convincingly to be called a failure. I repeat. Failing 0 times, 1 time, 2 times does not make you a failure. The number of times you fail does not matter. It's the time you fail to get up that counts. Remember however a man commits adultery not only when he sleeps with a married woman but the moment he winks an eye onto her. Adultery does not start with action but with imagination. So it is with prosperity and so it is with poverty.

The poorest of the poor will never get out of the pit unless they get to the bottom of the ladder. The upward movement starts at the bottom of the ladder. The thinking part or the planning part is the beginning of all wisdom. You can spoon feed poor men or you can forgive African countries of their foreign debts but they will never get out of poverty unless they start thinking on their own of what crisis they are in, how to overcome the crisis and what they want to be after the crisis. Man's greatest enemy has always been man himself. It is not the devil that devours man but the pride in man. Poor people are fond of saying, "I cannot do that" yet prosperous people say, "everything is possible...... (To those who believe)"To get out of your hardship you need to participate actively in the struggle. You cannot sit and stare. The time of "Pray for me" passed away two thousand years ago when the apostles of Jesus begged, "Teach us how to pray." (If you want to check out my story, go to Luke Chapter 11). I have bad news for every poor man and every poor woman. The upward movement starts at the bottom of the ladder but the thinking part comes before that and no one can do the thinking for you.

There is so much confusion in this world. I do not want to frighten you but there is a price to pay when you live on planet Earth. There are people who keep on shaking the ladder to stop others from going further up. You may hate such people. You may hate yourself. Welcome to planet Earth. Here you cannot change the environment. All you can change is your thinking. This is a crab race.

Have you ever seen crabs trying to climb a wall? They always fail to climb over it not because they do not have strong hands or legs. Each crab is pulling the other down!

This is a 'crab race' not a 'human race'. Should the human race be this silly? No. Humans being guardians of civilization as they are or claim to be, the strong should be lifting the weak to the ladder. Look around you and see what is happening. Poverty affects individuals, groups and is not confined to developing nations or to people with poor backgrounds. Life is not easy but you can make life easier by changing the way you look at it.

I am writing this book from a country where more than 60% of the people earn less than a dollar a day. More than half of the country has no electricity and more than half the population has never seen a mobile phone. I am not talking about having a nutritional diet. I am not talking about hospitals without medicine or doctors. I am not talking about schools without books. I am not talking about malaria or HIV. I am talking about a people where Moslems and Christians lie together like a lamb and a cub and none goes at the other or runs away from the other. Poverty breeds grievances but that is only when you think about it that way. I have seen Christians marrying Moslems and the other way round. I have seen Moslems with their veils in churches and Jesus healing them all alike without saying, "Change your name first." Life is not easy but you can make life easier by changing the way you look at it.

Think of this one. Case 1

(1) AIDS is rampant in Africa because Africa is poor.
(2) There are more AIDS cases in South Africa than in any other part of Africa.

(3) South Africa is the richest country in Africa.
Case 2
(1) AIDS is the disease of the poor.
(2) In Tanzania there are more AIDS cases among the rich than among the poor.
(3) Tanzania is not a poor country.

If you look at this country as one of the poorest places in the world you will see starvation, poverty and disease. You will think of supplying fresh water and toys for Christmas. You may perhaps donate your second hand clothes to your favorite charity and claim or not claim tax rebate. You will see a desperate people and you will find excuses for resigning on the fate of this race.

If you are lucky you may watch a TV program about marriage of underage children or recruiting child prostitutes and you will feel some bit of sympathy in your heart. However, if somebody told you that the people of this country might be poor but the country is rich you may think about this place with some degree of interest. Let me be that person to tell you. This country is rich. It is rapidly developing. Its main city is the third fastest growing city in the world. I may go this far at this moment to catch your interest but I could have added the third dimension here. Deuteronomy 8: 7-9. "The LORD your God is bringing you into a fertile land that has rivers, springs–a land that produces wheat barley, grapes etc. There you will never go hungry or even be in need. Its rocks have iron ore in them and from its hills you can mine copper". If this is a true description of this country would you like to invest in here?

You have read this far but still you may not be able to see yourself in the picture. You may not be able to define your position on the ladder. Your position might be like that of a man who had been sick for 38 years. He lay on the bank of the river in pain for all those years. Every year there was a specific time when the river water would turn medicinal. Whoever would fall in the river first at that specific time would have ones illness healed. He lay there, tried every time but never succeeded to be the first one because he was lame. He tried for 38 years but he never succeeded. In the 38th year he however succeeded. Watch your critics. Never allow them to walk away with your hope.

Before you leave however I want to encourage you with one story. There was a man who was so sick. He could neither talk nor walk. He could neither live nor die.

Reports came around that Jesus was in some house in the city. Relatives and friends carried him there only to find the whole place over-crowded. They tried to push through the crowds but they could not break through. They pushed 0 times, 1 time, 2 times, 3 times, 4, 5, 6, 7 times but they could not reach Jesus. Winners never quit, losers do.

They said to one another. "Let us lower him down through the roof."

I imagine they had no ropes. They had no reason for having come out with ropes. They looked for the ropes anyway. They climbed up the roof. I can personally see these men with hammers removing the roof of someone else's house. Wow, that was courage!

Piece by piece they removed the roof and lowered their patient through. They did no not drop him on the floor. They must have had long ropes.

You may be stunned at the driving power behind their success. Jesus was stunned too.

"Man, your sins have been forgiven. Your faith has healed you."

The Bible says, "The man was made whole."

He did not need further the assistance of his relatives and friends. He carried his own bed back home.

Now I say to you: A man is not judged brave by the number of times he falls but by the number of times he rises. It does not matter how many times you have been on that yoyo swing of yours. It does not matter whether you have tried 0, 1, 2, 3, 4, 5, 6, 7, 8, 9 or 10 times. It is your faith that heals. Do not let this go out of your head

I wanted to take you away from this figment of your imagination. I made another disturbing statement and you could hang me for it if I did not turn out to be right. I did renew my refund pledge and even extended it to cover page 13. Go back to Page 12, check what is written in italics. The offer was extended.

"We can overcome poverty and the entire human race is destined to prosper. This is another bold statement I made and called a true statement and throughout this book I said it again and again and I am going to urge you to believe and practice it and I promise you that your life will move from poverty to prosperity with no possibility of falling down again. I said there are no hidden secrets on the journey to prosperity and there is no hidden formula either. Prosperity is more than money, more than riches, more than wealth. It means to be whole. Prosperity therefore is more of a public asset than it is a property of the rich.

When you see trees swaying or when you see water swirling do not say you have seen the wind or the storm. What you have seen are the results of the storm or of the wind. The real wind or the real storm is that energy that empowered the water or the tree to move. Without that energy the water or the tree would have stayed in one place. In the same way do not count the cars, the beautiful houses, the jewels as prosperity. The real prosperity is that energy that enables you to move from misery to success. I thus exposed all there was in this book and all that was left for you was to make a choice whether to read on or not.

I withdrew one offer and created another one. It said: If within your heart you hear a voice telling you that you can never grow from your state of poverty to extreme prosperity particularly because prosperity is not for you, send an email to the author at *cares@kayiwa.com* with the words DISBELIEF in the Subject column and your money would be refunded. It could not pay you to read this book and I thought it would be corruption if I could charge for a service you could not get.

I say all this because I have come to believe (and belief is the central theme of this book) that if all gods came together, the only thing all would agree about is their desire to help the poor. All religions preach against poverty and have institutions designed in heaven to assist the poor. Look at the Koran. In the Book of the Cow, Chapter 1 verse 2 Article 110: "And keep up prayer and pay the poor-rate and whatever good you send before for yourselves, you shall find it with Allah; surely Allah sees what you do". Then look in the Bible. Luke 4:18 "The Spirit of the Lord is on me, because he has anointed me to preach good news to the poor. He has sent me to proclaim freedom for the prisoners and recovery of sight for the blind, to release the oppressed." What is the good news to a bankrupt? What is the good news to a hungry man? What is the good news to a prisoner? What is the good news to a sick man?

There are many more examples that can be quoted from other religions. The fourth Noble Truth of Buddhism says, "Everyone can be enlightened."

Let me continue with this theme. Deuteronomy Chapter 15 verse 4-7. "4 However, there should be no poor among you, for in the land the LORD your God is giving you to possess as your inheritance, he will richly bless you, 5 if only you fully obey the LORD your God and are careful to follow all these commands I am giving you today. 6 For the LORD your God will bless you as he has promised, and you will lend to many nations but will borrow from none. You will rule over many nations but none will rule over you. 7 If there is a poor man among your brothers in any of the towns of the land that the LORD your God is giving you, do not be hardhearted or tightfisted toward your poor brother". I guess what I am saying here is there in Verse 4 that prosperity is for all.

Let me quote the Koran again: The Family of Imran, Chapter 1, verse 3, Article 181 "Allah has certainly heard the saying of those who said: Surely Allah is **poor** and we are rich. I will record what they say, and their killing the prophets unjustly, and I will say: Taste the chastisement of burning."

I am saying these things because there are some people who want to keep the poor in the sorry state by quoting Jesus saying, : "Blessed are the poor" and justify laziness, lack of accommodation, hard life , suffering as if it were from the Lord. They preach that Jesus was humble and poor because he was born in a cowshed! Rubbish. Rubbish. Rubbish. How many poor men need treasurers to keep their finances? How can one who owns the universe be poor? Look at property owners. They own so little yet they are so rich! Those who say such things start and finish the argument themselves. Jesus could have started as a poor man but he died as a King (Undeniable. There was a banner on the cross).

And think again: Psalm 22:18 and John 19: 23 "When the soldiers crucified Jesus, they took his clothes, dividing them into four shares, one for each of them, with the undergarment remaining. This garment was seamless, woven in one piece from top to bottom.

24"Let's not tear it," they said to one another. "Let's decide by lot who will get it." This happened that the scripture might be fulfilled which said, "They divided my garments among them and cast lots for my clothing." So this is what the soldiers did".

My question to you dear reader: Did soldiers share out Jesus' rags? Was it rags they shared? No! He was dressed like a king. "They took his clothes, dividing them into four shares, one for each of them." These are historical records. The undergarment alone was better than what you or I are wearing today. Compare: This garment was seamless, woven in one piece from top to bottom.

Be deceived not. You can turn from poverty to prosperity. You were created to live a prosperous life. If God is on your side no one can be against you. Rise up and walk.

What I have told you is a life changing message. It is a strong message requiring changing your thinking. Every computer expert knows that before you do any editing to your computer registry it is critical that you make a backup of the current registry. The temptation to make "one little change" without backing up is great. It can also be deadly. I told you to back up your excuses all your reasons and thoughts that were keeping you in poverty because I did not want you to lose any argument. Now I am telling you to format that disk; you will not need that nuisance anymore. I am speaking from experience and most likely you are going to ignore this warning just as most people do. Hopefully you will be a little smarter.

INDEX

Abed,
Parking 74, 78, 79 Name 93,
   childhood 95, dog 99, church 103,
   security guard 105, justice 106,
   thief 107, Japan 111, business
   114, letter 130, grave 191, father
   192, mother 193, prison 223,
   word 232, kanga 251, chunya 291,
   gold 293, pray 294, 296, 297, dry
   bones 298, truth 304
Abimelech, 196
Abraham, obstacles 59, prophet 147,
   famine 196, blessing 203
Accountability, virtue 101, 105,
   police 270, reward 107, Solomon
   114
ACHIEVEMENTS, 89
acid, 300
accuse 53, 60, 64, 133, 136, 138, 142,
   144
AD, 67,
Adultery, 10, 106, Paul 215, God idea
   240,
ADVANTAGES, 78
Albert Roscher, 20
Aligato, 111
Allah, 14, 325, 326
ambassador, 87
angels, choir 3, guard 17, strangers
   68, human beings 216, church
   243, corrupt 288
anger 94, time 101, criticism 111,
   blocker 214, overcome 248,
   provoke God 278
anxiety, 17, 44
appreciate, 77, 94, 133

Arabs, 98, 21
ATM, 85
Attitude, 89, 123, 137, 144

Bad company, 453,
Bagamoyo, 143, 210
baggage, 83
Bail, 106
ballistic missile, 243
baptize, 98, 236
BBQ, 49
BC, 67
bean, 34, 76, 202, 261, 300,
beggars, 42, 55, 130,
belief system, 7, 49, 119, 151
Benz, 112
best girl, 19, 69, 81
Bible, 8, 13, 28, 36, 50, 73, 145, 156,
blame God, 35
Blessed are the eyes, 47
blessing blocker, 111, 114
Bob Marley, 72, 79, 115,
Bongo, 34, 46
Book of the Cow, 14, 169,
boundaries, 18, 66
Breed of Gentlemen, 44
bribe, 16, 70, 135, 144, 150
British, 8, 17, 55, 148,
Buguruni, 68, 79, 103, 118,
butterfly, 16, 43, 65, 79, 117, 143
Buxter, 45

Camp, 46, 55, 131
Canaan, 15
cardinal sins, 113, 115
cares@kayiwa.com, 2, 14, 70, 85, 169

Index

Caring, 58, 116
Carrots, 24, 78
Challenge God, 8, 164
Chang Doa, 31
Chinese, 46, 98, 115, 136, 157
Christians, 12, 52, 97, 133, 168
Christmas, 12, 40, 52, 168
City Garden, 90, 99
climb, 3, 11, 36, 42, 54, 59, 78, 123, 167,
Coban, 72
coffee, 24, 52, 58, 137, 157
Coma, 21, 142
Commission of Science, 135, 137
common causes of failure, 10, 166
condemn, 18, 25, 38, 47, 50, 62, 72, 73, 81, 88, 100, 120, 125, 161
confession, 60, 120, 159
Confidence, 10, 19, 46, 62, 76, 92, 109, 138, 166
continent, 25, 98
Corruption, 4, 70, 85, 114, 125, 131, 134, 139, 148, 150, 160, 169
Country Resort, 110
criminals, 62, 72, 77, 119, 151
Criticism, 28, 35, 62, 72, 79, 84, 142

Dar Es Salaam, 63, 78, 80, 82, 87, 96, 99, 110, 130, 144, 153
declaration, 18, 38, 116
demon, 52,
depression., 6, 15, 39, 119, 151, 162
Deuteronomy, 13, 58, 101, 123 , 145, 168, 170
Devil, 12, 29, 35, 40, 51, 60, 72, 101, 117, 128, 137, 139, 141, 144, 158, 167
dinner, 17, 37, 52, 87, 109, 121
Dionysius, 40,
Disbelief, 4, 14, 66, 117, 124, 144, 169
disobey God, 36
divorce, 10, 18, 29, 55, 61, 72, 81, 88, 89, 101, 122, 128, 138, 166,
Dodoma, 17, 19, 34, 126, 129,
dog, 57, 62, 80, 120, 124127
dollar, 90, 94, 98, 100, 108, 110, 115, 118, 129, 140, 148, 168

Dream, 115, 121, 128, 150, 156, 165

Easter, 40, 52, 124, 149
egg, 8, 12, 24, 29, 79, 137, 167,
Egypt, 15, 105, 145
Elisha, 143
Elvis Presley, 72
encourage, 2, 11, 13, 31, 47, 49, 78, 86, 88, 99, 100, 125, 165, 169
enemy, 12, 37, 58, 74, 93, 114, 120, 128, 131, 167
enjoy your life, 32, 43
enter a town, 37
Esau, 105,
excuses, 6, 12, 15, 20, 28, 38, 47, 51, 68, 82, 122, 126, 133, 139, 148, 157, 168, 170
exercise., 26, 28, 32, 49, 51, 66, 77, 85, 88, 100, 146, 157, 162,
exit strategy, 49, 63, 66, 69, 92, 144
Exodus, 145
Experience, 78, 82, 103, 109, 118, 120, 133, 134, 138, 166, 170
Ezekiel, 148, 149, 154, 158

Face to Face with Grief, 9, 29, 38, 47, 65, 77, 113, 165, 166
Faith, 128, 139, 142, 144, 153, 156, 157, 159, 165, 165, 167,
falling in love, 9, 19, 69, 79, 81
fear, 4, 8, 15, 19, 25, 30, 40, 48, 51, 60, 70, 76, 80, 86, 91, 99, 108, 111, 112, 127, 135, 142, 153, 158, 159
Feeling angry, 9, 165
first person, 36
fish, 16, 20, 24, 31, 67, 121, 124, 130, 132, 139, 153, 155
fool, 6, 9, 21, 27, 28, 49, 60, 67, 80, 96, 147,
Format, 18, 170
Freedom Road, 7
futile to serve God., 8, 164

game of cards, 76
Gazelle., 31, 111, 137
Gehazi, 144,

Genesis, 15, 66, 70, 145,
George W. Bush, 62
Gerar, 105, 108
Germany, 17, 29, 30, 66
gift, 4, 18, 37, 41, 70, 87, 121, 133, 137, 144, 148,
Goal, 3, 8, 29, 30, 38, 48, 54, 66, 85, 100, 122, 134, 166
God Bless, 45
God, Gold, You and Godless, 10, 156, 166,
good news, 14, 16, 51, 63, 112, 170, 170,
good-old days, 36, 72, 73
great wall, 11, 78, 166
greed of the rich, 29

happiest of people, 24
hard work, 45, 46, 57, 71, 75, 110, 115, 116, 127
heart, 8, 12, 17, 22, 24, 29, 39, 43, 57, 66, 75, 85, 101, 114, 123, 146, 147, 151, 156, 169
HIV, 12, 125, 149, 161, 168
homosexuality, 136, 137
Hosef, 84, 86, 89, 112, 130, 162, 166,
hours, 15, 22, 34, 52, 69, 95, 123, 136, 166
hunger, 55, 135, 160
hurt, 6, 9, 23, 28, 38, 40, 42, 64, 73, 77, 80, 84, 92, 112, 131, 136, 165,
hymns, 15

Ilala, 17, 33, 69
illicit relationship, 8
Iraq, 50, 62
Isaac, 54, 101, 105, 108, 109
Isaiah, 32, 39, 148, 158, 163
Israel, 17, 28, 69, 81, 104, 110, 125, 135, 143, 148, 155
italics, 6, 11, 13, 22, 78, 166, 169

Jacob, 54, 101, 105
Jane, 7, 25, 53, 77, 112, 121, 129, 133, 157, 163
Jane's prayer, 8
Japan, 8, 44, 56, 62, 72, 99, 120, 162

Jasper, 56, 57, 59, 127
Jeremiah, 30, 108, 148
Jerusalem., 7, 17, 28, 32, 53, 129, 148.
Jesus, 11, 14, 20, 28, 35, 36, 40, 51, 58, 63, 67, 73, 81, 94, 101, 125, 131, 149, 155, 158, 159, 169, 170
Jews, 54
John, 14, 23, 40, 45, 49, 62, 63, 82, 101, 116, 151, 153, 157, 163, 170
Joseph, 15,
Judge, 13, 23, 49, 60, 72, 93, 100, 120, 134, 146, 151, 169
junk, 52, 55

Kanga, 132, 133
Kariakoo, 17
Karibuni, 37
Kato, 62, 91, 123, 162
Kayiwa Foundations, 2, 47
Kenya, 17, 19, 34, 141
Kigamboni, 19
Kikwete, 50, 53, 64, 132, 139, 139, 140, 141, 144
King, 47, 51, 59, 65, 79, 82, 115, 143, 148, 170,
Kingdom, 15, 37, 51, 71, 81, 92, 114,
Kipepeo, 16, 30, 42, 43, 59, 68, 72, 109, 115
Know It All, 119
knowledge, 9, 15, 48, 50, 62, 92, 98, 103, 109, 112, 139, 141, 144, 145, 154, 165
Koran, 8, 14, 67, 117, 131, 161, 169, 170

labor, 33, 94, 95, 109, 125, 126, 130
lack of knowledge, 50, 63, 144, 145, 154
ladder, 12, 26, 32, 42, 68, 78, 94, 132, 163, 167, 168
landlord, 33
LandMark, 90, 92, 93, 94, 99, 104
Latvin, 40, 41, 42, 59, 64
Leprosy, 143, 144
Letty, 4, 40, 41, 65, 116, 153
lick one's own elbow., 9, 165

Index

Liiban Hotel, 34, 35, 59, 69
little girl, 128, 129
Look at your life, 36
LORD your God, 13, 14, 101, 106, 135, 139, 146, 168, 170,
Lord's Prayer, 48
lose my strength, 24
Lowassa, 140, 141, 142, 144, 152,
luggages, 49, 88, 114, 153
Luke, 11, 12, 14, 22, 37, 51, 58, 63, 66, 67, 150, 156, 157, 159, 167, 169

Mafia, 131, 132, 133, 159
Magomeni, 91
Majid, 17,
Malachi, 8, 9, 58, 150, 165,
Malapa, 68, 69, 79, 118, 163
malaria, 12, 56, 160, 161, 168
man of God, 143, 144
Mango, 87, 121
Maputo, 63, 67
Mark, 46, 47, 51, 57, 66, 68, 85,
Marriages, 18, 89
Master Card, 41
Matthew, 51, 66, 97, 158
MAU MAU, 17
Mbeya, 34, 92, 94, 95, 96, 98, 102, 109, 114, 127, 136, 152, 153
meditate, 9, 24, 33, 36, 50, 54, 99, 122
Mercedes Benzes, 112
millionaire, 11, 21, 161, 167
minerals, 87, 88, 126
Mnazi Moja, 69,
Momentary Insanity, 38
monkey, 56
moon, 27, 124, 125, 132
Morogoro, 34, 86, 87, 112, 161, 162,
Moses, 20, 81, 101, 122, 145, 147
Mozambique, 55, 61, 72, 80, 92, 103, 153, 162
Mwakiteme, 141, 142
Mwinyi, 142, 144, 162

Naaman, 143, 144, 145, 148,
needle, 36
Newton, 49, 56, 71, 163
Nicodemus, 80, 81,

not believe, 113, 121, 133, 134, 142, 153, 165, 166
Nyerere, 18, 35, 44, 50, 53, 135, 140, 142, 153

Oath, 103, 105, 106, 109, 124
Obey, 14, 18, 19, 60, 66, 78, 80, 93, 101, 105, 113, 123, 133, 137, 139, 159, 170
obstacle, 23, 29, 36, 46, 51, 52, 54, 63, 70, 139, 157
old age, 20, 39, 40, 81, 93, 128
Open yourself, 61
out of debt, 36, 122
Oyster Bay, 17, 34, 44

P.O.Box 91185 TST, 2, 47
Page, 7, 11, 13, 24, 25, 28, 38, 47, 54, 69, 73, 77, 91, 121, 127, 131, 135, 145, 166, 169
Paradise, 44, 86
partridge, 30, 67
Paul, 18, 23, 29, 30, 54, 72, 82, 114
peel, 156, 157, 159,
people perish, 50, 63
perseverance, 9, 85, 86, 165,
personality, 72, 86, 118, 126
Peter, 23, 39, 73, 112, 142, 150, 151, 158
Pharaoh., 15,
Philippians, 30, 40
phone, 12, 18, 36, 77, 83, 84, 88, 98, 120, 122, 126, 130, 162, 163, 168
pocket, 37, 42, 57, 67, 74, 95, 127, 139, 144, 149
police, 8, 23, 53, 60, 62, 77, 89, 113, 118, 119, 125, 130, 135, 139, 142, 162
poorest of the poor, 12, 78, 167
Pope, 40, 82, 158
Prados, 44, 112
Praise God, 31, 41, 118, 158
PRC, 56, 62, 67
President, 18, 39, 44, 50, 53, 56, 62, 139, 140, 141, 142, 144, 162
pretty, 48, 128, 149, 151, 164
Prime Minister, 15, 64, 140, 141, 142, 152

principle, 58, 61, 64, 71, 74, 78, 84, 97, 111, 114, 116, 121, 156
prison, 120, 124, 136, 139, 161,
procrusteanistism, 51
Promised Land, 59, 68, 69, 79
prophet, 14, 32, 47, 80, 133, 143, 150, 154, 155, 170.
prosperity as wealth, 32
prostitution, 4, 29, 61, 115, 124, 125, 126, 128, 130, 133, 134, 159, 160
Prune, 70, 87, 88
Psalm, 10, 14, 147, 170

Que Sera Sera, 128
quit, 8, 11, 13, 26, 32, 38, 45, 53, 75, 75, 86, 88, 128, 130, 163, 167, 169

race, 13, 32, 44, 47, 74, 79, 79, 85, 95, 125, 153, 167, 168, 169
rain, 112, 113, 166
real money, 15, 30
Rebekah, 104,
record of your miseries, 36
refund, 11, 13, 34, 98, 114, 166, 169,
Reject, 6, 22, 25, 51, 58, 108, 120, 170
rejoice, 32, 37, 48, 49, 143, 147, 158
religious, 53, 55, 64, 113, 121
restaurant, 29, 37, 52, 90, 101, 132
retire young, 50, 63, 66, 94, 162
Revelation, 80, 104, 151
rich man, 11, 22, 28, 35, 38, 44, 62, 104, 159
rich and the poor, 11, 47, 167
river, 13, 109, 131, 143, 144, 168,
ropes, 13, 169,
running in circles, 11, 167

Sabbath, 23
Samuel, 113, 146,
Santa Claus, 52
Sarah, 23, 54
SATAN, 35, 52, 54, 73, 73, 80, 119, 128, 131, 136, 139, 149, 157, 158,
scare, 8, 62, 72, 124, 146, 155, 157, 164
scheme, 11, 25, 39, 48, 52, 78, 84, 115, 135, 146, 166

scripture, 14, 155, 170
sense of hopelessness, 6, 22
seven times, 22, 143, 143
shelter, 15, 55, 74, 128, 132, 161
shilling, 28, 34, 43, 137, 141, 148
Shusha, 68
silent voice, 9, 165
sin, 22, 25, 36, 52, 73, 84, 113, 116, 127, 131,
siphon, 111
Sir Elton John, 62
skin, 8, 25, 49, 57, 62, 77, 106, 132, 136, 141, 151, 154
sleep, 15, 21, 23, 38, 59, 60, 73, 80, 91, 96, 115, 119, 132, 151, 158, 162, 163
smile, 15, 24, 56, 62, 79, 80, 83, 116, 127, 140, 163
Solomon, 31, 64, 65, 79, 112
son of God, 66, 145
spirit, 73, 75, 80, 81, 86, 88, 91, 115, 119, 121, 127, 128, 137, 144, 145, 150, 155, 156, 158, 159, 169
stammer, 22, 28
stinky and dirty, 44
stress, 15, 3948, 155, 162
suffering, 2, 9, 10, 14, 17, 19, 21, 35, 48, 49, 69, 97, 104, 134, 142, 161, 162, 165, 166, 170
surname, 10, 35, 146, 166
surrender 10, 86, 88, 104, 151
Swahili, 34, 35, 53, 68, 77, 82, 132

TANESCO, 140
TANU, 18
Taxi Driver, 34, 35,
thinking system, 9, 122, 148, 165
tongue, 18, 31, 45, 49, 87, 115
torture, 119,
tree, 42, 55, 56, 86, 87, 104, 109, 118, 121, 123, 127, 131, 149, 169
Treefrogs, 124, 131
Trial and Error, 76
Tribulations, 17, 19, 25, 60, 88, 91
Tsh, 34, 35, 41, 45
TV, 12, 15, 29, 46, 52, 133, 162, 163, 168

Index

Ubungo, 34, 35, 68, 82, 84, 86, 90, 92, 95, 96
Uganda, 17
United Nations, 62

virus, 118, 119, 122, 123, 139, 161
vision, 2, 10, 55, 66, 67, 72, 91, 156, 157, 166

Wife 101, 104, 105, 107, 108, 109, 113, 116, 118, 122, 129, 135, 143, 153, 164, 166

wisdom, 48, 58, 64, 65, 69, 74, 81, 93, 96, 113, 128, 141, 150, 157, 158, 161, 162, 163, 167
wives 5, 17, 52, 56, 125, 126, 132
wolves, 50, 99
worry, 10, 29, 32, 41, 70, 74, 97, 104, 136, 166,

Yes we can, 51

Zanzibar, 17, 18, 19, 53, 78, 142, 162,

www.ingramcontent.com/pod-product-compliance
Lightning Source LLC
Chambersburg PA
CBHW071619170426
43195CB00038B/1428